Catholicism and Catholicity:
Eucharistic Communities in Historical
and Contemporary Perspectives

Catholicism and Catholicity: Eucharistic Communities in Historical and Contemporary Perspectives

Edited by Sarah Beckwith

BLACKWELL
Publishers

Copyright © Blackwell Publishers Ltd

First published in 1999

Blackwell Publishers Ltd
108 Cowley Road, Oxford OX4 1JF, UK

and
350 Main Street
Malden, MA 02148, USA

British Library Cataloguing in Publication Data

A CIP catalogue record for this book is available from
the British Library

Library of Congress Cataloging-in-Publication Data

Data applied for

ISBN 0-631 21501 8

Printed in Great Britain By
MPG Books Ltd, Bodmin, Cornwall

CONTENTS

INTRODUCTION

SARAH BECKWITH

"Christianity", says one of the contributors to this volume:

> becomes simultaneously an infiltration of hope into the world and an overcoming of hope by the world. Such a civilization is disturbed and perturbed by its own hidden treasury of possibilities, embodied in icon and image, including the broken image of Christ who absorbed the tension in his own body. So the perturbation and the brokenness are represented and continually reenacted at the heart of Christianity, often under conditions of incongruous splendour.
>
> The problems which exercise such a civilization, insofar as it is Christian, have precisely to do with unity and its lack, including its potent absence amongst Christians, and with peaceability, and its lack.[1]

As an idea, an ideal, and a practice of unity and peace in the body of Christ, the Eucharist has always put the most pressure on that persistent, productive tension between Catholicism and Catholicity.

The following collection of essays provides you with the proceedings of the Homeland conference on the Eucharist held at Duke University, April 17–19th, 1998.[2] The conference took as its title and guideline: "Catholicism and Catholicity: Eucharistic Communities in Historical and Contemporary Perspectives" and invited a group of distinguished scholars in theology, history, and anthropology to meditate upon it. The essays offer fascinating and challenging reflections on Eucharistic signification, its inheritance, nature, and felicities and infelicities in enactment. Together, they make a vital contribution to a modern theology of the Eucharist.

In her essay, Mary Douglas returns to *Leviticus*, and examines the basis for sacrifice as it is laid down there as an important context for the early Christian Eucharist. Fergus Kerr considers the possibilities of a Catholic doctrine of the Eucharist without metaphysics and explores Elizabeth

Sarah Beckwith
Department of English, Duke University, Durham, NC 27708, USA

Anscombe's and Michael Dummett's Wittgensteinian exploration of tran-substantiation. In his essay, "The Eucharist as Language", Herbert McCabe proposes that "the body of Christ is present in the Eucharist as the meaning is present in the word". This emphasis on language is also explored in Catherine Pickstock's philosophical grammar of the words of consecration. Denys Turner uses J. L. Austin's distinction between perlocutions and illocutions to analyse the efficacy, abuse, and misunderstanding of Eucharistic language.

For William Cavanaugh, the Eucharist is a powerful counter-story to globalization, "not a place as such, but a story which performs certain spatial operations on place". David Martin explores the Anglican Prayer Book controversy in the 1980s and Sidney Griffith is likewise interested in liturgical performance, this time the liturgy of the lyrical Ephraem the Syrian, a fourth century Christian in the Syriac-speaking Church. Miri Rubin discusses the Eucharist from the point of view of a historian and from the twin perspectives of her own historical studies of the body of Christ in *Corpus Christi: The Eucharist in Medieval Culture* and in her more recent book, *Gentile Tales*.[3]

With the exception of David Martin's paper (and for reasons he himself explains) the essays presented here are longer versions of the papers delivered on the occasion of the conference. Eamon Duffy was given the difficult task of commenting on all the papers and graciously agreed at popular request to allow us to publish his afterword, which he expanded to discuss some pressing issues of liturgical reform.

We thank the Homeland Foundation for the generous grant that enabled us to bring together these exceptionally thoughtful scholars, and subsequently these essays. Taken as a group they make significant contributions to a theology and a history of the Eucharist and the communities made and unmade by means of it.[4]

NOTES

1   David Martin, *Reflections on Sociology and Theology* (Oxford: Clarendon Press, 1997), p. 16.
2   The conference was the culmination of a year in which we were privileged to hear a series of lectures (also sponsored by the Homeland Foundation) by Augustine DiNoia, Luke Timothy Johnson, and Daniel Lasker on the theme of the Eucharist.
3   *Corpus Christi: The Eucharist in Medieval Culture* (Cambridge: Cambridge University Press, 1991) and *Gentile Tales: The Narrative Assault on Late Medieval Jews* (New Haven and London: Yale University Press, 1999).
4   The Homeland Committee which helped to organize the conference consisted in Bruce Lawrence, David Aers, David Steinmetz, Julie Byrne, Dale Martin, Elizabeth Clark, Lillian Spiller, and in its earliest incarnations, Alastair MacIntyre and Mike Shagrue. Thanks to the Committee and especially to the indispensably good-humoured and efficient Lillian Spiller for her work over the year.

TRANSUBSTANTIATION AFTER WITTGENSTEIN

FERGUS KERR

"I could not possibly bring myself to believe all the things that they believe", Wittgenstein once remarked to Norman Malcolm, referring to his Roman Catholic friends Elizabeth Anscombe and Yorick Smythies.[1] No specific doctrine is mentioned. In saying this, Malcolm thought, Wittgenstein was "not disparaging their belief" but simply making "an observation about his own capacity". He regarded religious belief, Malcolm suspected, as "based on qualities of character and will that he himself did not possess". In *On Certainty*, in the context of considering the possibility of perhaps having to put up with someone's contradicting one's fundamental attitudes, Wittgenstein notes, in his only published reference to the doctrine of transubstantiation, that "Catholics believe ... that in certain circumstances a wafer completely changes its nature, and at the same time that all evidence proves the contrary."[2] Here as elsewhere, he is concerned to bring out the difference between contradicting what someone believes and finding someone's view of the world so incommensurable with one's own that contradiction would not be in order.[3]

No doubt, as Malcolm says, Wittgenstein connected the possibility of religious belief with qualities of character and will rather than with being intellectually open to persuasion by theistic arguments and the like. Religious belief, he once noted, "could only be (something like) passionately committing oneself to a system of co-ordinates"—which means that "although it's *belief*, it is really a way of living, or a way of judging life". Instruction in religious belief, then, "would have to be portraying, describing that system of reference and at the same time appealing to the conscience".[4] What is required, in effect, rather than metaphysical arguments for the general plausibility of theism, is the story of how the world looks from within the new co-ordinates,

Fergus Kerr
Blackfriars, 25 George Square, Edinburgh EH8 9LD, UK

told in such a way as to prompt conversion: philosophical theorising would only distort our understanding of religion. Wittgenstein even committed himself to the following remark: "If Christianity is the truth, then all the philosophy about it is false."[5]

Wittgenstein's hostility to "metaphysics" needs little documentation, though it is not always clear what he means. In 1930 he speaks highly of Leibniz and Schopenhauer: "Don't think I despise metaphysics. I regard some of the great philosophical systems of the past as among the noblest productions of the human mind."[6] In his *Blue Book*, on the other hand, dictated during 1933–1934, he inveighs against "metaphysics" on several occasions. He was not opposed to science, far from it, but he believed that philosophers "constantly see the method of science before their eyes, and are irresistibly tempted to ask and to answer questions in the way science does". Indeed, "this tendency is the real source of metaphysics and leads philosophers into complete darkness".[7] Against this "craving" he finds himself wanting to say that "it can never be our job ... to explain anything": "Philosophy really *is* 'purely descriptive'."

Wittgenstein's suspicion of explaining what needs only to be described goes deep. "If I could explain the essence of the ethical only by means of a theory," Waismann reports him as saying, "then what is ethical would be of no value whatsoever."[8] That is to say, if a theory is required to explain to someone "why" telling the truth is a good thing, the case is already lost. The "shallow, rationalist" conception in "theological ethics", Wittgenstein contends, is one that succumbs to the temptation to go behind moral judgements to lay bare rational foundations that explain them. In aesthetics and ethics, Wittgenstein would not reject a given explanation because it was false but simply "because it was an *explanation*".[9]

This leads to remarks about religion: "Is talking [*das Reden*] essential to religion?"[10] No, he says: he "can well imagine a religion in which there are no doctrinal propositions [*keine Lehrsätze*], in which nothing is said [*in der also nicht gesprochen wird*]". That strikes most people, believers and non-believers alike, as rather paradoxical, so captive are we in our culture to the picture of religious belief as nothing other than endorsing a set of doctrinal propositions. But it is surely not a religion in which no one would ever utter a word that Wittgenstein envisages—only one in which there need be no declarative sentences that express something true. After all, most of the speaking in characteristically religious contexts, such as worship, is intercessory, doxological, exhortatory, etc., rather than propositional. Waismann immediately notes the following qualification: "rather: if speech does occur, this itself is a component of religious behaviour and not a theory [*wenn geredet wird, so ist das selbst ein Bestandteil der religiösen Handlung und keine Theorie*]". This is why, Wittgenstein is quoted as saying, "it does not matter at all if the words used are true or false or nonsense"—perhaps misleadingly phrased, but Wittgenstein was familiar with William James's *Varieties of*

Religious Experience and must have been well aware of the immense range of linguistic phenomena in religious contexts, including speaking in tongues.[11]

Many people, including well-instructed Roman Catholics, think that the specifically Catholic doctrine of the Eucharist requires, and even depends on, a certain philosophical theory. True, *The Catechism of the Catholic Church* (1994), discussing the Eucharistic presence of Christ, makes no appeal to a metaphysics of substance.[12] Indeed, it has been criticised for *not* saying something about the various theories.[13] But consider what Ian Robinson takes for granted, in a recent essay in the journal of the (Anglican) Prayer Book Society[14]: "Transubstantiation depends on an idea of reality as *substance* which is hardly intelligible without some knowledge of the development of Aristotle's philosophy in the later middle ages." Roman Catholic doctrine of the real presence, Robinson believes, depends on the metaphysical theory that "appearances are absolutely and permanently deceptive". Natural philosophy, as inherited from Aristotle and taught in the medieval schools, took this for granted. Cranmer, on the other hand, so the article is out to show, "disposes once and for all of the Scholastic pseudo-physics demanded by the doctrine". Indeed, Aristotelian physics is unsound in much the same way as Aristotle's conception of language, Robinson goes on: a word is a sign of a previous mental event, and thus points to a meaning which is *elsewhere*. "The signified, the sense made in the understanding, is not in some place other than the signifier, also found in the understanding," so Cranmer held, and in this he was "much more Wittgensteinian".[15] However that may be, the fact remains that a well-instructed, traditionally minded Anglican like Robinson takes it for granted that the doctrine of transubstantiation incorporates a specific (and now obsolete) metaphysics of substance.

It is not long since Elizabeth Anscombe and Michael Dummett, two of the most respected philosophers in the post-Wittgensteinian tradition, who are also deeply committed Catholics, each published an essay on the doctrine of transubstantiation, seeking to rid it of the metaphysical theories with which it is still commonly associated in many people's minds.[16]

Anscombe: Transubstantiation for Little Children

"It is easiest to tell what transubstantiation is by saying this: little children should be taught about it as early as possible."[17] Professor Anscombe surely intends that wonderful opening sentence to provoke the reader, as I guess it usually does; and if it comes as a surprise, that is because we remain inclined to think that transubstantiation is one of the most sophisticated and difficult Roman Catholic doctrines—certainly not something to be taught to little children. If we are tempted to think that, of course, it would only confirm Wittgenstein's suspicion that instruction is regarded essentially as the imparting of *theory*. Anscombe continues: "Not of course using the word 'transubstantiation', because it is not a little child's word. But the thing can be taught, and it is best taught at mass at the consecration, the one part where a small child should be got to fix its attention on what is going on. I mean a child that is beginning to speak, one that understands enough language to be able to be told and to tell you things that have happened and to follow a simple story" (p. 107).

Anscombe describes how this happens: "Such a child can be taught then by whispering to it such things as: 'Look! Look what the priest is doing … He is saying Jesus' words that change the bread into Jesus' body. Now he's lifting it up. Look! Now bow your head and say 'My Lord and my God'"— and so on—"This need not be disturbing to the surrounding people" (p. 107). (A mother speaking from her own experience, obviously.)

Anscombe does not mention Wittgenstein; but this is a characteristically Wittgensteinian move. What he learned, evidently, during his years as a primary school teacher in mountain villages in his native Austria, was that all our concepts are rooted, not in intellectual reasoning but in *speaking*, and that means speaking as a component of an *activity*, such as (his examples) being told a story, being taught to sing, to guess riddles, to make a joke, to ask, thank, curse, greet and pray.[18] Of course, propositions with truth claims come into it, but many other, often much more primitive and instinctive, linguistic moves are established by that time. Of course, talk of transubstantiation may one day become necessary, but a good deal else will long since have become second nature to the child.

This is very much a Wittgensteinian thought. "The word 'God' is amongst the earliest learnt—pictures and catechisms etc.", he is quoted as saying.[19] This is obvious ("Look and see!"); but, not uncommonly, people are inclined to say that religious notions are so difficult, requiring so much intellectual machinery, that we must wait until children are much older, even until they are grown up, before they can be introduced to such sophisticated matters. Again and again, Wittgenstein ridicules such intellectualism. "A six-year-old boy knows as much about the foundations of arithmetic as Bertrand Russell does", he is cited as saying, rather provocatively—so much for *Principia Mathematica!*[20] Worship, similarly, is an activity, Anscombe suggests, that can be shared with a very young child; even, perhaps, if one has not been initiated into a certain practice of reverence at the Eucharist, one will never find theorizing talk of transubstantiation intelligible.

The time may come, sooner than the parent wants, for the child's questions to be answered: "Afterwards, or sometimes then (if for example it asks), it can be told what the words are which the priest says and how Jesus said them at the Last Supper. How he was offering himself up to the Father, the body that was going to be crucified and the blood that was going to be shed. So he showed that on the next day, when he was crucified, his death was an offering, a sacrifice. You can tell an older child how from the beginning priests have offered sacrifices to God (and to other, false, gods too) bringing animals, the best that people had, and offering them on altars: that this was how gods were worshipped, for sacrifice is the principal sign that something is being worshipped as a god." And much else in the same vein.

Professor Anscombe's paper first appeared in 1974. By that time, as she no doubt knew, in the wake of Vatican II's liturgical reforms, many Catholics would have had problems with her account—doubting that the consecration is a high point during the Mass; accusing her of centring attention on the elements instead of on the presence of Christ in the community; probably horrified at her teaching the child about sacrifice, relating the Christian sacrifice to pagan sacrifices, and so on. Paradoxically, the new emphasis on making the Eucharist more intelligible to worshippers favoured an intellectualization of the liturgy which reduced, and even excluded, the practices of reverence in which Anscombe expected concepts of real presence, transubstantiation, holy communion, and so on, to be rooted. The clergy in particular were sometimes licensed to indulge the craving to explain, which (Wittgenstein would have expected) simply distracted attention from what must be allowed the freedom to be itself.

By this sort of instruction, Anscombe observes, "the little child learns a great deal of faith". First, "it learns in the best possible way: as part of an *action*; as concerning *something going on* before it" (p. 108, my italics); and second, the child learns "as actually *unifying* and *connecting* beliefs" (my italics again)— which, as she says, "is clearer and more vivifying than being taught only later, in a classroom perhaps, that we have all these beliefs".

It is a second Wittgensteinian point. Our beliefs have their roots in practices which we share; but no single belief can be isolated from a cluster of others. To have even the most rudimentary concept, let alone to have a relatively sophisticated and controversial one, presupposes having a battery of other concepts—and a great deal more besides.[21]

Anscombe never uses the word metaphysics in her essay. She does say, however, that "it was perhaps a fault of the old exposition in terms of a distinction between the substance of a thing (supposed to be unascertainable) and its accidents, that this exposition was sometimes offered as if it were supposed to make everything intelligible." Here, certainly, the Wittgenstein of the *Blue Book* would have agreed with her: to think that "the thing can be understood, sorted out, expounded as a possibility with nothing mysterious about it" (p. 109), would be an example of exactly the kind of would-be scientific reductionism that he denounced there. Anscombe, with that "perhaps", is quite cautious; but in effect she is conceding that the concept of transubstantiation was, not uncommonly, mistakenly regarded as having explanatory force.[22] Correctly understood, however, the concept of transubstantiation does not *explain* but rather *protects* the mystery: "For in the philosophy of scholastic Aristotelianism in which those distinctions were drawn, transubstantiation is as difficult, as 'impossible', as it seems to any ordinary reflection. And it is right that it should be so. When we call something a mystery, we mean that we cannot iron out the difficulties about understanding it and demonstrate once for all that it is perfectly possible" (p. 109). That is to say: the "old exposition", presumably the standard line that recently prevailed among the simple faithful, was understood as an explanatory theory; but, with "greater learning", it should be plain that the language of substance and accidents, exploited far beyond its origins in Aristotle's philosophy, simply enabled theologians to locate the mystery—the language breaks open and this nonce-word designates this unique and incomparable event.

The rest of Anscombe's essay asks why we celebrate the Eucharist— "Because the Lord told us to. That is reason enough" (p. 109). But there is something on which she invites us to reflect: that is to say, "the mysterious fact that he wanted to nourish us with himself". This, she says, "is the greatest mystery of all about the Eucharistic sacrifice, a greater mystery than transubstantiation itself". In another Wittgensteinian move, that is to say, she shifts the focus from what seems the great problem to something connected with it but actually of much greater importance. "We Christians are so much accustomed to the idea of holy communion that we tend not to notice how mysterious an idea it is" (p. 110). Highlighting this forgotten truth, so to speak, brings Anscombe to an interesting ecumenical insight: "There is the now old dispute between Catholics and Protestants whether we eat what only symbolises, or really is, the flesh of the saviour when we eat the bread consecrated in the eucharist; drink his blood only symbolically or really. Because of this dispute, it appeared as if only the Catholic belief were extravagant—the Protestants having the perfectly reasonable procedure of *symbolically* eating Christ's flesh and drinking his blood! The staggering strangeness of doing such a thing even only symbolically slipped out of notice in the dispute about transubstantiation. But let us realize it now" (pp. 110–111). As Wittgenstein remarked: "One is unable to notice something —because it is always before one's eyes."[23]

Anscombe devotes a paragraph to theologians who, "in modern times", "have tried to explain transubstantiation as trans-signification" (p. 111). Some of them might protest that they were not trying to "explain", but rather to place the Eucharistic change in a different context (as we shall see below). Her summary of the theory is brief: "The 'substance' of some things is the meaning they have in human life." She agrees that some things, like money, are what they are because of their use. These theologians "have wished to say it is true of bread and wine". Their argument is that bread and wine are not "chemical substances, but mean human food and drink". Anscombe concedes that they are not "single substances"—assuming, no doubt, that, in terms of modern physics, they are conglomerates of substances (molecules, etc.). "The bread and wine that are fit to use at the Eucharist", however, "are defined by the natural kinds they are made from, by wheat and grape." This is "defined", she must mean, by the tradition of the Church, as expressed in the Code of Canon Law. Her point is that it is not the "meaning" that bread and wine have in human life that confers on them their character, as the transignificationists are assumed to maintain, but the wheat and grapes—which, while certainly cultivated, count as what philosophers call, not uncontroversially, *natural kinds*. Rather, it is easier to identify natural kind *terms*, such as mass terms, like "gold" and "water", as well as certain sortal terms, like "tiger" and "apple", than to say what, ontologically speaking, natural kinds themselves actually are. Loosely, they are types of naturally occurring stuffs and things. Anscombe's point is that, however transignification is held to improve on transubstantiation, bread and wine owe their nature to things that grow out of the ground, and not just to the significance that we human beings confer on them (as the theorists are suspected of thinking). "For the rest, what is said may be very true", Anscombe says, a little brusquely—agreeing, it appears, that bread and wine, granted their dependence on things that do not owe their nature to human beings, are what they are because of their place in human life. But the "odd thing"—"which is apparently not noticed"—is that "what gets trans-signified in the Eucharist is not the bread and wine, but the body and blood of the Lord, which are trans-signified into food and drink" (p. 111). *That* is "the mystery", Anscombe concludes. Once again, it is a typically Wittgensteinian move: it is obvious, of course, once it is pointed out. So often the theories concentrate on what happens at the consecration to the bread and wine—on "the old exposition", perhaps, on explaining how; whereas, for the worshipper, it is the coming of the Lord as food and drink, bread of life and cup of salvation, that is the focus.

A philosopher, schooled by Wittgenstein, may thus encourage us to "reflect" on the fact of what happens in the Eucharist, thereby highlighting aspects often or hitherto neglected and left aside. (The difference between "reflecting" and "theory", in philosophy, calls for further investigation.) But the Wittgensteinian philosopher out to clear the ground on which the houses of cards stood[24] has the last word—Anscombe's paper concludes as follows: "It is the mystery of faith which is the same for the simple and the learned. For they believe the same, and what is grasped by the simple is not better understood by the learned: their service is to clear away the rubbish which the human reason so often throws in the way to create obstacles."

The "learned", there, must be (among others) the post-Wittgensteinian philosophers who can serve the faith by destroying the would-be rational explanations which the irrepressible metaphysician among us—*in* us[25]—keeps inventing. "What *we* do", as Wittgenstein remarked (his italics), "is to bring words back from their metaphysical to their everyday application".[26] Religion, Eucharistic worship, and so on, are, of course, for Wittgenstein as for Anscombe, matters of everyday life and concern—not esoteric and minority interests. She does not speak explicitly of metaphysics; it is safe to say, however, that the "rubbish" which philosophers have to clear away, in this context, would include some versions at least of substance/accidents metaphysics as well as modern transignification theories.

Dummett: Transubstantiation without Metaphysical Baggage

Michael Dummett concentrates on the doctrine of transubstantiation as formulating the rationale of the practice of reservation of the consecrated bread.[27] To start with, he tells us that he assumes that the use of the word "substance" in connection with the doctrine "carries with it no commitment to any specific philosophical thesis" (p. 234). What the doctrine means is that, when we ask of either of the consecrated elements, "What is it?", the answer is "The Body of Christ" or "The Blood of Christ". The doctrine, so understood, bare of philosophical commitments, simply formulates, in the most natural manner, what the New Testament and early Church commonly say about the Eucharist.

The natural sense of a passage in the New Testament can, however, be open to dispute, Dummett argues. Thus, the doctrine of transubstantiation "requires more grounding than just the language of the New Testament and of the early Church concerning the eucharist" (p. 235). He focuses on "the practice of reservation", which "touches the lives of lay Christians" (p. 236), at the liturgy of the presanctified in the West, every Wednesday and Friday in Lent in the Byzantine rite; in viaticum; in the case of privileged individuals like Mary Queen of Scots, early hermits, and "almost everyone in the times of the early persecutions".

Next, in his exposition, Dummett highlights the "enormous change" (p. 236) brought about at the Reformation. When Orthodox and Catholic Christians, including Anglo-Catholics, speak of "going to church", he says, they mean, primarily, attending the celebration of the Eucharist *with or without receiving communion*. For Protestants, on the other hand, including moderate Anglicans, going to church means taking part in some service of prayers, hymns and psalms. This is an enormous difference, Dummett holds. Some differences of practice are different ways of doing the same thing; other differences, however, are differences of principle. "Radically different beliefs may be expressed in the same words, while different words may express what, upon close analysis, amounts to just the same thing" (p. 237). No imaginable future reunion of Christian churches, however, could accommodate "those for whom the eucharistic liturgy was the principal communal act of worship and those for whom it was a mere communion service, attendance at which would be pointless for those not intending to receive the sacrament" (p. 237).[28]

It is with a *practice*, then, that Dummett initiates his reflections: the practice of reserving the sacrament. The Catholic doctrine of transubstantiation is "an attempted verbal crystallisation" (p. 240) of this practice. From now on, Dummett will be concerned with "a strictly philosophical examination of transubstantiation, understood as I have said, as unburdened with metaphysical baggage" (p. 241). This is the first use of the phrase "metaphysical baggage", but presumably he is thinking of the remark about assuming that the term "substance" carries with it "no commitment to any specific philosophical thesis" (p. 234). Rephrasing what he has just said, he next asks "from the standpoint of contemporary philosophy" (p. 214) where the problem of making sense of transubstantiation lies. "The primary philosophical question", he contends, "is how it is possible to deny propositions that pass all the normal tests for truth, namely that this is bread and that wine, and affirm in their place propositions that pass none of these tests". Curiously, he thinks that "scholastic writers" on the eucharist were not troubled by this question; but philosophers[29] who have been subjected to logical-positivist verificationism, "withered" as it may now be, have become "more chary of assuming that we may indulge in mystery in an unlimited degree without incurring the penalty of altogether depriving our statements of sense" (pp. 242–243).

So what accounts of transubstantiation might there be, which involve philosophical theory? The first is the neo-Cartesian theory, according to which "God systematically induces sensory illusions in us after the consecration" (p. 242). If God did not do this we should see Christ's flesh and blood on the altar as they really are, which would expose us to the charge of cannibalism; but God conceals them by making them appear to us like the bread and wine that were placed on the altar. This account employs "a degenerate use of the notion of substance"—"On this view, all we ever truly know are appearances: whenever we judge, on the basis of what we see or hear or feel, that an object of any given kind is present, we are making an act of faith, essentially in the mercy of God: for, save for our trust in that mercy, we should never have any reason for inferring, from the fact that something gives rise to those appearances that we associate with, say, tables, that it is not, for instance, a hippopotamus" (pp. 242–243). On this "neo-Cartesian theory", it is not difficult to accept that the bread and wine, after the consecration, should really be something else—after all, it is always an act of faith that anything is as it appears. This story should be dismissed out of hand, Dummett says; but it continues to haunt the rest of his essay.[30]

Dummett make the now familiar point that the Council of Trent used the word *"species"* instead of "accident", no doubt to avoid a commitment to "a metaphysics of substance and accident" or, for that matter, any other philosophical jargon.[31] He goes on to discuss the "genuine scholastic doctrine", "the scholastic theory" (p. 243), which slides into "Aquinas's theory", "the thomistic theory, in the form in which we are now considering it" (p. 245). In his allotted space, of course, Dummett cannot expound Aquinas at length and in detail: what he focuses on is the "extraordinary theory" (p. 244) that, among the particularized qualities of the bread and wine that persist after the consecration, one of them, their dimension, acts as a subject for the rest.[32] After airing possible mitigations of the theory, Dummett concludes that Aquinas "is coming perilously close to adopting the degenerate conception of substance which we rejected above" (p. 246). The accidents of the bread and wine that persist after the consecration are carried, so to speak, by certain regions of space, but the Body and Blood of Christ, now present, do not exactly occupy these spaces. The problem that Dummett sees here is that the theory does not secure any connection between the persisting accidents and the miraculously given substances: "The consecrated elements are, as it were, merely the discarded husk of the bread and wine earlier present, and have no more intimate connection with the Body and Blood of Christ than that. It is as if the bread and wine have stepped aside to make room for Christ's Body and Blood, which could not otherwise be present, and, in so stepping aside, have, so to speak, left their mortal remains behind" (pp. 246–247). This lack of connection is the kind of "conceptual incoherence" which it is the philosopher's task to identify, as a service to the theologian or, as it might be, the physicist or the psychologist (cf. p. 232).

It is the same incoherence that Dummett will now find in "the relatively recent theory of the Eucharist known as 'transignification'" (p. 248). He apologises for knowing it "only in the version expounded at one time by Charles Davis", thus "cannot be sure that this is representative", but understands that the fundamental idea—"said to be derived from Heidegger"—is that "the character of an object depends upon our attitude towards it and the use we make of it". More particularly, "since we *treat* the consecrated elements as being the Body and Blood of Christ, that is what they are". This account, he says, comes "near to being correct", though requires correction: Davis makes the mistake of "generalizing without warrant a principle that has only limited application" (p. 248).

This promises an example of how a philosopher can help to repair a theologian's theory. Dummett gives no reference to any publication by Davis; he may be relying on his memory of a lecture.[33] In his classic paper on transubstantiation, at all events, Davis does not use the word, let alone expound a transignification theory, nor does he attribute the fundamental idea to Heidegger, or to any other philosopher.[34] In fact, Davis gets most of the way to what he wants to say by insisting, as a theologian much concerned at the time with liturgy and sacramental theology, that transubstantiation is a "religious event", "an action by which Christ establishes a new relation with us through the use of bread and wine", requiring, for intelligibility, only to be "replaced in the human, religious and sacramental context to which it belongs".[35]

The difficulties people have (or had) with transubstantiation, Davis argues, come from regarding bread as a substance, in the Aristotelian sense of substance, that is as an entity existing in itself and not in another, whereas bread, once we recall that we live in a human world, "exists as bread only in relation to man".[36] We make bread, as we say, it does not grow on trees; but that it is bread depends on its physical and chemical composition, which can vary a good deal though within limits. But it is bread, Davis holds, principally because of the use it has in a human community—on its relation to the human beings who eat it.

Dummett agrees that there are some objects which are what they are in virtue of the use to which we put them. This is the principle that Davis unwarrantedly generalizes, or so Dummett claims. A coin, for example, though it must have certain physical properties, "must be or have been treated as a token of monetary exchange in some society having the institution of money" (p. 248). Davis would be happy with that—"we give things a conventional status, assign them a particular meaning and use them for a particular purpose".[37] Dummett next cites the Pyrex dish, "intended by the manufacturers for use in cooking", which he bought to use as an ashtray because it was "far cheaper than anything of the size advertised as an ashtray" (pp. 248–249). "It *is* an ashtray, not merely because it is so used, but because I use it as such and permit those who call on me to do so." That, on the other hand, would sound pretty arbitrary and Humpty-Dumptyish to Davis: while agreeing that the purpose for which a manufactured object may be used can change its status, he insists that we cannot change a man-made thing into something else by decree: "if we take a saucer and say that this is an ashtray, we may use it as an ashtray, but everyone will always recognize it as a saucer".[38]

Moving on, in his survey of how a thing's nature may be changed by how it is used, Dummett notes, less controversially, that a dog is a sheepdog if it has been trained in certain ways, but whether an animal is a dog or not has nothing to do with how it is treated. "The concepts of bread and wine, and of a human body and human blood, are of this latter kind, and not like those of a coin or an ashtray" (p. 249). Crucially, while, within limits, how we, or some other animal, treat a substance will determine whether it is food, and it is part of the concept of bread that it is used as food, bread itself (or wine) does not owe its nature simply to the purpose to which it is put by human beings. It is a mistake, in transignification theories, if they are intended to improve on transubstantiation ones, to say that the "substance" of a thing like bread or wine simply *is* its "meaning" in our human world: "We cannot make a thing bread by simply treating it as if it were bread", as Davis says.[39]

The philosophical mistake which Dummett finds in the transignification theory, in "the version expounded at one time by Charles Davis", was identified by Davis himself: bread does not owe its nature simply to the use to which it is put by human beings—*a fortiori* it is not how believers treat the bread and wine after the consecration that brings about the change in their status and character. Transubstantiation, reinterpreted as transignification in *that* sense, indeed becomes a human *work*.

The conceptual incoherence that Dummett identifies in "the thomistic theory, in the form in which we are now considering it" (p. 245), turns out to be the same as in the transignification theory that he knows "only in the version expounded at one time by Charles Davis" (p. 248). On the first theory, the lack of connection between the persisting accidents and the miraculously given presence of the Body and Blood of Christ means, Dummett thinks, that it would be intelligible to say that Christ's Body and Blood might be present, instead of bread and wine, "quite unknown to us" (p. 250). Certainly, if we bring in "the degenerate conception of substance—to which, as we saw, the thomistic account is driven uncomfortably close" (p. 250), you might conceivably believe Christ's Body and Blood to be still in existence, in a range of accidents, "without believing even in the existence of God, let alone in the Incarnation". The possibility that Christ's Body and Blood should be present, in place of bread and wine, quite unknown to us, could be ruled out "only by appeal to the improbability that God would allow us to be so woefully deceived".

The transignification theory, relying on the unwarrantedly generalized philosophical principle that the nature of things like bread and wine is determined by the meaning they have for human beings, allows—even requires—us to say that, since the bread and wine, after the consecration, are *treated* differently, as being the Body and Blood of Christ, that is what they *are*. Even an atheist could understand that, Dummett says; indeed, given the way in which the consecrated elements have been treated and are still treated in many churches, an atheist, on this theory, would be "committing a conceptual mistake" if he failed to acknowledge their sacred nature.

To sum up. On the neo-Cartesian theory, since we never know whether how things appear to us is really how they are anyway, there is nothing all that odd about bread and wine really being Christ's Body and Blood. On the degenerate substance-and-accidents theory, it is logically possible to suppose that, if the accidents persisted without a subject, they might do so in the presence of any substance whatever; that might include, for one who denied his divinity, Christ's Body and Blood (mummified, dried, for all we know). On the transignification theory, as Dummett expounds it, bread and wine, both before and after the consecration, are what they are because of how they are treated—and even an atheist would have to concede, if that is how the consecrated elements are treated, that is what they must be. The first theory supposes that appearances are always deceptive; the second that the substance, understood as the inner reality of a thing, is always inaccessible to the senses; and the third alleges that what a thing of the relevant kind is, is decided by how it is treated in our culture.

One way or another, Dummett suggests, each of these theories misrepresents the dependence of one item of the Christian faith on another. He does not work this out as regards the neo-Cartesian theory: the story would be that the doctrine of creation reflects nothing of the nature of God.[40] The scholastic theory allows the possibility of believing in the presence of Christ's Body and Blood in the consecrated elements without believing in his divinity. The transignification theory would require even an atheist to believe in the presence of Christ in the sacrament.

Philosophers like such paradoxes. Any belief about what might happen in the Eucharist must hang together, Dummett argues, with a belief in the Incarnation, which the scholastic theory cannot secure. Similarly, what happens in the Eucharist, if it is to be intelligible, must depend on belief in God as well as in the Incarnation, and this the transignification theory cannot ensure. Very much the same, or anyway an analogous, conceptual incoherence is identified in the two theories with which Dummett is principally concerned. Philosophers also like finding the same error in what seem disparate theories. This, we might think, is a philosopher schooled in the post-Wittgensteinian tradition, clearing away "rubbish".

Dummett rescues the transignification theory by appealing to the concept of "deeming something to be so" (p. 250). We deem the consecrated elements to be Christ's Body and Blood, but the authority for our doing so is Christ himself. Even he could not be recognised as having such authority if he were not God made man (p. 254). The consecrated elements are Christ's Body and Blood in virtue of being deemed to be so, of course, rather than naturally: "if we did not recognise this, we should be back with the neo-Cartesian theory that God subjects us to mass illusion" (p. 254). But since, as believing Christians, we take ourselves to have God's word that the bread and wine after the consecration are Christ's Body and Blood *in God's sight*, though of course not in ours, "it would be presumptuous, if not blasphemous, to say that, all the same, they were not *really* so" (p. 254).[41]

It would not only be blasphemous to question whether the reality was as God's word says, it would be *unintelligible*: "We are impelled by a drive to discover how things really are in themselves, that is to say, independently of the way they present themselves to us, with our particular sensory and intellectual faculties and our particular spatial and temporal perspective" (p. 254). Here speaks the philosopher who, more than any other, has brought the issue of realism back into metaphysics.[42] "I doubt whether it is possible", he goes on, "to represent this notion of reality as it is in itself as even coherent, save by equating how things are in themselves with how they are apprehended by God: without that identification, there is only the description of the world as it appears to us and as how we may usefully represent it to ourselves for the purpose of rendering its workings and regularities surveyable." In effect, without theism, realism is incoherent and anti-realism prevails. Time and again, throughout his work, and certainly in this essay on transubstantiation, Dummett keeps returning to the difference between how things are and how they appear to us, and in the end it is the believer who speaks: "However this may be, anyone who believes in God must equate the two things: there can be no gap between how God sees something and how it really is in itself" (p. 255).

Both Elizabeth Anscombe and Michael Dummett clear away philosophical theorizings to allow religious events to stand on their own: the moment of consecration, the reservation of the consecrated elements. In this respect they are destroying houses of cards, in a Wittgensteinian manner. But a theologian is left with some disquiet, particularly with respect to Dummett's essay. The two theories which preoccupy him are analyzed and criticized in much less than the best available versions. Does the traditional scholastic theory always involve a "degenerate" notion of substance? Does the modern transignification theory necessarily contain a voluntaristic epistemology according to which the character and status of things in a relevant category are decided by how human beings choose to use them? At best, bad theories have been removed to allow certain religious practices to stand free. That does not show, however, that *all* philosophizing about religious doctrine need be "rubbish".

NOTES

1   Norman Malcolm, *Ludwig Wittgenstein: A Memoir* (Oxford: Oxford University Press, 1984), p. 60; a remark made sometime in 1946–47.
2   Ludwig Wittgenstein, *On Certainty* (Oxford: Basil Blackwell, 1969): § 239 (noted in 1951). In 1938, at the beginning of the first lecture on religious belief, Wittgenstein told the students that, during the First World War, when he fought in the Austrian army against the Russians, he saw consecrated bread being carried in chromium steel, presumably by a Catholic priest—"This struck him as ludicrous"—which perhaps reveals something of how Catholic his sensibilities were at that time, *Lectures & Conversations on Aesthetics, Psychology and Religious Belief* (Oxford: Basil Blackwell, 1966), p. 53.
3   Ibid., pp. 53–59, and discussion by Hilary Putnam, *Renewing Philosophy* (London: Harvard University Press, 1992), pp. 141–157.
4   *Culture and Value* (Oxford: Blackwell, 1998), p. 73 (noted in 1947).
5   Ibid., p. 89 (noted in 1949).
6   *Recollections of Wittgenstein* edited by Rush Rhees (Oxford: Oxford University Press, 1984), p. 105.
7   *The Blue and Brown Books* (Oxford: Basil Blackwell, 1958), p. 18.
8   *Wittgenstein and the Vienna Circle*: conversations recorded by Friedrich Waismann, edited by Brian McGuinness (Oxford: Basil Blackwell, 1979), p. 117.
9   Ibid., p. 116: "If I were told anything that was a *theory*, I would say, No, no! That does not interest me. Even if this theory were true, it would not interest me—it would not be the exact thing I was looking for."
10 Ibid., p. 117.
11 As his friend M. O'C. Drury reports: "This book he told me [in 1930] had helped him greatly. And if I am not mistaken the category of *Varieties* continued to play an important part in his thinking", *Recollections of Wittgenstein*, pp. 93 and 106.
12 *The Catechism of the Catholic Church* (London: Geoffrey Chapman, 1994), §§ 1371–1381.
13 Raymond Moloney S.J., *Commentary on the Catechism of the Catholic Church* edited by Michael J. Walsh (London: Geoffrey Chapman 1994), p. 269: "In particular one will notice the absence in the *Catechism* of any reference to the controversies concerning real presence which, though not discussed in the documents of Vatican II, were much spoken of at that time and were the occasion of Paul VI's encyclical *Mysterium Fidei* … The absence of any reference to these approaches in the *Catechism* fits in with its tendency to avoid theological theories, but since these approaches have been widely discussed and can be the source of questions in people's minds, some mention of them seems necessary today."
14 Ian Robinson, "Thomas Cranmer on the Real Presence", *Faith and Worship* 43 (1997), pp. 2–10; Robinson has a valuable chapter on "Religious English" in his unjustly neglected book *The Survival of English: Essays in Criticism of Language* (Cambridge University Press, 1973).
15 Ibid., p. 4.
16 Several other philosophers in the analytic tradition, who are Catholics, have discussed transubstantiation, e.g., William Charlton, in *Philosophy and Christian Belief* (London: Sheed & Ward, 1988), speaks of "sterile debate", p. 210; P. J. FitzPatrick, in *In Breaking of Bread: The Eucharist and Ritual* (Cambridge: Cambridge University Press, 1993), at much greater

length, conducts a very radical critique of theories of transubstantiation ancient and modern.

17 G. E. M. Anscombe, "On Transubstantiation", Catholic Truth Society (London, 1974), reprinted in *The Collected Philosophical Papers of G. E. M. Anscombe* volume 3: Ethics, Religion and Politics (Oxford: Basil Blackwell, 1981), pp. 107–112; cf. p. 107; henceforward cited in the text. Born in 1919, Elizabeth Anscombe studied classics and philosophy at Oxford, moved to Cambridge to do research, and there met Wittgenstein; they became friends, he made her one of his literary executors, and she translated his posthumously published *Philosophical Investigations* (1953). With *Intention* (1957), *An Introduction to Wittgenstein's Tractatus* (1959), and many papers, she established herself as one of the leading philosophers in England. In 1970 she was appointed to the chair of philosophy in Cambridge which Wittgenstein once held. She has long been known as a firm and occasionally forthright adherent of traditional Catholicism.

18 *Philosophical Investigations* (Oxford, Basil Blackwell, 1953): § 23.

19 *Lectures & Conversations*, p. 59.

20 Cited by H. L. Finch, *Wittgenstein* (Rockport, Massachusetts: Element Books, 1995), p. 160.

21 To quote Wilfrid Sellars's formulation, *Science, Perception and Reality* (London: Routledge, 1963), p. 148.

22 As is conceded in the Anglican-Roman Catholic Agreed Statement on Eucharistic Doctrine (Windsor, 1971), where at § 6 on the real presence the word "transubstantiation" is assigned to a longish footnote, concluding with the following guarded admission: "In contemporary Roman Catholic theology it is not understood as explaining *how* the change takes place."

23 *Philosophical Investigations*, § 129.

24 Ibid., § 118.

25 According to Anthony Kenny, in a good discussion of Wittgenstein's views about philosophy, he regarded philosophy as "a tool which is useful only against philosophers and against the philosopher in us", citing a note dated 1932–33, see "Wittgenstein on the Nature of Philosophy", in *Wittgenstein and His Times* edited by Brian McGuinness (Basil Blackwell: Oxford, 1982), p. 13.

26 *Investigations*, § 116.

27 Michael Dummett, "The Intelligibility of Eucharistic Doctrine", *The Rationality of Religious Belief: Essays in Honour of Basil Mitchell* edited by William J. Abraham and Steven W. Holzer (Oxford: Clarendon Press, 1987), pp. 231–261; references in the text. Born in 1925, Michael Dummett has spent most of his life in Oxford, apart from military service; his interpretation of Frege's philosophy of language and mathematics and renewal of the realism/anti-realism debate make him the most important philosopher in Oxford during the last thirty years. Well known for opposition to British immigration policies, he has also published severe criticism of post-Vatican II Catholic theology and biblical scholarship.

28 Just as Anscombe's practice could not be followed by families who have to worship in certain new styles of Eucharistic liturgy, Dummett's point here is affected by the disappearance, particularly in middle-class parishes, of worshippers who do not always receive holy communion.

29 Like himself: Dummett inherited A. J. Ayer's chair at Oxford.

30 J. H. Newman, insisting that the doctrine of transubstantiation is not difficult to believe, asks: "Why should it not be? What's to hinder it? What do I know of substance or matter? Just as much as the greatest philosophers, and that is nothing at all", *Apologia pro Vita Sua*, chapter 5. Karl Barth, in his doctrine of creation, argues that it is only because we have God's revealed word for it that we know that created reality is not an illusion: see Fergus Kerr, "Cartesianism According to Karl Barth", *New Blackfriars* 77 (1996), pp. 358–368.

31 The point is made most accessibly by Edward Schillebeeckx, e.g., in *The Eucharist* (London: Sheed and Ward, 1968); P. J. FitzPatrick, *In Breaking of Bread*, pp. 125–130, brings evidence against it.

32 *Summa Theologiae*, III, 77, 2: "the dimensive quantity of the bread or wine is the subject of the other accidents in the sacrament."

33 From before 1966, presumably, when Charles Davis left the Roman Catholic Church.

34 Charles Davis, "The Theology of Transubstantiation", *Sophia* 3 (1964), pp. 12–24, and "Understanding the Real Presence", in *The Word in History: The St Xavier Symposium* edited

by T. Patrick Burke (London: Collins, 1968), pp. 154–178, where transubstantiation is discussed in the same way, never mentioning transignification, or Heidegger.

35 *Sophia*, p. 15; *The Word in History*, p. 176.

36 *Sophia*, p. 16.

37 Ibid., p. 18.

38 Ibid., p. 19.

39 Ibid., p. 19.

40 Or that our knowledge of the reality of the created order depends on divine revelation, cf. Barth note 31.

41 Charles Davis says much the same thing, in different words: "It is not a question of our altering the conventional status of the bread and deciding to give it a new meaning in the context of the eucharist. Christ alone can make the bread his Body, he does so by the efficacious words of consecration. These do not merely tell us of the change but they bring it about in the real order", *Sophia*, p. 21.

42 "Metaphysics" in a non-pejorative, non-Wittgensteinian sense: with his William James Lectures at Harvard in 1976, published as *The Logical Basis of Metaphysics* (London: Duckworth, 1991), Dummett has played a key role in the revival of metaphysics in Anglo-American philosophy—whatever his suspicions of "metaphysical baggage" in the theology of the Eucharist.

THE EUCHARIST AS LANGUAGE

HERBERT McCABE O.P.

Plainly, the Eucharist can be studied in the light of a great number of disciplines: anthropology, history, sociology and so on. It seems reasonable, however, to suppose that, first of all, it is a matter of theology. By theology I do not now mean a study of religions but rather a study within a religious tradition. In other and more classical words, it means "Faith seeking understanding". I shall be looking at the Eucharist from the inside, so to speak, rather than as a detached observer.

> In many and various ways God spoke of old to our fathers by the prophets; but in these last days he has spoken to us by a son whom he appointed heir of all things, through whom he also created the world. (Heb. 1:1–2)

This tremendous claim in the Epistle to the Hebrews, I take as my starting point. I am not concerned, for present purposes, with whether this Epistle falls short of Chalcedonian Christology or even that of John, but simply with the notion that God "spoke to our fathers" and that he has "spoken to us" by the Son.

In what I would call the mainstream Catholic tradition, (elegantly set forth in Eph. 3:1–10) God's revelation of the "mystery of his will, according to the purpose he set forth in Christ as a plan for the fullness of time (is) to unite all things in him, things in heaven and things on earth".

This revelation is presented to us by the prophets (in the words of Scripture) but most definitively in the Word made flesh dwelling amongst us; and the dwelling amongst us which took place historically in the life, death and resurrection of Jesus, giving rise to the preaching of the New Testament, thereby takes place sacramentally in the mysteries that constitute the institutional Church. These are the continuing presence/absence of the Word of God, centring on the Eucharist.

Herbert McCabe O.P.
Blackfriars, Blackfriars Hall, Oxford OX1 3LY, UK

Of course, all these propositions are highly debatable but my purpose is not an apologetic in defence of this view, but simply to admit to what I am taking for granted as background to the proposition that I do want to discuss. This is the proposition that the body of Christ is present in the Eucharist as the meaning is present in a word.

Three or four decades ago a number of Roman Catholic theologians, uneasy with what they took to be the traditional doctrine of transubstantiation as an account of the real presence of Christ in the Eucharist, proposed to substitute a doctrine of "transignification", according to which it was not that the *being* of the bread and wine became the being of Christ, but that the *meaning* which the bread and wine had as a symbol of our unity in a common meal, became through our faith a sign of deeper unity in the body of Christ. This presented as an *alternative* to transubstantiation sounded suspiciously close to the proposition that a piece of fabric with the necessary number of stars and stripes on it should be the national flag and, on ceremonial occasions be saluted as an expression of patriotism. This is perfectly reasonable behaviour but it makes of the flag an emblem whose meaning is supplied by the opinions and aspirations and bonds of friendship in the human society in question. The proposition that the Eucharist is something much the same seemed to empty it of its mystery, not to say its interest. It is true, as I shall be trying to argue, that human language itself, whether of flags or words, is a kind of mystery, something that in a way transcends our understanding even while being the means of our understanding. But, of course, for the tradition from which I speak, the mystery of the Eucharist is much deeper than this. For the Church is not founded on the opinions, aspirations and friendships of its members, rather it creates and sustains these; and "the Church's one foundation is Jesus Christ the Lord ...".

The Eucharist is the creative language of God, his eternal Word made flesh. The *aspirations* are the hope engendered by the resurrection, the *opinions* are the faith which is the word of God, and the *friendship* is the *agape* that God has given to us that we might share it with all humankind. The "society" whose "emblem" it is (I put both those words in scare-quotes to indicate that they are both being used analogically) is the society which is "the body of Christ" whose emblem is, (in yet *another* analogical sense) "the body of Christ".

A word, now, on the philosophical background to talk of transubstantiation. For Aristotle, as for Aquinas, a substance exists by being a certain kind of thing, having an essence which distinguishes it from other kinds of things. ("No entity without identity" as Quine used to say; "It is form that gives *esse*" as Aquinas used to say.) To say that Fred exists is not to attribute to him a property called "existence", there is no such property, it is to say of him that he truly *is a human being*; being a human being *is* what it takes for him to exist. This predication, they would say, is in the category of substance (simply answering the question: What is it?). True statements in other, accidental, categories (such as: he is sitting down ... or has a cold ...) although they presuppose, they would say, the existence of Fred, do not *directly assert* that he exists. Material substances exist (as does everything other than God) by being some kind of thing, and exist over against the possibility of changing into other kinds of things—for this is what being "material" implies. They are contingent, not in the later rationalist sense, (that we can conceive them not being), but in the medieval sense of being contingent on how they will be affected by the other things in the universe. That such substances (and, for that matter, non-material, imperishable "necessary beings" like Angels) should also exist over against the deeper possibility of there not being anything at all, nothing to be made out of, nothing to be made into, would be a thought quite foreign to Aristotle. And of course, that it *is* a real thought is something that needs to be demonstrated. Aristotle had a metaphysics of *substance* and form; Aquinas developed a deeper metaphysics of *esse*, and creation.

Etienne Gilson was, I think, quite right to argue that the notion of *esse* (existence over against the possibility that nothing whatever might have existed) came to medieval European thought not from classical Greek philosophy, but from the biblical doctrine of creation. Since it was generally agreed by advocates of both transubstantiation and of transignification that the consecration of the bread and wine made no chemical or physical or other scientifically detectable difference to these elements, the choice seemed to be between a deeper metaphysical transformation of the elements or a change in *our* interpretation of their significance. Of course, for transignificationists this change in our perception was an act of faith, a supernatural activity in us of the Holy Spirit, but it seemed to be something that had to do with us, in us, rather than with the bread and wine themselves. It sounded like nominalism—this was, of course in a period when "metaphysics" was not a respectable word but a term of abuse (like "theological" today).

The most coherent exponent of transubstantiation, Thomas Aquinas, was quite clear that it was a matter of metaphysics. He argues that the Eucharist is not a question of the substance of bread becoming the substance of a human body (this kind of substantial change is familiar enough and takes place whenever we eat a slice of bread); it is a miraculous transformation at a deeper level, which Aquinas compares to creation, in which the *esse* (the existence) of this piece of bread and this cup of wine becomes the *esse* of Christ. This transformation of a substance into another *particular* existent, as distinct from a different kind of thing (as in ordinary substantial change) would have been completely unintelligible to Aristotle as, of course, was the notion of creation and, indeed, the whole notion of *esse* in Aquinas's sense.

My next task, then, is to give some account of "meaning". This philosophical task may seem rather distant from doing theology as such, but if faith is "seeking understanding" it had better not be confused about understanding. I shall be arguing that meaning is never subjective "just in the mind" but nor is it "objective" in the sense that most people would reckon that leopards and trees are objectively there (or not).

"When I use a word", Humpty Dumpty said in a rather scornful tone, "it means just what I choose it to mean—neither more nor less …". "The question is", said Humpty Dumpty, "which is to be master—that's all". He was, of course, talking nonsense. Words are for communication, which means common use, and cannot function unless there is a conventional agreement about their meaning. As Wittgenstein has convincingly shown, there can be no such thing as a private meaning. Meaning *belongs to the language itself.* Though, of course, in the development of language throughout a human history, there is the creation and appreciation of new meanings, which is the intellectual life of a human society and is the intellectual life of particular individuals who share in the task. This is a point well brought out by Peter Geach (in *Mental Acts,* London, n.d.) in criticising the form of behaviourism he detected in Gilbert Ryle's *Concept of Mind* (London, 1949). The same point was made by Thomas Aquinas in the *De unitate intellectus contra Averroistas.* The understanding of meaning is the work of human intelligence, by which we transcend our individuality: but this intelligence is nevertheless itself a power of the human soul which is always the substantial form of an individual human body. I found a fascinating parallel here with Bill Kavanagh's account of the authentic *Catholica* arising from local churches but refusing to be limited by localisation itself (unlike the devil's caricature: the standardisation that belongs to the ethos of the market economy). For Aquinas, concepts, unlike sensations, are not the private property of individuals but do arise from individual material animals transcending their individuality and hence their materiality. As Aristotle knew, thoughts, unlike sensations, have no corporeal organ. Brains do not think; they are the co-ordinating centre of the structure of the nervous system which makes possible the sensual interpretation of our world, which is itself interpreted in the structure of symbols, language, which we do not inherit with our genes but create for ourselves in community.

Britain had, fairly recently, a prime minister who notoriously said, "There is no such thing as society; there are only individuals and their families." I will argue that there is a kind of objectivity to meaning just because there *is* such a thing as society and, moreover, that there is a symbiotic relationship between language and society; one cannot exist without the other. And both are essential to (of the essence of) being human. I shall claim that the sacraments which centre upon the Eucharist are the language which makes a certain "society" possible, and that it is this society that makes this sacramental language meaningful, and what makes *this* language distinct from others is that the society in question is the mystery of the People of God. Of course, anything that is actual is "of God", created and thus kept in being by the creative act of God, but the people of God are not simply God's creatures but the outcome of his personal convenantal love, the Holy Spirit, so that we are *children* of God sharing by grace in his own divine life. The sacramental language is the language granted to us in which this mystery is to be expressed and lived out in human and material terms.

The word "sacrament" is, like so many theological words, used *analogically* (as with "sin" and "love" and all the words we use to speak of the unknown God). The first and greatest sacrament is the culmination of scriptural revelation (in the perspective of *Hebrews*) in the Word made flesh, the humanity of *Christ*, the image of the invisible God. Secondly, we speak analogically of the *Church* as "sacrament", "a sign and instrument, that is, of communion with God and of unity amongst all humankind" (*Lumen Gentium 1*). The document of the Second Vatican Council from which these words come is in a medieval tradition which sees sacraments not simply as "outward signs of inward grace" but as taking in the whole sweep of salvation history, past, present and future, and sees this unity of humankind as something mainly for the future: "while people of the present day are drawn ever more closely together by social, technical and cultural bonds, it still remains for them to achieve full unity in Christ." That seems to me the ecclesiastical understatement of the century.

After the humanity of Christ and, then, the Community of the Church, the third analogical use of "sacrament" we use is when speaking in the plural, of the *"sacraments of the Church"*—Baptism, Eucharist, etc. My own view, which I do not have a chance to expound here, is that discussion of these has to be a discussion of the constitution and structure of the People of God, which is neither political nor invisibly "spiritual" but precisely *sacramentally* visible. But we do not have time for this. Sufficient to say that the Eucharist in my view, (which is not at all original), is the centre of the sacramental life and other sacraments are sacramental by their relationship to the Eucharist.

But, back to the objectivity of meaning. In order to understand this, we first need, I think, to distinguish clearly between *sense experience* and *understanding*. Aquinas said that to make this distinction was one of the great achievements of Aristotle; but since then the blight of empiricism, amongst other things, has badly obscured it. To elucidate it, I think we need to think first about animal life.

It seems to me characteristic of animals that, unlike lifeless things like bits of glass and computers and volcanic rocks, they have purposes and a point of view and they *interpret* and *evaluate* from their own point of view the world in which they live. They find bits of their world frightening or edible or pleasurable or sexually attractive … or whatever. Animals do not have to be taught to groom each other; lambs do not have to learn to run away from wolves. Moreover, they manifestly do some things willingly and some things, under coercion, unwillingly.

It was by way of Avicenna (Ibn Sina, the eleventh-century Persian philosopher) that the medieval Europeans learnt of what they called the "interior sense powers". These were, first the *sensus communis*, the power of coordinating the deliveries of the different exterior senses, to produce what in the early twentieth century we began to call the Gestalt as the meaningful object of sense experience. Secondly, there was the *imaginatio* or phantasma, the power of retaining such experience for future reference. Thirdly, was the *sensus aestimativus* (or *cogitativus*) that I have called the evaluative sense-power, by which the animal feels that something is dangerous or edible or whatever. Finally, there is the *sense-memory*, the awareness of time and temporality, the power of recalling experiences as past. In linguistic animals there is also a quite distinct power which is not a sense but the "intellectual memory", which is not concerned with time as such but is the power of *recall* by which what we have learnt and not forgotten is brought to mind when we are not at the moment thinking about it—like your address or the capital of Spain or Newton's second law.

So I want to argue that the sensuous bodily life that, broadly speaking, we share with non-linguistic animals, is primarily about finding *meaning* in the world. This *is* sense-experience: not simply being struck by some mythical "sense data", but being struck by the *significance* of surrounding things for the animal itself "from its own point of view". Such an experience gives rise to animal behaviour (if a bit of its world strikes an animal as edible it will tend to try to eat it). Not all such response is as simple as this. If, for example, a male animal perceives a fellow male of the species as threatening and aggressive, his response may be the performance of a ritual action of, say, submission, which will divert the other's aggression. Ritual behaviour amongst non-linguistic animals is extremely common in moments of crisis, both in danger situations and in courtship, and it is one of the features of behaviour that we should be careful *not* to confuse with language. The reason for this is that it is genetically determined by the animal's inherited DNA and quite as automatic as any other triggered response.

But in any case, every non-linguistic animal's response to its world is mediated by, and determined by, the meaning it discovers in it by its senses. What it *desires* to achieve or avoid (which is to say what it will *tend* to achieve or avoid) is conditioned by, indeed is *defined* by, its sensual interpretation of its world. Meaning can only be understood in terms of the larger notion of structure.

Meaning, in a perfectly general sense, is, I would maintain, always the role or place or function that some part of the structure has within that structure. What does it *mean* to be President of the United States? To answer this you have to give some account of the *structure* of U.S. government and society. What does "perhaps" *mean*? It is a word, an adverb, qualifying a statement to express possibility with uncertainty. (O.E.D.) You have thus placed "perhaps" within the *structure* of language in which it has a part to play.

Now consider seeing. It begins with light of some kind falling on the retina of the eye, in consequence of this, because the eye belongs to the structure of the bodily nervous system, certain things occur in the brain and, in consequence of *this*, certain tendencies may arise in the muscles of the animal's limbs and so on. The point of this is that the eye, because it belongs to the structure of the nervous system, is *relevant* to other parts of the animal's body. What happens in the eye is *meaningful* for the animal. It is this meaningfulness of the eye that we call "sight". The eye does not see; it is the whole animal that sees because of what has happened in the eye and elsewhere. The eye is an instrument of seeing (so the Greeks called it an "organ", which means instrument). Animals see and hear and feel because the behaviour of parts of them is relevant to the whole. We call it an *organic* whole.

The non-linguistic animal's interpretation of its world is expressed in its behaviour, and only in its behaviour. There is a superstitious view that the brain is what sees. This is quite false. The brain is the coordinator, the "nerve centre" of the nervous system (and even this is not true in all animals). The notion that the brain sees is only a degree less absurd than the notion that the brain understands or thinks. The brain is not even the organ of understanding but rather part of the sensitive infra-structure necessary for understanding.

So: the non-linguistic animal's interpretation and evaluation of its world is expressed in its behaviour and *only* in its *behaviour*. The linguistic animal's interpretation of its world is expressed also in *language*. So we must now turn to language and understanding.

The extraordinary thing about human animals is that besides the inherited, genetically supplied nervous system which not only is the structure that makes meaningful *sense-experience* possible, it also provides an (enormously more complex) brain structure which will serve as the necessary infra-structure of meaning that *we do not inherit but create for ourselves*, the structures of language. Nobody could have a gene for the Polish language, and if she could, Polish could not be a language.

As when we and our fellow animals *experience* our world we take it up into our inherited, more or less *genetically determined* bodily structures, so when we *understand* we take this experience up into our socially created structures of language. So our understanding, our use of language, requires sense-experience as *that which* we interpret and "comment on" but also because, in order to use the meanings we understand, we need what Aquinas calls the "*conversio ad phantasmata*": a reference back to the interior sense-power of "*imaginatio*" in order to recall and actually reflect upon what is latent in our intellectual memory but which needs bringing to mind. This selective recall of what we have in the intellectual memory is, for Aquinas, at the heart of the unique human capacity for free choice. The necessity for the *conversio ad phantasmata* shows us why what we have called the "bodily infra-structure" of human linguistic intellectual life is so important, and it is why, for example, brain-damage inhibits thinking. This is not, as I have said, because the brain is an organ of understanding, but because the brain is an important part of the "infra-structure" upon which human understanding depends.

To make a language is to take certain material things (noises, marks on paper or cuts in stone ... etc.) and use them not as tools for their causal efficacy, as we might a hammer or a sword, but as symbols, as having an externally imposed meaning, imposed by our *convention*. Of course, no amount of study of the *intrinsic* meaning (the *natural form*) of the material thing which happens to be used as a symbol will reveal what its *linguistic* meaning is. You have to go amongst the community who use it and share their life so that you will come to appreciate how it is to be used in accordance with their conventions.

That assertion demands a very important qualification. It is not true that it is only the *conventional* and not the *natural* properties of our symbols that matter in a language. The full complete and perfectly precise use of language is what we nowadays call poetry. In listening to or reading or writing a poem, we pay attention not only to what I shall call the conventional "dictionary meaning" of a word but also its sensual value, how we interpret it through our natural bodily nervous system, its rhythm and how it sounds and feels along the nerves. And this is not only true of the limited area *we* call poetry but also of normal human conversation. In fact to use language attending *only* to its dictionary meaning demands a special skill, but a very important one, for on it depends the development of all the scientific disciplines— indeed, it is largely this that defines our use of words like "scientific" and "logical". (But poetry is language trying to be bodily experience, as music is bodily experience trying to be language.)

It is when our language is stripped down to its dictionary meanings that we can confidently say that all human languages are intertranslatable, so that when we learn "our own" language we are not simply fitting into the customs of our tribe, but potentially hearing or speaking to the whole human race, past, present and to come. To understand a meaning at the human linguistic level is just to have a skill in using a symbol, let us call it a word. Now, there is an important difference between understanding a linguistic meaning and having a sensation, even though both are a matter of meaning, though at different levels. I can reasonably expect another member of my species to have roughly the same sensations as I have. It must be much the same for him or her as for me to be hungry or angry or frightened—if this were not so we could never learn the words "hunger", "anger" or whatever.

Now it is not so with understanding linguistic meanings: here it is necessary not simply that another should have *similar* meanings in mind; it is necessary that he or she should have *identical* meanings in mind. It is necessary that we should agree on at least the "dictionary meaning" of the words, otherwise we shall be at cross purposes.

Fortunately it is not difficult to resolve such misunderstanding because it is a feature of language that we can talk about talking. In our sensual interpretation this is not possible, or at least not in the same way. (The interior evaluative sense (the *sensus aestimativus*) come close to sensing a sense—as the alternative medieval name for it—*sensus cogitativus*—implies.)

Sensations remain my private property or yours. Thought, however, transcends my privacy. To repeat myself, in the creation of language we reach beyond our private material individuality to break into the non-individual, non-material sphere of linguistic meaning. This does not, of course, mean that we cease to be material animals, but we are the material animal which has a way of transcending its individuality so that the community it forms with others is something entirely new.

The human polis does not rest upon interacting self-interests—as Aristotle thought our international relations did—and Thatcherites thought all human community did. But the polis itself rests, as Aristotle thought, on philia (*Pol.* III.9). What distinguishes citizens from foreigners in the true polis is that our moral bonds with the foreigners are those of a particular kind of commercial justice, whereas what unites citizens is *philia*, friendship, which involves the capacity to transcend our individuality and our individual interests. And with this we are not far from "Greater love hath no man than that he lay down his life for his friend".

And here we come to the central meaning of the Eucharist. With the irony or paradox typical of the New Testament, it is a celebratory feast which is about a defeat and death. It is both about the world of sin and about the redemption of this world within, but from beyond, this world by grace. It is misunderstood if either of these is forgotten or played down. It is an *agape*, a love feast, but it is saying that love is best represented in our kind of world by an acceptance of death, indeed—an acceptance of murder. But this is not presented as a philosophical or sociological discovery. It is not presented as a doctrine at all. The festival celebrating liberation from slavery takes place under the shadow of the imminence of Calvary, and these irreconcilables like presence/absence cannot coexist on paper but only in a person, in the human person of Christ. Not in what he illustrates or what *he stands for* but in *himself*. That is why transubstantiation is right. The Christian Church as I see it does not first of all preach a doctrine—as Paul said, we preach "Christ crucified". Sure, over the centuries we have quite rightly developed doctrines, but these have been articulated to prevent misunderstandings, especially facile simplifications.

Like Karl Marx, Thomas Aquinas thought that the Christian religious cult belongs essentially to an age of alienation, or as he put it, of sin. And by the use of this word "sin" he indicates that the alienation is something deeper than anything Marx understood. For sin, for Thomas, was an option for some perceived good which, in the circumstances would be *incompatible* with *friendship*, *agape* with God, and that means alienation from the very roots of our existence and from our sharing in divinity. For Marx, religious cult was merely a symptom, certainly not a cause, of human alienation. It was neither the cause nor the cure, but simply "the painkiller of the people" giving an illusion of well-being. With the elimination of the market economy, which has to treat human beings as commodities, religion, Marx thought, would simply fade away much as being greedy for sweets fades away as we grow up. Aquinas would have seen this as too optimistic; his thought is more complex. He sees the sacramental order as essentially God's word in our symbolic linguistic mode but, like Paul, he sees it also as a possible occasion of sin. In the famous passage from 1 Cor. 11, Paul tells them roundly:

> When you come together it is not for the better but for the worse. For in the first place, when you assemble as a church, I hear that there are divisions among you ... When you meet together it is not the Lord's supper that you eat. For in eating, each one goes ahead with his own meal and one is hungry while another is intoxicated ... do you despise the church of God and humiliate those who have nothing?

and Paul goes on

> It was on the night he was *betrayed* that the Lord Jesus took bread and having given thanks broke it and said "this is my body". (my emphasis)

Like the historical death of Christ, the sacramental commemoration (and even celebration) of it takes place in a world of sin.

A church which is not a challenge to the values of such a world is one which, as Paul says, "does not discern the body", but the body is there to be "discerned" and they are "profaning the body and blood of the Lord" which is there to be profaned. For the Eucharist is the Word of God and not the word of man. We *make*, as well as *being made by* our human language, but we do not make the meaning of the Eucharist; if it is anything of interest it is the Word of God and thus a word of power: the creative word that says "light be"—and there was light. The re-creative word says "this is my body and my blood"—and so it is. What the bread and wine have become is clearly not an icon, picture, reminder of Christ but Christ himself, and him crucified, the only one who can reconcile the opposites, who can bring life out of death.

A church which celebrates the Eucharist while ignoring what we should nowadays call "the fundamental option for the poor" is "eating and drinking judgement upon herself", as Aquinas thought; it is using the language of God to tell a lie.

Medieval Eucharistic theology distinguished three levels of meaning in the Eucharistic language. There was what was simply a sign *sacramentum tantum*, visible to anyone, a ritual meal, like a party which could be studied as well by atheist anthropologists as by Christians. This sign, however, is a God-spoken word which reveals itself to our faith at two levels. First there is the significance for *this* world of both grace and sin, this still-alienated world. The sign is that of the Church witnessing to this world and challenging it with the revelation of the gospel of love. This the medievals called the "*res et sacramentum*". This "*res*" means what is signified by a sign; "*sacramentum*" means a sign itself. So at this level of meaning we have what is signified by the ritual meal, our human word of friendship. For now it signifies and thus realises the incarnate Word of God at the moment of his supreme expression of love for us (what John calls his "hour" and his "lifting up") when his body is broken in death (as symbolised by the separation of body and blood). Here he reveals his loving and obedient faithfulness to his mission from the Father, the mission to be the first totally human being, living by love, by transcending his individual self and self-interest and thereby being totally vulnerable, not seeking to evade or resist whatever his brothers and sisters would do to him. It was this loving acceptance of defeat at our hands that won for this first really human being his defeat of death and our being given a sharing in such resurrection.

This real presence, then, of the incarnate Word of God in his meaning of victory-through-accepted-defeat for himself and for us, is the *res*, the thing directly signified by our Eucharistic token meal. But this *res*, the sacramentally real presence of the body of Christ, is also itself a sign, a *sacramentum*, of a deeper *res*, a deeper reality, indeed the deepest reality.

The sacramental order of this world points towards and partially realises a further third level of meaning, the ultimate mystery that is signified-and-not-a-sign of anything deeper (*res tantum*). This is the *agape*, the *caritas*, the love which is the Godhead. The liturgy of the Eucharist and its attendant sacraments, our life in the Church, is itself a sacramental sign and realisation of our life in the Kingdom.

Then there will be no more Eucharist, no more sacramental religion, no more faith or hope; all this will wither away, there will be simply the unimaginable human living out of love which is the Spirit of God in eternity.

THE DARKNESS OF GOD
AND THE LIGHT OF CHRIST:
NEGATIVE THEOLOGY AND
EUCHARISTIC PRESENCE

DENYS TURNER

I know that we are all apophatic theologians now, mystery is back in theological business and we are reassured by our knowledge that we do not know what God is. I do not suppose that this is *merely* a fashion, though I wonder how much of it is just that; and in any case, though there are plenty who will acknowledge the claims of "negative theology" in what, it is thought, is its own sphere—located safely in the territory of "the mystical"—I do not see a great deal of evidence that this passion for "unknowing" and "deconstruction" has much tendency to realise its potential across the whole theological field. No more than at any time previously within the period of "modern theology" is there much acknowledgement of the need to do *all* theology under the constraint of this apophatic parsimony, this restraint of speech and of knowledge. Much in recent theology, in comparativist and historiographical scholarship, serves to reinforce a notion of a distinct territory marked out by the name "mysticism", which is the proper homeland of the apophatic, where disruption and subversion of speech can go its riotous way untrammelled, on condition that, thus confined, its capacity for generalised theological mayhem is thereby contained.

My own academic experience reinforces this impression with another, distinctly Christian, anxiety. I can guarantee nowadays that whenever I read a paper on some account of the "apophatic", among the first participants in the following discussion will be someone who wonders how I, or the authority I have been expounding, will, within all this negativity and unknowing of God, take account of the positive revelation of God in Jesus

Denys Turner
Department of Theology, University of Birmingham, Birmingham B15 2TT, UK

Christ. For surely, it is said, Christ is the *visibility* of the Godhead, the source of all theological affirmativeness; so that, as it were, whatever license may or must be given to the apophatic in the meantime, in the end is the Word as it was in the beginning, therefore in the end there is speech, not silence. Occasionally I get as an elaboration of this a connected thought—it is an ancient doubt which is drawn on here, stretching back into the earliest years of Christian intellectual history—that "negative theology" is really but an alien import into Christian theology, a concession made to pagan, and especially neo-platonic sources, mainly to Plotinus and Proclus. Then a whole cluster of thoughts falls into a pattern of complex linkages: that negative theology equals "mysticism", that "mysticism" equals platonism, and that theologies which mix Christian revelation with platonic mysticism produce an unacceptable, distorting theological hybrid, unrecognisable in the thorough-bred purity of a gospel Christianity.

Stock questions get stock answers on these occasions. Until recently I would respond on behalf of the medieval traditions by pointing to a counter-example in Bonaventure's *Itinerarium Mentis in Deum*.[1] Here, I would say, we find a complex interweaving of at least three strands of theological tradition. First, his own Franciscan piety and devotion, which places centrally within Christian thought and practice the human nature of Christ, but very particularly the passion of Christ. Secondly, a rampantly affirmative theology of exemplarism, in which, in classically medieval style, he constructs a hierarchy of "contemplations" of God, beginning from the lowest *vestigia* in material objects, upwards and inwards to our perception of them, through the *imagines* of God in the human soul, especially in its highest powers, further "upwards" and beyond them to "contemplations" through the highest concepts of God, "existence" and "goodness". In just such an ascending hierarchy constructed in the first six chapters of the *Itinerarium* does Bonaventure construe the whole universe as the "book of creation" in which its author is spoken and revealed; all of which theological affirmativeness is resumed in the human nature of Christ, only there no longer is it merely the passive "Book of Creation" in which the Godhead can be read, but now the "Book of Life", who actively works our redemption and salvation.

But in the transition from the first six chapters of the *Itinerarium* to the seventh Bonaventure effects, thirdly, a powerfully subversive theological *transitus*, from all the affirmativeness with which creation in one way, and Christ in another, speak God, to a thoroughgoing negative theology. For beyond the knowing of God is the unknowing of God; nor is this "unknowing" merely "beyond": through the increasing intensity and complexity of its internal contradictoriness this knowing *leads to* the unknowing. As one might say, the very superfluity of the affirmativeness sustained by the books of Creation and of Life collapses into the silence of the apophatic: and chapter seven consists in little but a string of quotations from the more apophatic sayings of the *Mystical Theology* of the Pseudo-Dionysius. But the organising symbolism of that theological *transitus* from the visibility of the Godhead in Christ to the unknowability of the Godhead brings Bonaventure back to his Franciscan starting point; for that *transitus* is also effected through Christ—more to the point, through the passion and death of Christ. For in that catastrophe of destruction, in which the humanity of Christ is brought low, is all the affirmative capacity of speech subverted: thus it is that through the drama of Christ's life on the one hand and death on the other, through the recapitulation of the symbolic weight and density of creation in this human nature on the one hand, and its destruction on the Cross on the other, is the complex interplay of affirmative and negative fused and concretely realised. In Christ, therefore, is there not only the visibility of the Godhead, but also the invisibility: if Christ is the Way, Christ is, in short, our access to the *un*-knowability of God, not so as ultimately to know it, but so as to be brought into participation with the *Deus absconditus* precisely as *unknown*. Then, finally, I slip in a little reference to Thomas, by way of reassurance to those unconfident of Bonaventure's authority: "In this life what God is is unknown to us [even] by the revelation of grace; and so [by grace] we are joined to him as to something unknown".[2]

Now all this did for the purposes, except for one thing. The structure of Bonaventure's *Itinerarium* is in one respect very misleading, and works to the opposite effect that I call on him to achieve. I suppose it is a consequence of the medieval passion for hierarchical structures of thought—I mean, the obsession with theological construction modelled on the metaphor of ladders of ascent—that as Bonaventure sets out his argument in the *Itinerarium*, you would have the impression that affirmation and negation are successive theological moments, that, as it were, you have first to climb the ladder of affirmation only to throw it away into the gulf of unknowing after you have reached the top. First, we unproblematically affirm; then, as if in a distinct theological act, differently and separately motivated, we deny. I suppose the consequence is not *as such* to suggest—though I have the impression that many a modern takes this view anyway—that affirmative and negative theologies are alternative theological strategies, even optional strategies, but that at the very least they are *successive* strategies. In any case, Bonaventure's metaphorically generated structure of exposition would certainly appear to imply that affirmation and negation are theologically linked not so as to interpenetrate at every level of theological discourse, but as hierarchically ranked. It is as if there is an ascending scale of affirmativeness which is rounded off with the top doh of negativity—even, heaven help us, of "mysticism".

But then, there is an equally marked tendency in late medieval thought to construe the hierarchy to the opposite effect as far as ranking order goes, even if with the same outcome of successiveness. In the fifteenth century, a resolute follower of the Pseudo-Dionysius, Denys the Carthusian, is as "apophatic" a theologian as you might wish, but is quite sure that you could not let the silence of negation have the last word. For, when all our denials of God are said and done, he comments, "there is still a remainder of affirmation and positive meaning which is implied by and presupposed to [those denials]".[3] Well, you might at least admit the problem which leads Denys to say such a thing. How, if there is no theological discourse at least *ultimately* untroubled by the destabilisations of the negative, will it be possible to distinguish the negative theologian from the atheist—for sure, there must be some way, he seems to think, of distinguishing between the atheist, who will not climb the ladder at all because he says there isn't one, and the theist, who insists that it must be climbed if only to throw it away. Both will conclude with Thomas that "it is better to say that God does not exist" but they will mean the opposite: and for Denys, the only grounds on which his conviction of this negativity will be distinguishable from the atheist's, is if, *in the end*, the ladder props up on a stable residue of affirmation.

But whichever you think this ascending scale ends in, affirmation or negation, the common mistake—as I should think it to be—is in the shared misconstrual of the relationship between the moments of affirmation and the moments of negation; for that relationship structures theological utterance at every stage: indeed, it is this interplay of negativity and affirmation which structures all theological discourse *precisely as theological*. You can put this point in all sorts of ways, of which this is just one: if, in a quite general way, theology will be characterised as "mystical" by its acknowledgment of the apophatic; and if you have already identified the apophatic as some distinct strategy of negation spinning off into disorderly, if no doubt terribly exciting, post-thought, post-experience or post-speech at the end of your orderly theological knowing; then you will, naturally, conclude that the "mystical" is to be identified as some distinct strategy of thought, or experience, or discourse—distinct, that is to say, from the ordinary business of theological thought, experience or speech, a sort of "after-*non*-thought", an "after-*non*-word", an appendix of experientially blank pages. In post-medieval times— and the late modern theories of William James and a host of contemporary theologians and anthropologists reinforce just this notion—this is exactly how the "mystical" is construed by so many today—as ineffable *experience*.

But here is another way of putting it. Many students of the medieval "mysticisms" broadly categorise them into "apophatic" and "cataphatic" forms. Eschewing altogether the question of how they come to be called "mysticisms" in the first place, Bernard of Clairvaux is obviously going to have to be a "cataphatic" mystic on the strength of the floridly erotic affirmativeness of his *Sermons on the Song of Songs*; so too is Julian of Norwich, whose exuberance of affirmative metaphor is unrivalled in the medieval period even by Bernard. But then by contrast, the *Cloud of Unknowing* will have to be typically "apophatic", characterised as that text is by "unknowings" and "nothings", "nowhere's" and "darknesses"; so too Eckhart, for his "deserts", "abysses" and "no why's, no whatnesses and no things". Well indeed, but since when was a negative metaphor not a metaphor? Since when was the preference for negative metaphors any less or more a vote of confidence in speech than the preference for affirmative? The fact is that Julian's riotous prolixity of affirmative metaphor is no less apophatic than the *Cloud's* astringency; nor is the language of the *Cloud* any the less dense of metaphor than is Julian's. Though the metaphors differ and the apophatic strategies approach from different directions, they converge in a common perception that all language of God fails all the way along the line (or up the ladder): and in fact, this sense of the simultaneous necessity and deficiency of language is in some way exhibited more sharply in Julian's habit of constructing metaphors which subvert themselves in the act of their very utterance; as when she shatters the imageries of gender precisely in the exploitation of their full potential: "In our *Mother* Christ," she says, "we grow and develop; in *his* mercy *he* reforms and restores us".[4]

So, then, speaking now quite generally, if the "mystical" is in some way tied up with the moment of theological negation, and if, on an adequate account of the apophatic dimension of theological discourse, it has to be understood as determinative of that discourse as *mystical in principle and as such*; then this can be so only insofar as we have abandoned a whole raft of accounts of the relations between the "apophatic" and the "cataphatic". For we are diverted from this account insofar as we suppose that there is some such *discourse* as "apophatic discourse". The apophatic is not given in some negative vocabulary which takes over from the affirmative when we get a mystical urge; it is not engaged in some chasing game with the affirmative up the ladder of speech about God, thus at the top either to win or lose out to the affirmative. Rather it is that the tensions between affirmation and negation within all theological speech are, precisely, what determine it to be theological speech, and to be, in the only worthwhile sense of the term, "mystical". Moreover, those tensions are finally unresolvable: the necessity of our linguistic resources of theology can never supply their deficiency; nor can the perception of their deficiency ever reduce the necessity for them. We know both the need for, and the failure of, theological talk simultaneously in the one act of its utterance; we both say and unsay in the same theological word. And if these constraints of thought and speech hold for theology generally, they will hold *a fortiori* for any account of Eucharistic presence, whether formally theological or materially realised in liturgical or architectural symbolisms.

II

In this last connection, in the once medieval Catholic, now Calvinist-maintained Cathedral at Bern in Switzerland, one is confronted by a visibly Calvinist architectural revision. Altars are stripped, niches empty, walls whitewashed, the glass plain, the orientation is reversed, the stalls facing

West not East. The effect is dramatic, not merely because of the powerful but *relative* impact—relative, that is to expectations which derive from our historical knowledge of what is missing, its former ornateness of iconography, lurid colour schemes, its architectural orientation towards a high-altar; for the overwhelming sense of "absence" is reinforced by the more absolute and architecturally organic effect of the gothic style itself, which, I suppose, could be said to give priority to the engineering and organisation of space rather than to the articulation of solid mass. Bern Cathedral is, one might say, a place of absence, indeed a holy place of absence or a place which "sacralises" absence, a place fit for a community witnessing to absence. It "speaks" absence as a theological—and still to some degree as a theological-polemical—and liturgical statement.

Now turn history back to, say, the year 1500. Reconstruct the former condition of the Cathedral, fill its niches with statues of saints, the virgin Mary, Christ, the windows with glass representing Moses and the prophets in the north transept, the apostles in the south, the Ascension in the west end and the Resurrection in the east; daub the walls with colour and picture, and above all refocus the building upon an elaborate triptych behind which stands an ornate and elevated tabernacle at the east end, in short re-equip the Cathedral with all that, I guess, was stripped from it forty years later. Then ask for the theological-liturgical statement which in that condition the appointments of the Cathedral make. Well, it is obvious, is it not? Here you have a statement of "holy presence", a fullness of theological affirmation, a space filled with presence and with a community *in* that presence.

And is it not obvious in what the contrast between the present condition of the church and its former state consists? Now it is architecturally apophatic, then it was cataphatic; now it witnesses to a Zwinglian theology of Eucharistic absence, then to a Catholic theology of Eucharistic presence. Well, yes, these things *are* obvious. Indeed, I think they are even, in a way, true, so let us spell them out a little more fully.

Return then to the cathedral in 1500. It is full. But what it is full of is sign. Therefore, of course, you might say, on a certain account of signs with which I shall say I am unhappy, that it is full of absence. I once facetiously explained to a student that you could account for the difference between the Catholic and the Protestant view of the presence of Christ in the Eucharist by analogy with a conference meal-ticket which he had been showing me. The Protestant, I said, thinks that the meal-ticket represents the meal you can purchase by means of it; the Catholic eats the meal-ticket thinking that that's what you are getting for lunch. Of course, this is a travesty of the difference, indeed a common sixteenth century Protestant travesty of it, for this version of what Catholics believe entirely ignores what Catholic theology had always been fully aware of, namely the distinction between the material reality of the signifier and the formal character of the sign precisely as signifying. And of course in that formal character the sign signifies the body and blood of Christ precisely insofar as they are "absent", where "absence" is defined by contrast with the material presence of the sign itself; and so, insofar as by signifying the body and blood of Christ the appearances of bread and wine make them present in one way, they do so only insofar as in another, that is, in the manner in which the sign itself is present, they are absent.

Which is why Zwingli is, of course, right, and in agreement with Thomas Aquinas on this single point of convergence, when he says that Christ cannot be present *in* the Eucharist in the way in which the sign itself is present in its material reality. And Thomas and Zwingli agree on this notwithstanding the difference that for Thomas the bread and wine *become* the body and blood of Christ which they signify, whereas for Zwingli they only signify the body and blood of Christ. For both, however, the material sign—the bread and wine—are present in a time and place, here in Bern in 1500. And if Christ is anywhere locally in 1500 it is not, as Thomas agrees, where the bread and wine are in Bern in 1500. For Christ has risen and is ascended into heaven, seated at the right hand of the Father.[5] In fact, Christ is absent in the Eucharist along two dimensions of time: he is absent in respect of his historical existence pre-mortem and he is absent as he will be for us in the beatific vision in heaven. If, therefore, the Eucharist makes Christ present by signifying, it does so only on a double condition of the absence of what is signified: the Eucharist is time past and time future insofar as they can be present in the present, as it were in a kind of "nostalgia for the future".

Now for Zwingli all you need to say about the presence of Christ in the Eucharist is that he is there in the sign only; and all you need to say about the absence of Christ is that Christ's not being there is in the Eucharist's character *as a sign*. For Thomas the position appears to be quite different and fraught with much tougher problems, and for reasons which show that his agreement with Zwingli about the meaning of "absence" is at best super-ficial. Thomas wants to say that Christ is really present, but *also* absent. But, whereas Zwingli thinks this absence simply follows from the nature of a sign as such, I rather doubt if Thomas maintained that view of signs at all. On the other hand, for him sacramental signs constitute a set of special cases, in which the conditions of absence follow not as such from the *nature of signs* but from the nature of *a sacrament*, and in the very special case of the Eucharist the necessity of Christ's absence does not *exclude* the real presence of Christ, but rather lays down conditions for the description of that real presence. For Thomas, in other words, if you are going to say that Christ is really present in the Eucharist, your account of the word "real" is going to have to meet at least the following conditions: Christ is not there as he was in his historical pre-mortem existence; Christ is not there as, in the kingdom, he will be seen by us at the right hand of the Father; yet the Christ who is there is numerically one and the same Christ as he who walked the shores of lake Galilee and is now at the right hand of the Father. From this it follows that if Christ is really present in the Eucharist then he will have to be present in the Eucharist in his body. For no sense of Christ's presence which evacuates it of bodiliness will have the force of being "real", since numerical identity of persons requires sameness of body. Hence, to capture the force of the word "real" as said of Christ's presence in the Eucharist, we will have to say that he is present in his body but neither as known to Peter and James and John two thousand years ago, nor as they now know him in his and their condition as raised. So the question for Thomas is not whether Christ is present in the Eucharist as in a sign *as opposed to* his being present there "really"; it is, rather that, given that Christ is present in the Eucharist as in a sign, how can we find a sense for the word "real" which is consistent with the Eucharist's eschatological temporality? And this is because the real problem for Thomas' account of the Eucharist is the problem of how the future—the kingdom of our communication with the risen Christ—can be present now in our fallen and failing powers of bodily communication.

Zwingli, on the other hand, thinks that he has no such problem, nor that any Christian ought to have it. But in this he appears to be mistaken. For turn again to the stripped-down cathedral of 1535. Here the relations of "presence" and "absence" are worked out along altogether different lines. Whereas in 1500 the repleteness of signs works its power of signifying only in the medium, as it were, of the absence of what is signified, in 1535 it is absence which is the very sign itself. Now emptiness of sign *is* the sign, its emptiness in no way diminishing the cathedral's character of being a sign, for negative signs, for all their negativity, are still signs. Note that the 1535 cathedral can effect its negative signification only if it contains *no signs at all*. It could not do its work of signifying absence if there were a single sign *in* the cathedral, for the incomplete emptiness would simply have the effect of focusing attention upon the signifying power of that one sign: the cathedral would then be full of that single sign. As a matter of fact, the cathedral *is* possessed of one sign which draws attention to itself in that way, but that sign only reinforces the sense of absence, for it is itself empty, being a vacant cross. So here too the cathedral is "full of sign", now making "absence" present whereas before it made "presence" absent.

Hence, if the 1535 condition of things signifies by means of absence, if, to repeat, it is absence which is the sign, that absence can possess no less the materiality of a sign than does the fullness of sign in 1500. It may be a mistake to eat the meal-ticket thinking it is the meal; but if that is the case it is exactly the same mistake to identify the physical, material absences of Zwingli's cathedral with the absence of Christ which they signify. For if our analogy between the two conditions of the cathedral and the relations between affirmative and negative theology holds in general it holds very particularly here. Just as affirmative and negative metaphors are equally metaphors; just as affirmation and negation are equally *language*; just as the "mystical" is characterised by its transcendence of both affirmation and negation, so too are the signs of presence and the signs of absence equally *signs*. Hence, if it is possible materialistically to displace the signified by the reification of the sign in the one case, so it is possible in the other. In short, "absence" as a sign is but a material state of affairs—specifically, an architectural and decorative state of affairs—which signifies only on condition of the absence of what it signifies. So Zwingli's empty cathedral is not *itself* the absence of Christ which it signifies, but is only the sign of it, making that absence present only on the condition that it is not the thing itself.

And this seems to be important. Zwingli seems to think that he can overthrow the arguments of the papists simply by appeal to the bodily absence of Christ since the Ascension. Constantly in his polemic *On the Lord's Supper*[6] he appeals to John 16:5–11, where Jesus tells his disciples that it is to their advantage that he go away, "for if I do not go away the Counsellor will not come to you" (John 16:7). So, Zwingli comments,

> if he has gone away, if he has left the world, then either the Creed is unfaithful to the word of Christ, which is impossible (for it affirms that he will be with us always) or else the body and blood of Christ cannot be present in the sacrament.[7]

So, for Zwingli, what is present is the *sign* of absence, a presence of Christ in the sign, on condition that Christ is not present in body and blood. But, to repeat, a negative sign, signifying absence, is not itself the absence it signifies. To maintain that would be to maintain that the meal-ticket is the meal, for again, on his account signs signify only in the absence of what they signify. And what holds for signs in general must hold for negative signs as well. For the sign of absence to make that absence present Zwingli needs, as much as Thomas needs, a force for the word "real" such that the Eucharist can be said to "realise" what it signifies consistently with its doing so *as sign*. And yet on his own account he cannot have one. For his starting point is an account of sign such that the presence of a thing in a sign *excludes* its being present as "real"—a word the force of which Zwingli, like the Catholics, takes to mean "in his body". Thus he says:

> A sacrament is the sign of a holy thing. When I say: 'the sacrament of the Lord's body', I am simply referring to that bread which is the symbol of the body of Christ who was put to death for our sakes ... But the very body of Christ is the body which is seated at the right hand of God, and the sacrament of his body is the bread and the sacrament of his blood is the wine ... Now the sign and the thing signified cannot be one and the same. Therefore the sacrament of the body of Christ cannot be the body itself.[8]

To which it seems enough simply to reply: if we cannot, in the fallen condition of our bodiliness enter fully into communication with the presence of the absent, because raised, person of Jesus, then neither can we enter fully into communication with that absence. For as we cannot yet know that kingdom which one day we will see and fully enjoy, so neither can we have any grasp of how far we fall short of communicating with it. We fail even in our calculation of the degree to which our Eucharistic communication fails. Hence, if there is a problem about how Christ is present in the Eucharistic sign there must equally be a problem of accounting for how that absence is present within it; and that problem is not to be resolved on any account of the nature of signs, but only on some account of the relationship between the apophatic and the cataphatic, the relationship being itself defined only under the constraint of the eschatological.

III

Now what seems to me to be missing from Zwingli's account of Eucharistic absence is its theological source. What the Eucharist realises, or makes present, is the future, the kingdom. It does so necessarily under conditions of absence, for the kingdom, as such, is not yet with us; necessarily, therefore, insofar as it is present among us, it is so as anticipated, as not yet; therefore also as absent. And this absence of Christ, to which the Eucharist gives witness, is, we might say, constitutive of the Eucharist precisely as *sacrament*, for the character of the Eucharist as sacrament both derives from and constitutes the very nature of the Christian historical reality. The Christian times just are the times "between", when Christ is present to the Church in the mode of absence, but for all that really; in his body, but not as it was when Jesus was among us as the historical individual 2000 years ago—more present than that—nor yet as it will be after our own resurrection—less present than that. They are those times which are constituted by two foundational facts, namely that Jesus has been raised and that we have not. If, therefore, Jesus will always be with us, present, it can only be as he who is raised can be present to those who have not been raised—and being raised and not being raised are conditions of embodiment. Hence, if we are to say *how* Christ is present in the Eucharist, we have to say, as McCabe tells us, that "he is present in his body". But if we ask, "How is Christ's body present in the Eucharist?", we can give an answer for which we have only a name and a set of constraints, of presence and absence, on that name's meaning: Christ's body is present "sacramentally".[9] The position theologically is rather like that common in scientific explanation, when we know what needs to be explained, we know therefore what conditions an explanation will have to meet to explain it, but otherwise know nothing of what it is that does explain it: we can give a name to it, as nineteenth century scientists did to the virus, long before any viruses had been observed. So too here: we know what we are theologically constrained to say about the presence of Christ in the Eucharist and we have the name for that presence—it is "sacramental"—but we cannot know what we mean by the word, for it is and must be utter mystery.

I think what follows from this is that if we are to get some sort of Christian ontology of "presence"—that is to say, some account of how the world is shaped and formed by the presence of Christ to it—this will be possible only insofar as we can provide with it some kind of Christian account of that failed communication which is our consort with the Father through Jesus, in other words, we need some account of that partial and inadequate presence among us of the future kingdom—the other name for which is "grace". You might say that this requires a sort of ontology of absence, a way of finding a sense for the expression "the *real absence* of Christ". But I prefer to say that what is really needed here is an adequate account of what we call an "apophatic theology" of the Eucharist, a notable oxymoron, you will observe, at least etymologically. For theology, I take it, means something like "speech about God". Whereas "apophatic" means something more like "the failure of speech", so that the conjunction yields "that speech about God which is the failure of speech". And that, as it seems adequately to capture the whole tendency of theology as such, also seems to meet the need we are encountering here, epistemologically, if we are to capture the full force of what we mean by Eucharistic presence. For if there is a sense in which the Eucharist is that divine communication of the risen kingdom which is given to us in our condition of not yet being raised, then we can enter into that communication only on the condition of its ultimate failure; and on the further condition of our acknowledgement of its failure. So that in the Eucharist we are sharing in a "failed communication" *precisely as* failing.

Now Zwingli's account of Eucharistic absence does not capture the full theological force of this sacramental absence and this, I suspect, is because he has got his absence in the wrong place. He has his absence placed not, that is to say, in the theological character of the Eucharist itself, but in what he, wrongly as I believe, thinks of as the nature of sign as such. Consequently he is caught in a double polarisation, which, we might somewhat impertinently say, "overthroweth the nature of a sacrament", as the Thirty Nine Articles put it: that between "real presence" and "presence as a sign", and that between "present in the body" and "present as a sign". For that "absence" is a modality of the risen Christ's presence in the world; neither is adequately grasped except through the other, for it is a present-absence and an absent-presence. We can no more describe that presence without the modality of absence, and vice-versa, than we can affirm without denying or deny without affirming anything of God. The "real" is, as it were, constituted by that dialectic: Christ is not absent *really* in order to be present *in a sign*, as Zwingli would have it; nor is it much more adequate to say, as Trent in an early draft decree came near to saying, that Christ is not present *merely* in the sign, but *rather* "really"[10]—as if, in addition to being present in the sign, you had to bolt on some other sense of the word "real" to get at what is signified. For it is by means alone of the sign that Christ is really present, communicated to us: the sign becomes, really, the body and blood of Christ and being present thus in the sign, and so by means of absence, is *how* Christ is really present. It is in the nature of human communication that it is bodily. And it is in the nature of unraised bodies in which we communicate, that the communication of the risen body of Christ should also fail of presence; but it is not in the nature of either that this presence/absence should fail of *reality*.

IV

Which brings me to the issue of sacramental efficacy. Since the twelfth century it has commonly been said to be in the nature of a sacrament to "effect what it signifies". And while I have no quibble with this formula as such, I have to say that, largely because of post medieval and distinctly empiricist notions of causality, it is now a highly misleading formula. For these reasons.

I have suggested that we ought to distinguish between the formal character of a sign in virtue of which it signifies and its material existence as an event or thing in the world. Now I propose to abuse a famous distinction of J. L. Austin's between "illocutionary" and "perlocutionary" speech acts so as to distinguish, in analogous fashion, between what one might call the formal and material efficacy of a performative utterance, between what you are doing *in* saying something—for example, promising in uttering the words "I promise"—and what you are doing *by means of* saying it—for example, misleading the promisee when you have no intention of carrying the promise out.[11] We might, even more generally, distinguish between what it is that your words effect in virtue of what they mean and what it is that your act of saying those words effects in virtue of being uttered. This distinction is easiest to see in the case of what we might call "performative contradictions", where the two fall apart: arguing at tedious length in favour of maximum participation in the seminar means one thing which the prolixity of your saying it inhibits; reading the Riot Act, as in 1922 the British army officer did to a peaceful assembly of striking Welsh miners, means: "behave in an orderly fashion, or else", but the intended (and actual) effect was to provoke the riotous behaviour it prohibits, thus to justify employing the force the Act then permits; or, more recently, creating racial conflict in the manner of the late British member of Parliament, Enoch Powell, by means of lurid warnings against its dangers; these are all cases in which people refute what they are saying by the act of saying. They say one thing: but what their saying of it does says the opposite.

Now this last formula may need a little explanation. You might balk at the notion of an utterance being "contradicted by" its being uttered, since only meanings can be in relations of contradiction with one another, not actions with meanings. But the notion is not after all so problematic. We are, since Austin, accustomed to the notion of a performative utterance. We ought to be as used, since Wittgenstein, to the notion of an uttering performance, that is to say, of an action's bearing meaning. For sure, we all know that actions "speak", and, obviously, utterings are actions. There ought therefore to be little difficulty with the notion that utterances not only utter what the words uttered say, but also, being actions, can speak *qua performances*. That being so, there ought to be no difficulty in the analysis of the recursively contradictory behaviour say, of the parent who smacks the child in order to teach her not to solve problems by means of violence.

Now rituals and liturgies are, *par excellence*, complex behaviours constituted by their interactions of performative utterances and uttering performances. Every liturgical action gets it *rationale* from what it means, which is to say, every liturgical action is a sign; and the central utterances of a Eucharistic liturgy are performative utterances: they are signs, as theologians have said since the twelfth century, "which effect what they signify", they *do* what they *say*. The utterance "I baptise you ..." *baptises*; the priest's saying "This is my body" over what appears to be bread makes "this" *to be* the body of Christ.

These distinctions are, at least theoretically, fairly clear. All the same, there lies in them a source of very common confusion. I have suggested that Austin's distinction between an "illocutionary" and a "perlocutionary" speech act roughly corresponds with my distinction between what an *utterance* effects by virtue of its meaning and what *the action of uttering* effects by virtue of that action's meaning. There is, of course, a distinction between my uttering the words "I promise ...", which, *by virtue of the meaning of the utterance* enacts a promise, and the *effect which flows from* my uttering it, for example, your being persuaded that I mean what I say. An illocutionary act performs what it says by virtue of what the words mean; the words of a promise do not *cause* a promise to be made, they *are* a promise made. On the other hand, a perlocutionary effect is *caused* by an utterance; by promising I have caused you to have confidence in my word. Now there are many who confuse the two, and I suspect that Zwingli is one such. But then, I suspect that many contemporary Catholics are no less confused.

For the *effects* of a liturgy's system of signs being enacted are not to be confused with what those signs realise *as sacramental signs*. For Aquinas, the efficacy of a sacrament is guaranteed by God and is brought about, in the sign, by God alone. But God does not guarantee, for any ritual whatever, that the empirical effects it gives rise to as perlocution are just those which, as sacramental sign, the ritual act signifies and effects.

Let me give a somewhat stereotyped, if not entirely fanciful, example, which may serve to illustrate, by analogy, some of the complexity with which illocutionary and perlocutionary forces interact with one another. Let us suppose a preacher delivering his sermon, as it were, from the height of his authoritarian pulpit, on the equality of all the people of God. Now we should not, on the strength of the distinction I have made between the formal message of a speech act and the perlocutionary message of its being uttered,

analyse these elements into separate, unrelated factors, the egalitarian communication and the fact that, as it happens, it is delivered from an authoritarian pulpit. For the point about authoritarian pulpits is that they are
already sermons: as I said, actions also speak, as does this pulpit, which
communicates quite effectively enough within the words of the egalitarian
sermon. We might suppose it is adequate to say that the pulpit is but part
of the *materiality* of the preacher's act of saying, as if thereby to suggest that
it can play no part in the total communicative act. But this would be to
misdescribe the distinction. For the pulpit communicates too, for it both
internalises and exhibits the character of the preacher's relationship with the
congregation, and the significance of that materiality practices its own
hermeneutic upon the explicit formal meanings of the preacher's words.
Hence those words become the bearer of a condensation of conflicting meanings which, precisely insofar as it lies outside the intended communication
of the preacher, exists independently of those intentions, while at the same
time subverting them. The total result is a social reality constructed upon the
contradictoriness internal to the communicative act.

For it is in the facts of this contradiction that the members of the worship-
ping community are socialised. They perceive their relationship to the act of
worship via the condensation of contradictory meanings, for at one level they
attend, perhaps with approval, to the egalitarian message of the preacher
and *in so doing* they reciprocate the authoritarianism of his act of saying it.
Consequently, the preacher and the congregation enact a relationship constituted by the contradiction in which they are jointly socialised. Thus as
they live out their relationship with the egalitarianism of the preacher's
message through the authoritarian structures of its communication, so they
live out their relationships with the authoritarianism of those structures
through mystified categories of egalitarianism. In short, what such rituals
effect is a rupture between what the ritual signifies and what it effects. And
when a ritual effects this rupture as a routine, when, in other words, it social-
ises the participants in this rupturing, then we can say that such rituals have
the character which Marxists, when there usefully were any to own the
terminology, used to call "ideological". In more theological terms we can also
say that they parody the sacramental character which they are supposed to
exhibit. For they are rituals whose effects *contradict* what they signify: thus
do the participants, as Paul says, "eat and drink judgment on themselves"
(1 Cor. 11:29).

Now these phenomena of bastard liturgies all have to do with the perlocutionary effects of the enactment of liturgical signs, in other words with
what, as perlocutions, the signs effect under certain empirical conditions of
their reception. The issues which arise here are altogether different from
(if not entirely unrelated to) the issue of the *sacramental* efficacy of a sign. For
if the Eucharistic "presence" is to be seen, as I have suggested it must, as an
act of radical communication given to us by the Father through Jesus, then

the signs which "effect" that communication must be seen as more like Austin's *illocutions* than as his *perlocutions*, and the causal language of the traditional formula as in some way obscuring that distinction. For the way in which the Father communicates with us in Jesus through the eating of bread and wine is efficacious of that communication rather more in the way in which to say the words "I promise ..." *is* to promise, *is* to communicate in that way, not, as Austin says, as being the *cause* of some mysterious "promising event" over and above that communication. Thus too, the uttering of the words "this is my body" and the subsequent eating and drinking of what appears to be bread and wine is not in a quasi-perlocutionary fashion the *cause of* something miraculous *by means* of a communication: it *is* the communication, or, as we say, the communion, in the body and blood of Christ. That is how Christ is present, not the less "real" because it is a communication through signs, as if by saying it is a "communication" one had denied that it was "real". For that is pure Zwinglianism.

But if that is how Christ is present to us—in an act of radical communication—it is also how Christ is absent. For until we too are raised that communication with the risen Jesus can only fail of ultimacy. The Eucharist is not yet the kingdom of the future as it will be in the future. It points to it *as absent*, not because, as a sign, it is in the nature of signs to signify in the absence of the signified, but because by means of the Father's action this human sign of eating and drinking acquires a depth, an "inwardness" of meaning which realises the whole nature of our historical condition: what, in its essential brokenness, the Eucharist haltingly and provisionally signifies, can be fully realised only by its abolition in the kingdom itself. The Eucharistic sign thus caught up in this eschatological two-sidedness becomes thereby and necessarily a two-sided sign: it is affirmation interpenetrated by negation, presence interpenetrated by absence: *that* is what is made "real" in the Eucharist.

In this perspective it is now possible to see just what is wrong with Zwingli's "absence". It is a one-sided absence which gets its meaning by reaction against a rather mechanistically causalist account of Eucharistic efficacy: as if the doctrine of real presence he denies maintained that the sign "effects what it signifies" in a perlocutionary manner, such that the uttering of the words pulls off the effect of Christ's presence in the way in which a provocative remark pulls off a provocation; so that, if you are to deny that account, the only thing you are left with is sign, with no "reality" effected. As we have seen, this is not in any case what the formula means, even if there are indeed Catholics who appear to have thought it. But then Zwingli does not reject that position in the name of any less mechanistic an account of sacramental efficacy, since for him no account of Christ's presence as "real" is possible other than in such mechanistically causal terms. As a consequence, for him, what the sign effects is merely the negative significance of absence in the minds of the Eucharistic community.

And this, in the end, is what in Zwingli's account, "overthroweth the nature of the sacrament", namely that he supposes the efficacy of the sacrament to lie in what it causes to occur "in the mind" *by contrast with* what occurs "in reality". Catholics, of course, will only reinforce the error of Zwingli's ways if they affirm, as Zwingli thought they did, that what the sacrament effects is something "in reality" *by contrast with* its occurring "in the mind". And Catholics still might be tempted to say such things when they hear it said, as, following McCabe I have said here, that what the sacrament effects is an act of "radical communication"; at any rate, they will be so tempted insofar as they suppose, as many a liberal Catholic nowadays seems to suppose, that communication itself is something which occurs "in the mind" rather than "in reality". But is it not time that we were finally done with such epistemologies, if only for the sake of a decent theology of Eucharistic presence—which theology, to conclude, is where the dialectic of affirmation and negation, of the darkness of God and the light of Christ is first, that is to say, primordially, located and sourced? Our doctrines of the Eucharistic presence are not *formed by* that dialectic—as if those relations of affirmativity and negativity stood preformed in some platonic or pagan philosophy of language about God thus to determine the shape of Eucharistic theology *a priori*. Rather it is the reverse: it is in the eschatological dynamic of the Eucharist, in its complexities of presence and absence, of realisation and failure, of its multi-faceted temporalities, that those dialectics of affirmation and negation are forced upon us as theological necessities of thought, the philosophy yielding to, and not imposing, the radicalness of faith's claims upon it.

NOTES

1 In Philotheus Boehner and M. Frances Loughlin (eds), *The Works of St Bonaventure*, vol. II (New York, NY: The Franciscan Institute, 1956).
2 *Summa Theologiae*, 1a, q. 12 a. 13 ad 1: "...per revelationem gratiae in hac vita non cognoscamus de Deo quid est, et sic ei quasi ignoto coniungamur".
3 *Difficultatum Praecipuarum Absolutiones*, a. 2 (Appendix attached to his *Commentary on the Mystical Theology of the Pseudo-Dionysius*), in *Doctoris Ecstatici D. Dionysii Cartusiani Opera Omnia*, vol. XVI (Tournai: Typis Cartusiae S.M. de Pratis, 1902), p. 484C.
4 *Revelations of Divine Love*, c. 58.
5 *Summa Theologiae*, 3a, q. 95, a. 2, corp. where Thomas argues, exactly as Zwingli, that Christ could not be present *locally* in the Eucharist, else he would have left heaven: *corpus Christi non incipit esse in hoc sacramento per motum localem ... quia sequeretur quod desineret esse in coelo ...*
6 *On the Lord's Supper*, The Library of Christian Classics, vol. XXIV (ed. and trans. G. W. Bromily, London, 1953), pp. 195–238.
7 Ibid., p. 214.
8 Ibid., p. 188.
9 Herbert McCabe, "Transubstantiation and the real presence" in *God Matters* (London: Geoffrey Chapman, 1987), p. 117.
10 Schema of 5 May, 1547, quoted in E. Schillebeeckx, *The Eucharist* (London: Sheed and Ward, 1968), p. 33.
11 J. L. Austin, *How to do things with Words* (Oxford: OUP, 1962), pp. 7–11.

THOMAS AQUINAS AND THE QUEST FOR THE EUCHARIST

CATHERINE PICKSTOCK

In his speculation on the noun-phrase "landscape" in Paragraph 65 of the *Pensées*, Pascal explains how language fixes or designates reality and at the same time surrenders to the indeterminacy and flux of signifieds: "A town or a landscape from afar off is a town and a landscape," he writes, "but as one approaches, it becomes houses, trees, tiles, leaves, grass, ants, ants' legs, and so on *ad infinitum*. All *that* is comprehended in the word 'landscape'."[1] A single noun-phrase is shown at once to conceal and yield an infinite asymptotic analysis of reality, and here Pascal intimates how our words remain always undefined until we actually use them, even though there is always *something* we know of a word's meaning which enables us to use it in the first place. However, it is clear from Pascal's analysis that even when we have used a particular word, we can never be entirely certain of its exhaustive definition.

In the Port-Royal treatise on the categorical theory of propositions, *Logic or the Art of Thinking*, Antoine Arnauld and Pierre Nicole invoke precisely this discussion of the infinite divisibility of the world and the difficulty this presents for our use and understanding of words. They explain how every word we use summons at best a confused idea of the signified, which will always be accompanied by what they call "incidental ideas" which the mind perforce adds to the meanings of words. Such confusion is at an absolute maximum in the case of the demonstrative pronoun *hoc*, "this", used instead of a proper noun. When the supremely indeterminate pronoun "this" is used to display, say, a diamond, the mind does not settle on conceiving it as a present apparent thing, but adds to it the ideas of a hard and sparkling body having a certain shape, besides connotations of wealth, beauty, romance and rarity.[2]

Dr Catherine Pickstock
Emmanuel College, Cambridge, St. Andrew's Street, Cambridge CB2 3AP, UK

This qualification of our certainty regarding the meaning of words forms the basis of Arnauld and Nicole's attack on the Calvinists' metaphorical interpretation of the Eucharist. The Calvinists, they argue, assume in full nominalist fashion (probably influenced by the French Calvinist humanist Petrus Ramus), that the word "this" establishes a firm attachment to a determinate referent, namely, in the case of Jesus's assertion, "This is my body", a firm attachment to the bread. If one detaches the demonstrative pronoun from its obvious referent, as is the case, the Calvinists claim, when Jesus says "This is my body", then it must be intended metaphorically. Arnauld and Nicole argue against this by drawing attention to the Calvinists' error of assuming that the demonstrative pronoun "this" is anchored to a determinate specificity. To the contrary, they argue, specific application is only made possible in this case because of the term's maximum of indeterminacy, its unlimited transferability. For the word "this" always remains susceptible of further determinations and of being linked to other ideas.[3] In addition, even when something apparently determinate is invoked by the pronoun "this", that specificity is itself infinitely divisible and in consequence retains an open-ended and mysterious character. One might think, in the case of the bread to which the pronoun "this" refers in Jesus's assertion, that there is at least some limit to the open-endedness of our mental compassing of the bread. But later in the *Logic*, again invoking Pascal, Arnauld and Nicole protest that even "the smallest grain of wheat contains in itself a tiny world with all its parts—a sun, heavens, stars, planets, and an earth—with admirably precise proportions; that there are no parts of this grain that do not contain yet another proportional world."[4] Thus, even the most literal-seeming reference in fact preserves an infinity of mystery even as it seems to command or delimit that extension.[5]

It should of course be added that behind these assertions of the infinite divisibility of matter lies the seventeenth century disciplining and enhancement of the senses provided by such devices as the microscope, telescope and air-pump, which revealed things that were previously invisible, and cautioned against relying upon the observations of unassisted sense.[6] Thus Pascal and his allies deployed aspects of the New Science *against* nominalism and the cruder variants of empiricism. And they brought into apologetic alignment the scene of experimentation with the scene of sacrificial offering to the extent that both are read as exposing and releasing unexpected depths within seemingly brute matter.

For the Port-Royal grammarians, therefore, there is a triple bond between the theory of physical matter, the question of how language operates and the theology of the Eucharist, and in particular the doctrine of transubstantiation. Echoing this threefold concern I will demonstrate in this essay how discernment of the Body and Blood of Christ in the material species of bread and wine in the Eucharist allows for—even demands—the greatest inexhaustibility of meaning, but at the same time, overcomes the problem of a sheer indeterminacy of sense.

But before going on to consider this oxymoronic status of meaning and language in the Eucharist, one should perhaps ask why, having referred to the Port-Royal critique of how the Calvinist "fixing" of language ignores language's indeterminacy, one should regard "sheer indeterminacy" without qualification as a problem—for surely the attempt to secure meaning is inherently futile. Is not this view, after all, a key feature of postmodern—especially Derridean—philosophy which hails *différance* and the eruption of flows and postponement of meaning as the ineliminable outwitting of metaphysical attempts to secure present truth from the ravages of time and indeterminacy. Such a position exalts the release of language into a play of traces which, far from being "commanded" or fixed by the person wielding signs, rather ensures that that person is commanded *by* those signs.[7] Moreover, this command is a strange anarchic sort of command, which never finally declares *what* is commanded, since meaning is held forever in abeyance by the postponing protocol of *différance*. So, given this rigorous release of language, why should one reinvoke a nostalgia for even the relatively determinate? There is not time to investigate at length the Derridean sign within the compass of this essay, but, put briefly, the problems, as I see them, with the Derridean sign as they relate to my theme are as follows.

In the first place, by cleaving to absence, Derrida leaves the metaphysical correlation of meaning and presence in place, even as he claims that presence is that which is perpetually postponed. For the vehicle of Derridean *différance*, namely the sign, must perforce remain the same in its repeatedly pointing to something which never arrives. This renders both signification and repetition transcendentally *univocal*, precisely because they point to the nothing of postponed presence—and it should perhaps be noted that nothing is more identical than nothing is to nothing. In this way the very unmediability of an absolute radical difference, immune to any likeness, must collapse into its opposite, into identity, sameness and indifference. It resolves, as a transcendental category, into absolute equivalence which comprehends or measures each difference after all.

The second problem with the Derridean theory is that when difference is held at such optimum pitch, each assertion of discontinuity is identically superlative and attains a kind of homogeneous heterogeneity. Indeed, in the third place, for all his high talk, this in some way reduces the Derridean sign to the ideality of a perennially available and wordless thought which overcomes its own mediations and cleaves to presence. In the logic of deconstruction, there is no mediating relationship between *différance* and the various appearances of meaning which it organises or disorganises. In consequence, the universality of the "grammatological flux" is perhaps to be seen as a saturation of language which empties language of itself. As John D. Caputo explains, meanings are allowed "to slip loose, to twist free from their horizons, to leek and run off".[8] Thus, the Derridean sign relinquishes commitment to any specific epiphanies of meaning, or preferences for the lure of certain metaphors, and substitutes a universalised, autonomous and impersonal *mathesis* for language as such (as Gillian Rose rightly argued). For true difference and openness to the Other demand a sensitivity to the fact that some things are more alike than others, or are driven by the provocation of preference or desire which celebrates that difference all the better.

In the fourth place, one might even say that, grammatically-speaking, the Derridean sign, in privileging absence which becomes after all the superlative present object, is cast in the indicative mood of the present tense, which is the very prototype of all language, only for a specifically *Cartesian* linguistics. One should add here that Derrida invokes the category of the middle voice to suggest that *différance* nonetheless does exceed the dichotomy of active and passive. However (as I have argued elsewhere), because for Derrida the sign commands the subject bespeaking or inscribing language, however much a speaker or writer intends a meaning, the infinite play of autonomous "corridors of meaning" by definition always arrives over-against the subject to cancel the specificity of his or her desire.[9] In this way the impersonally objective rules, but such a notion of the objective, from Descartes onwards, is only available for the dispassionately representing *subject*. Hence any suggestion of postmodernism that the Cartesian subject has been erased is a ruse: in fact what it removes is the situated, embodied, specifically desiring historical subject, whereas it must secretly retain a transcendental subject who merely knows, since otherwise the indifferent rule of the sign would never "appear" as a transcendental truth.

Finally, one should perhaps say a little more about the *subject*, as Derrida sees him or her. Insofar as Derrida hastens to undo any substantiality on the part of the subject's intention or desire when he or she elects a meaning in language—by insisting upon meaning as being withheld in an abstruse realm of postponement and by subjugating the speaking self to the sway of the grammatological flux—he after all assumes that the subject's intentionality is something that *requires* cancellation. In other words, he simply repeats the assumption that human will can only be construed as something that issues from a self-identical subject which commands all that it wills. He here enthrones a voluntarist subjectivity which wields dominion over all that it surveys, even as he insists upon the inevitable abdication of that subjectivity. His fear of the engulfing power of human desire—that same fear which forces Derrida to deny the giving or receiving of a gift, or any reciprocal relationship with the Other—too much equates desire with exhaustive *acquisition*, and suggests that there are no modalities other than that of the indicative and the imperative, even if these modalities are consummated through deconstruction in Derrida's sceptical discourse. And if one can have no intimation at all of the postponed meanings of a sign through anticipation or desire—just as one cannot for Derrida ever present oneself, as oneself, to the Other, either with one's gifts, praise or prayer— then, like the air which surrounds us, that postponed meaning has in fact no distance from us at all. In refraining from every risk of reducing meaning to presence, one in fact finds that meaning is accorded a kind of hyper-presence which surrounds us with its untouchability. The preciosity of Derrida's demur accords absent meaning a stifling inaccessibility and un-mediable enclosure within a revered guarded fortress. Such a construal renders absence dialectically identical with an all-too-metaphysical fetish-ization of presence.[10]

Now, the foregoing critique of Derrida's account of the sign is by no means exhaustive, but what I have been trying to show is that it is neither presence as such nor absence as such which is culpably metaphysical, but rather the dichotomy itself, and that for all Derrida's exaltation of the in-determinacy and flux of meaning, by simply inversing the metaphysical structure of the sign, he stays within its paradigm, and ends up fetishizing presence after all.

At this point, we must return to the theme of the signs of the Eucharist and ask whether by contrast they in any way outwit this difficult dichotomy of presence and absence. If *all* they do is render explicit the indeterminacy of a sign, then there would be no contribution that Eucharistic theology could make to semiotics surplus to that of a sceptical philosophy. However, one might also entertain an opposite anxiety: a cursory glance at the history of post-mediaeval Catholic theology, and its focus upon transubstantiation and "real presence", might seem to suggest that the Eucharistic signs clearly privilege presence over absence. But if one looks further back to mediaeval theology and some of its later refractions, such as the work of the Port-Royal grammarians already mentioned—despite their Cartesian aspects—one can construct a different account of the theological signs of the Eucharist which—beyond the postmodern—genuinely outwits the metaphysical dichotomies of presence and absence, life and death, continuity and discontinuity and so forth. In order for such an account to be possible, however, one must understand the Eucharist, following the work of Henri de Lubac, as an essential action within the Church which constantly reproduces the Church, and not simply as either an isolated authoritative presence or merely illustrative symbol, which came, following the early modern period, to be the dominant readings.[11]

Briefly, the key to the transcending of the dichotomy of absence and presence in the Eucharist lies in the "logic"—if one can here use such a term —of *mystery* which, according to patristic negotiations of the word *musterion*, implies a positive but not fetishizable *arrival* in which signs essentially participate, but which they cannot exhaust, for that mystery arrives by virtue of a transcendent plenitude which perfectly integrates absence and presence. Thus, a more positive account of the sign is suggested, for the sign here is neither emptily "left behind" through postponement, nor is it the instru-mental Ramist sign which secures the real in an artificial exactitude.

What this amounts to is an ontological coincidence of the mystical and the real, a coincidence which, as de Lubac shows, lies at the heart of mediaeval

Eucharistic theology. If this coincidence becomes fissured, the Eucharistic signs perforce become either a matter of non-essential, *illustrative* signification which relies upon a non-participatory and conventional (if mimetic) similitude between the bread and the Body, and the wine and the Blood, or else the site of an extrinsicist miracle which stresses the alienness of bread from Body, and wine from Blood. These alternatives, in disconnecting the symbolic from the real, in an attempt to prioritize either one or the other, are *both* equally reducible to a synchronic mode of presence which fails to allow the sacramental mystery its full, temporally ecstatic potential within the action of the *ecclesia*, namely, the continuing coming-to-be of the Church as Christ's body through an ingesting of this same body which is at once a real and a symbolic consuming. Without such a context, the merely static localized presences of instrumental sign or intrusive miracle are ultimately situated within the order of the sign mentioned already in association with philosophical privileging of either presence or absence, for, in being disconnected from ecstatic ecclesial action, the Eucharistic signs must implicitly separate the signifier from the signified.[12] Even in the case of an arbitrary miraculous presence, the exclusive prioritization of the "real" over the merely "symbolic" gives rise to a tendency to think of the Eucharist as an arbitrarily present sign concealing an equally present meaning (the giving of a merely extrinsic "grace") subsisting within a synchronic or rationalised realm of logical demonstration on the basis of certain authorized assumptions.

So, by stressing the *ecclesial* and *relational* context of the Eucharist, and its character as linguistic and significatory *action* rather than extra-linguistic presence, one can start to overcome the logic of the secular Derridean sign. But in doing so, one finds also that one has—almost by default—defended an account of transubstantiation. For it is when the Eucharist is hypostasized as either a thing or a sign in separation from ecclesial and ecstatic action, that it becomes truly decadent. Thus, Jean-Luc Marion, implicitly building upon de Lubac, convincingly argues that transubstantiation *depends* upon the idea that Christ's Body and Blood are "present" only in the sense of the ecstatic passing of time as gift, and *not* in the mode of a punctual moment abstracted from action, under the command of our gaze. And he shows furthermore that modern theories of transignification presuppose a mundane temporality in which Body reduced to meaning is fully "present" to us, rendering such theories crudely metaphysical in a way that transubstantiation avoids.[13]

To explain further how one can construe the theory of transubstantiation in terms of a theory of the sign as mediating between presence and absence, two points can be emphasised. First, following Louis Marin, there is the question of the relation between this theory and a general philosophical scepticism. On the fact of it, transubstantiation seems to collude with the sceptical notion that the way things *appear* to be is no guarantee as to how they really are. For here, it seems, we have an absolute denial of the apparent presence of bread and wine, and an affirmation, by faith, of the presence of the Body and Blood of Christ, despite the fact that none of the normal sensory indicators of such phenomena is present at all.[14] Does one have here then, a fideistic denigration of vision, and of the reliability of sensory evidence as indicators of truth? It might seem so, since there is discontinuity and rupture between the bread of the Body, or between wine and Blood. However, the sceptical disruption of normal certainty in the case of tran-substantiation is balanced by the certainty of the affirmation of faith: here *is* the Body and Blood. Moreover, the appearances of bread and wine are *not* disowned as mere illusions. To the contrary, it is allowed that they remain as accidents, and indeed as accidents which convey with symbolic appropri-ateness their new underlying substance of Body and Blood. One might say that only the symbols of an outpoured body nourishing us, give us an *expanded* sense of the character of this divine body: disclosing it as an imparted and yet not exhausted body quite beyond the norms and capacities of an ordinary body.[15]

Hence although one passes here through a moment of the most apparently extreme philosophical scepticism—this thing is not at all what it appears to be; its reality is radically absent—this is only to arrive at a much more absolute guarantee of the reliability of appearances. For now it is held that certain sensory phenomena mediate and are upheld by a divine physical presence in the world (though this is invisible). The extreme of scepticism has been entertained in one instant, only comprehensively to overcome all possible scepticism and to arrive at a more absolute trust in our material surroundings. Through the faithful reception of the Eucharist we can now experience these surroundings as the possible vehicle of the divine. And the only mode of scepticism thereby finally endorsed is a benign, doxological one. If bread and wine can be the vehicle for the divine Body and Blood, then we must now assume that nothing exhaustively is as it seems.[16] But instead of this unknown surplus being construed as the threat of deception, it is now the promise of a further depth of significance: of a trustworthiness of appear-ances even beyond their known, everyday predictable trustworthiness. And since the fact of an unknown depth behind things is unavoidable, it really is *only* this benign scepticism upheld by a faith in a hidden presence of God which could ever fully defeat the more threatening scepticism of philosophy.

In the second place, one can note that there is still a rupture here of the normal functions of sense and reference. Under ordinary circumstances, one can present a sense or a meaning in the absence of any anchoring refer-ence (at least of a specific sort): for example, one can speak of an imaginary town, and still make sense. Inversely, of one is to *refer*, there has to be something palpable one can point to: if one says "London", then one knows that this is a place one can visit, somewhere one can point to on a map of a real place, "England". However, in the case of the words of institution, it seems that sense and reference peculiarly change places, or collapse into each other. Thus, pointing to a piece of bread and saying "This is my Body" does not even make fictional or imaginative sense, as we do not imagine an unknown body as bread. The phrase only makes sense if it does, however absurdly, actually *refer*: that is, there is only a meaning here if the words *do* point to the Body via the bread; only a sense if the bread has been transubstantiated. Inversely, however, the phrase "This is my Body" does not refer in the normal sense, because it does not indicate anything palpable which fulfils the expectation of the words—as would be the case if one used them while pointing back at oneself. In the latter case, "reference" would be satisfied because one could then look at the Body and say "ah, it's like that": one would have *identified* it. But in the case of the reference of the words of institution, no ordinary identification can take place, since there is no immediately manifest Body: reference is here affirmed without identification, since sense—the imaginative supposition of 'Christ's Body'—must continue to do all the identifying work. Thus while sense is drained of its usual absence, since there is only sense via specific reference; equally reference is drained of its usual presence, as we are presented with no palpable content.[17]

This second point about the collapsing together of sense and reference (in such a way that both appear to be missing) can now be brought together with the first point about a faithful trust in the bread and wine as disclosing an invisible depth of Body and Blood. Combining both points, it can now be seen that "this is my Body"—as said while pointing to bread—means that a missing sense for Body (how can it be bread?) and a missing identifying reference for Body (we do not see it) are both simultaneously supplied when we take the bread as symbolically disclosing an inexhaustible Body (or wine as disclosing the Blood); in other words, when we re-understand Christ's divine-human body as what nourishes our very being.

However, this does not mean that sense and reference are exhaustively supplied. To the contrary, if we say that the real sense and reference of this bread and wine are the Body and Blood of Christ, then since the latter are ultimately mysterious, sense and reference here are only supplied in being simultaneously withheld. Yet once again, this faithful trust is the most guarantee of sense and reference one could ever obtain. This is the case because, ontologically-speaking, for anything to be "here" it must be in excess of here; for something to arrive, it must withdraw. And the strange effect of such withdrawal into the inaccessibly real is to return reference to the "surface" of signification, to the realm of interpretation of senses or of meanings. For this reason, the Eucharistic collapse of sense and reference into one another only dramatises a situation which always obtains: sense and reference are *never* discrete, since even the fictional city is only imaginable because we identify it by reference to some *real* cities, while inversely London will be diversely identified according to the different senses we make of its appearances (including where we draw its boundaries). Thus reference is not denied, but secured in the only way possible, when, in the case of transubstantiation, it ceases to be that "other" of language which anchors all signs, but instead becomes that which folds back into sense, into language. For here, instead of the referent being confirmed by our glance towards the bread, it is confirmed by Jesus's phrase itself, uttered with a simple authority which kindles our trust.

So, whereas, according to Derrida, Christian theology privileges something pure outside language, it is on the contrary the case that the Eucharist situates us more inside language than ever. So much so, in fact, that it is the Body as word which will be given to eat, since the word alone renders the given in the mode of sign, as bread and wine. Not only is language that which administers the sacrament to us, but conversely, the Eucharist underlies all language, since in carrying the absence which characterizes every sign to an extreme (no body *appears* in the bread), it also delivers a final disclosure, or presence (the bread *is* the Body), which alone makes it possible now to trust every sign. In consequence we are no longer uncertainly distanced from "the original event" by language, but rather, we are *concelebrants of that event* in every word we speak (the event as transcendental category, whose transcendentality is now revealed to be the given of the Body and Blood of Christ).

We have discussed how the use of the word *hoc* or "this" hovers between specific designation and an open expectancy of infinite arrival. Such a hesitation brings together a specificity of presence—*this* tomato, etc.—with a generality of absence, where "this" may denote anything whatsoever. This point can be further elaborated by realising that this indicated hovering is in fact a linguistic presentation of the general epistemological problem of the aporia of learning, namely the question first articulated in the *Meno* as to how, if one is ignorant of something and *knows* one is ignorant of that thing, one can already know something of it in order to know that one is ignorant of it. At what imperceptible moment is the barrier of ignorance pierced? And once one has reached the stage of knowing one is ignorant of something, how does one know that there is more to be known, beyond this initial revelation? One of the ways in which Augustine resolves the aporia of learning is by recourse to the mediations of desire which not only provoke the knower ever forward without quite knowing what he or she is looking for, but also issue from the thing to be known, drawing the knower towards it, as if electing to be known by a particular person. But it should be noted that desire—which is divine grace in us—offers a resolution to the conundrum of knowledge only insofar as it lets it stand *as* a conundrum. For the provocations of desire reveal that the truth to be known is never exhausted, but is characterised by a promise of always more to come. Now, one can suggest that there is a linguistic variant of this Augustinian thematic, for when one uses words, one perforce uses them without quite knowing the true proportions of their referent, for those true proportions lie ever beyond our grasp. To a certain extent, they imply, words remain undefined until one elects a particular path for them, until one *uses* them, and yet this indeterminate or half-arbitrary specification is not wholly defined by us, for there always remains in the words we use some *lure* by which we can infer the paths of their meaning.

In a similar way, the simultaneous indeterminacy and specificity always involved in the deployment of the word "this" is mediated by the desire provoked by an initial indeterminacy in pronouncing the word "this" which yet requires a specific instantiation. Moreover, this work of mediation is doubled in an instance where one uses the word "this" in a seemingly redundant way by saying "This is" of something which is manifestly bread. And yet again, this element of desire is here trebled because if one continues by saying "This is bread from the bakery", the dimension of desire would drop away with the satisfaction of one's curiosity about what was going to be said. However, where one pronounces a seemingly bizarre identification, desire *remains*, partly because one wishes forever to penetrate this mystery, and partly because the specification is itself of something infinite, and therefore not exactly specific at all. So whereas in every specific use of the word "this", the indeterminate horizon remains, in this instance that is all the more the case.[18]

One can further illuminate this peculiar situation by mentioning an alternative use of the phrase "This is". Not only might it precede a statement of identification, which can often include an element of derivation as in "This is my grandmother's ring", it might alternatively precede a statement of re-identification or unmasking, as in "This painting is a forgery". However, in the case of "This is my body", neither of these seemingly exhaustive alternatives pertain. As we have already seen, one is not here giving accidental information, as in the first example, where the fact that the ring used to belong to my grandmother does not displace its essential and visible ringness (which does not require to be identified, except in the initial learning of language). This contrasts with the Eucharistic scenario, because when the priest says "This is my body", although he is not saying "This bread is not really bread", he is not attributing an accidental property: instead it would seem that he is providing an absurd identification, where actually no identification at all need be rendered. On the other hand, there is no suggestion of exposure of false appearances, as if Jesus had said "This bread is really Body". Thus when Aquinas claims that transubstantiation has been effected in such a way that the accidents of bread and wine nonetheless remain, one could say that he is strictly adhering to the peculiar linguistic pragmatics of this New Testament usage.

Nevertheless, there does seem to be one major problem about Aquinas's interpretation, namely that it runs counter to common sense. The natural reaction to the claim that the bread is more essentially Body is one of tremendous shock, because no Body can be seen.[19] Why does this shock not lead to rejection? The answer here is manifold, because it has to do with the complex circumstance in which this phrase is uttered. For one thing, the sheer plainness of the phrase tends to produce trust, and for another, the circumstances in which it is uttered—the ceremonial context, the priestly authority, the echoing of the original institution at an evening banquet, the choice of simple elements—which as Aquinas says possess a natural sweetness —all tend to ensure our consent. Although the shock could not be greater, it nonetheless concerns the conjoining of the supernatural with the ordinary in such a way that we are persuaded of a certain analogical continuity which makes us *desire* the claimed presence of the Bread and Body of Christ. In short, the shock is acceptable because desire, instead of being cancelled, as in the case where one's expectations are fulfilled, as when one says "This was my grandmother's ring", is here sustained and intensified. Aquinas repeatedly observes that it is actually desire *for* the Body which ensures discernment of the presence of the Body.[20]

Thus in Aquinas's description of the liturgy surrounding the Consecration, it seems that there is a determined effort to *incite* passions. These allusions to emotion can be divided into two categories, (1) relating to preparing the right *sort* of feelings during the liturgy leading up to the Consecration, in keeping with the solemnity of the mysteries about to be celebrated; and (2), related to the first kind, a more intense, even physical, stirring of emotions, which, as we will see later, is closely linked to Aquinas's theology of the Eucharist.

The first set of allusions can be surveyed quite briefly. Aquinas introduces the theme of emotional preparation with an invocation of the Old Testament injunction to "Keep thy foot when thou goest into the house of God" (Eccles. iv:17). The celebration of this mystery, he writes, "is preceded by a certain preparation in order that we may perform worthily that which follows after",[21] which would seem to suggest that liturgy is not an end in itself, but an act of preparation, very closely allied to human desires. The first stage of this preparation, he writes, is divine praise, and for Aquinas, this meant the singing of an *Introit*, usually taken from the Psalms; this is followed by a recalling of our present misery, and an invocation of divine mercy, through the recitation of the *Kyrie*. Next, heavenly glory is commemorated in the *Gloria*, so that, as Aquinas puts it, such glory becomes that towards which we might incline ourselves or tend. And finally, before the next main stage of this long act of preparation, the priest prays on behalf of the people that they may be made worthy of such mysteries. What this final prayer amounts to is in fact a prayer for emotional preparation, a preparation for preparation, a desire for there to be desire. What one might call this incipient stage, then, is a liturgical liturgy.

The second advance towards preparation is, as Aquinas puts it, the instruction of the faithful, which is given dispositively, when the lectors and subdeacons read aloud in the church the teachings of the prophets and apostles. At this point, we notice a slight change in the provocation of right desire. Whereas in the first stage, as we have already seen, the desires provoked were immediate responses or solicitations of joy, misery, glory and so on, now the passions of the people are lured via the mimetic enactment by choir or priest of certain spiritual or elevated emotions: for example, a sense of progress towards God, which is a sense of spiritual delighting or, sometimes, of spiritual sorrowing, according to Aquinas. Thus, after the Lesson, the choir sings the Gradual, which Aquinas says is to signify "progress in life"; then the Alleluia is intoned, and this denotes "spiritual joy"; or, if it is a mournful Office, the Tract is intoned, which, he writes, is "expressive of spiritual sighing". So, it seems that having first elicited the raw and uninstructed passions of joy and sorrow, the liturgy then provides a spiritual model whereby these emotions might be guided to make the people worthy of the mysteries to come. It is as if desire is at first fulfilled only by a reinforcing and increasing of desire which we must learn from the desired goal itself. It might at first sight seem strange that liturgical progress here runs from initially spontaneous and authentic emotions towards feigned and borrowed ones. For this inverts the normal assumed sequence whereby first one learns by copying and then one grows into authentic possession. However the placing of *mimesis* in this case ahead of the autonomous, suggests that, for the liturgical point of view, a borrowing *is* the highest authenticity that can be attained. For where all desire for God and praise of God must come from God, imitation is no mere pedagogic instrument which subserves a more fundamental self-originating substantiality. Here, to the contrary, one must copy in order first to begin to be, and one continues to be only *as* a copy, never in one's own right. However, as has been seen, what we first imitate and copy in the divine is desire or love. And here again normal expectations are subverted. For just as being does not here precede copying, so also the apprehension of the thing copied does not precede our copying. We do not first apprehend and *then* desire and imitate; rather we first apprehend in acts of desiring which alone begin to disclose, through mimesis, that which is imitated. This liturgical logic of imitation in fact performs a theology of creation for which it is the case that outside participation in the divine, the creature is, of itself, precisely "nothing". Later in this essay I will show how the narrative logic of imitation in the liturgy is underpinned by a metaphysical logic of participation, and how the culmination of the Mass in the transformation and reception of the elements displays the fusion of these two levels. For now, one can note that Aquinas's logic of imitation both anticipates and surpasses in advance a postmodern treatment of mimesis. For the latter also, imitation is constitutive of the imitator and precedes the original. And yet postmodernism, as if still echoing negatively a suspicion of all mimesis which it (falsely) attributes to Plato, regards these circumstances as entirely disruptive of all identity. More radically, Aquinas thinks of identity *as* reception, and of perception *as* receiving.

The third stage in preparation of emotions is to proceed to the celebration of the Mystery, which, as Aquinas explains, is an oblation and a sacrament.

Both of these dimensions of the mystery, the sacrificial and the sacramental, entail their own respective passions as well. Regarding the Mystery insofar as it is an oblation, the peoples' praise in singing the Offertory is now realised as they imitate in turn the mimetic performances of the choir or priest, for, as Aquinas says, this expresses the joy of the offerers. Insofar as the Mystery is to be seen as a sacrament, he declares that "the people are first of all excited to devotion in the Preface ... and admonished to lift up their hearts to the Lord, and therefore when the Preface is ended the people devoutly praise Christ's Godhead, saying with the angels: Holy, Holy, Holy; and with His humanity, saying with the children, Blessed is He that cometh."

Now one might think that after all this elevating and instructing of the passions, the people would finally be ready to receive the Mysteries. And we have seen how this involved a turning away from the rawness of spontaneity and a sublimation to a higher kind of passion. This would surely seem an appropriately elevated moment for proceeding to the Mysteries. But not so. At this most mysterious of moments, just prior to receiving God into one's body, the people are reminded of more earthly emotions; far from this being a moment to look into a spiritual and abstruse realm of higher desire, the people are now reminded of their desire and love for one another. This is done by the communal recitation of the Lord's Prayer, in which the people ask for their daily bread and by the exchange of the *Pax* which is then given again with the concluding words of the *Agnus Dei*. In this final intrusion of community, we can see a further elaboration of the logic of *mimesis*. The doubling of the choir's imitation of God and the angels by the peoples' imitation of the choir, reveals that the inversions of copy and original involved in relation to God are repeated at an interpersonal level. For our existing only as first created, as first an imitation of God, is repeated through the passage of time, as we exist (naturally and culturally) only through first receiving our specific mode of human existence, the mediation of our forebears and contemporaries. They indeed give birth to us, and speak us into articulate being. Hence *metaphysical* participation extends to the political domain, ensuring that here a participation in the *social* sense precedes the individual self. Thus once the people have been restored to themselves in earthly proximity to one another, after the earlier elevation of desire, they are now ready to receive the sacrament.

When Aquinas has thus narrated the modulations of desire during the liturgy, he then turns to more local observations in his replies to the various objections. And one or two of these replies are relevant to our theme. In his Reply to the Sixth Objection, Aquinas notes the way in which the liturgy seems to involve a great many different genres and perspectives, and that each of these seems to have a corresponding purpose linked to the provocation of desire. He writes that the Eucharist is a sacrament which pertains to the entire Church, and consequently, every different quarter of the Church must be included. Consequently, "some things which refer to the people are sung by the Choir, so as to inspire the entire people with them" and there are other words which the priest begins and then the people take up, the priest then acting as in the person of God, and so on. And even when the words which belong to the priest alone, and are said in secret, are to be uttered, he calls the people to attention by saying "The Lord be with you" and waiting for their assent by saying "Amen". At all times, it seems, the desire of the people is provoked, channelled and maintained. This is no automatic ritual, but one which, like the order of ancient sacrifices, must be accompanied by the right devotion in order to be acceptable to God.[22] So much is this the case, in fact, that at the Consecration, the priest does not seem to pray for the consecration to be fulfilled, but, as he says, "that it may be fruitful in our regard". Here Aquinas cites the words of the priest, "That it may become 'to us' the body and blood".

But just why is the Body of Christ so desirable? I have already mentioned that this is partly to do with its infinite absence and inexhaustibility, but it would be a mistake to suppose that this is the only reason. To do so would be to associate the instigation of desire with lack and frustration. On that account, desire is primarily a *possibility*. However, this account of desire, although a common one, is false, because if desire is primarily instigated by frustration, it reduces to the mere epistemic imagining of a *possible* satisfaction. But in order for desire to be felt at all, it must be granted at least some scope of expression, which amounts to some measure of fulfilment, since desire expresses itself only in response to some reception of the desired object. Were such reception to be withheld, then no desire could be expressed, nor any desire felt. Moreover, while it is true that we may appear especially to want the impossible, the knowledge that something *is* impossible always in some fashion blocks the spontaneity of desire in such a manner that one is not really relaxed in desiring, and remains self-conscious in a way which inhibits ecstasis or else forces one to contrive an artificial or rational mathesis of desire. In the opposite situation of a desire that can be fulfilled, it is true that familiarity can breed a slackening of interest. But all that this implies is that for desire fully to operate, there must be both the possibility of fulfilment, and a sustained strangeness and distance. In this optimum and therefore defining situation, desire is something primarily *actual* rather than *possible*, because it is maximally in existence when flowing freely, as well as being continuously provoked.

Such a construal of desire as primarily actual accords with a Thomistic understanding of desire in relation to the Eucharist. For us to desire Christ's Body in the Eucharist, according to Aquinas, it must not only be withheld but also, in a measure, be given. Thus Aquinas places great stress on the analogical appropriateness of the elements of bread and wine right down to the details of the multiplicity of grape and grain being compressed into a unity and so forth.[23] He also stresses how the elements of the Eucharist taste and smell good, and regards this as part of a complex rhetoric whereby the

Eucharistic presentation of Christ is made attractive to us.[24] Indeed, one could argue that Aquinas implies a Eucharistic re-working of what it is to know. On the one hand, it would seem, as we have seen, that transubstantiation accords with an optative scepticism about sensory evidence. Normally this would preface a spiritualizing or idealist philosophy which takes refuge in the certainty of ideas or logic. However, Aquinas denies sensory evidence only to announce that the real concealed substance is nonetheless manifest in sensory appearances if these are now reconstrued as both metaphors and sources of delectation. The elements are reduced to accidents, and yet their accidentality is then seen as all-important. One can go so far as to say that having denied knowledge by sensory evidence, Aquinas then affirms a knowledge by sensual enjoyment. Beyond the disciplining of desires by reason lies a higher desire for God only made possible when God conjoins Himself with the seemingly most base forms of sensory delighting in the form of bread and wine. There is no induction of God *a posteriori* and there is no deduction of God *a priori*, and yet there is a tasting of God through direct physical apprehension, conjoined with a longing for the forever absent. Thereby, one can see that the ultimate reason for the acceptance of the shock of the phrase of institution is that it is one's body which here guides one's reason in the name of an infinite reason. Such a pedagogic order is, for the patristic inheritance which Aquinas received, strictly in keeping with the kenotic logic of salvation history: since it was the higher, Adam's reason, which first betrayed the lower, his body, redemption is received in reverse order through the descent of the highest, God, into our bodies which then start to re-order our minds.

So far, in the foregoing, we have seen how one can read the Eucharist as a particularly acute resolution of the aporia of learning in terms of the category of desire. This reading also has the advantage of showing just how fundamentally in line with Augustinianism Aquinas's thinking about transubstantiation really is. Something similar can be glimpsed in a fourth example of mediation between presence and absence, namely the persistence of the accidents after the event of transubstantiation. This phenomenon, it turns out, is only comprehensible for Aquinas in terms of his somewhat Neo-Platonic ontology of participation in Being which surpasses Aristotelianism in seeking to do justice to the doctrine of creation.

Not often noted in Aquinas's account of the Eucharist is the way in which, besides transubstantiation, at least two subsidiary miracles are involved, although they are all part of the same miracle.[25] One of these is the conversion of water—representing the people—into wine, as at the wedding feast at Cana, occurring before the transubstantiation of the wine into Christ's Blood.[26] This is important, because it shows that the Body of Christ is a nuptial body which is always already the unity of Christ with the Church, His people; in a similar fashion, Aquinas emphasizes that bread and wine include a vast synthesis of disparate human labours, including the labour of transport and trade.[27] All these features tend to confirm the idea that, in the Eucharist, God is only made apparent in a sensual fashion which involves the mediation of all human physical interactions. Now, this exaltation of the sensual runs parallel with the glorification of the accidents which is the second subsidiary miracle involved.[28] It might seem that if bread and wine are reduced from substance to accident, that their natural materiality is thereby degraded. However, one can only think this if one remains ignorant of just how transubstantiation relates to Aquinas's most fundamental ontology. This is a matter ignored, for example, by P. J. FitzPatrick. I shall elaborate this presently. The miraculous character of the remaining accidents is patent for Aquinas in the fact that since the persisting accidental properties of bread and wine go on having a generative effect—for example, nourishing and delighting us, God causes the accidents to act *as if* they were substantive. This means that here the operation of matter in a *normal* fashion has been rendered miraculous. It is as if Aquinas is here saying that the rendering of the normal and continuous as miraculous is the greatest miracle of all, and helps us to re-understand the miraculously created reality of the everyday.[29]

Under normal circumstances, the accidents of bread and wine—for example, their shape and their taste—would manifest the substance of bread and wine, but now they have to be taken as directly manifesting God in whom they subsist. However, they are not accidents *of* the Body and Blood of Christ, since Christ being God, and therefore being simple, cannot be the subject of accidents. Nor, however, does this mean that they are simply *signs* of the divine, as if they were mere persisting miraculous appearances. This cannot be the case because Aquinas insists that the bread and wine remain as ontological accidents even though they are no longer accidents of any substance.[30] This is the point objected to by FitzPatrick on the grounds of its utter incoherence in terms of Aristotelian philosophy.[31] But what he ignores is that Aquinas's metaphysic is not ultimately Aristotelian.[32] Aquinas is quite explicit; in question 77, article 1 of the *Summa*, he raises the question of whether free-floating accidents are not utterly simple and therefore blasphemously like God in character.[33] But the answer he gives is that although they are torn away from the composition of substance and accident, they still retain a composition of existence and essence, since their essence, unlike that of God, does not cause them *to be*. This invocation of the real distinction between essence and existence constitutive of all creaturehood explains how it is possible for accidents to persist without substance, for they possess a ground in which to inhere, namely created being, *esse commune*, which is nonetheless only ever displayed in specifically characterised formations. The real distinction displays a deeper ontological level than that of substance and accident, because substance is always present in its own right as this or that kind of creature which can be accidentally qualified; whereas created being (*esse commune*) is not present in its own right at all, but only as this or that kind of being, whether substance or accident, since created being is really only a participation in Being as such, which belongs to God alone. Hence, para-doxically *beyond* substance, which is self-standing, lies something, for Aquinas, *not* self-standing, namely *esse commune*, which only exists in an improper borrowed fashion, just as earlier we saw that the human creature is imitative without remainder.[34] But since participation in being is the most fundamental ontological dimension of creation, the real distinction of essence and existence can in theory sustain finite reality before and without the division of substance and accident. And this explains why free-floating accidents are possible, although it would probably be better to say that the remaining accidents have passed beyond the contrast of substance and accident. They are neither essential—since they are not God—nor are they non-essential—since they manifest God and are His creation.

Once one has understood that the remaining accidents exceed the contrast of substance and accident, one can also see that they are not relegated beneath the level of substance. On the contrary, they are now promoted to a character that most essentially reveals the condition of createdness, and they are accorded the honour of directly subsisting in Being which is the most immediate divine created effect. For this reason, one can say that merely accidental bread and wine have become more themselves than ever before, and this coheres with the fact that they have also become completely attuned to a signifying and spiritually active purpose.[35] So much is this the case that Aquinas insists that partaking of the Body and Blood of Christ under the species of bread and wine has become the means of deification. It is as if one is saying that bread and wine now remain eschatologically alongside God in such a way that the most ordinary is here exalted, and it becomes not absurd to adore a mere piece of bread.[36] This is especially the case because the remaining accidents are no longer like food that only becomes food when we take it up and eat it, and otherwise is only *potential* food. Rather, to exceed the contrast between substance and accident is to attain to createdness as pure transparency, as pure mediation of the divine. At this point the under-lying metaphysical logic of participation as it were surfaces or erupts into the narrative logic of *mimesis* which it supports. For as purely subsisting in the divine, the accidents also achieve a pure flow of ceaseless and self-sustaining creative mimicry. Thus, the bread and wine which persist as accidents, have become always and essentially *food*—figurative food which shapes our imitative humanity—and, in this way, they are the appropriate vehicles of the Logos, since like the Logos, they now exist in a pure passage, or relationality. For this reason, Aquinas repeats Augustine's statement that the Eucharistic food is not like ordinary food which is cancelled as food by being incorporated into our nature when we eat it. It is rather the other way about: we are incorporated into the food.[37] This implies that we are speaking here about an essential food which never starts to be food and never ceases to be food, because it is entirely the mediation of a God who is in Himself mediation.

The fifth way in which the contrast of presence and absence is outwitted by the Eucharist concerns the operation of desire. We have already seen how desire mediates the usage of the word "this" in the case of the Eucharist; now I will show how for Aquinas the central role of desire helps to ensure that for the whole phenomenon of the Eucharist and the liturgy there is no fetishization of presence or absence.

First of all, the Eucharist might seem to risk a fetishization of presence if all that mattered for the sake of salvation were to receive the elements, since this is authorized by the Church. And indeed such a fetishization was risked by many Counter-Reformation approaches. Aquinas, by contrast, insists that what is primarily salvific, even if one does receive, is *desire* for the Body and Blood of Christ.[38] And this tends to make sense of the fact that we can never receive once and for all, and have to go on receiving. If there is no end to receiving the Eucharist, and we have never received enough, this does indeed imply that desire is as good as receiving, just as receiving the Eucharist in the right desire is essential.[39] Thus Aquinas repeatedly suggests that the whole of the liturgy is primarily directed towards preparing in people a proper attitude of receptive expectation.[40] Everything is intended to affect us in an appealing manner directed towards every aspect of our common humanity, including the more sensory aspects; and as we have seen, if anything, an appeal is made to our minds *through* our bodies, *rather* than the other way around.

Indeed, Aquinas construes the circumstances of the instauration of the Eucharist—the drama of the late evening supper, the unexpected directness of the words used—as deliberate rhetorical means deployed to fix truths in his disciples' and our memories, and incite true desire in our hearts.[41] Nevertheless, Aquinas insists that the primacy of desire does not mean that abstention is as good as reception, for it is in the very nature of desire that it should want what it desires, just as we have already seen that desire is only actualized when it is in part fulfilled and can flow freely, not when it is frustrated or contrived. Thus while avoiding a fetishization of presence, and insisting that it is the personal desire for God which is salvific, rather than adherence to ecclesial authorities, Aquinas nonetheless avoids an opposite fetishization of absence and postponement.[42] Thus God does provide us with a foretaste of His eschatological presence, and indeed Aquinas insists that we only *have* desire for Christ, not because of some *abstract* promise, but because our imaginations have been engaged right from the outset of the first Maundy Thursday by the use of beguiling verbal and sensory devices.[43]

It will be recalled that in the background of this interest in desire lies the Augustinian deployment of desire to resolve the aporia of learning. Desire is the answer to this aporia, but not desire alone. It has to be desire *for God*, for only if God is real, can we trust that a desire for further knowledge will be fulfilled and that signs are not empty. However, the question of desire for God should not be taken merely in an individualistic way, but rather in collective and historical fashion. Human beings have only been able to believe in God through the mediation of signs conveying His reality which they believe they can trust. Indeed, one might describe our fallenness as a situation of the absence of such trustworthy signs. The Passion of Christ drives that situation to an extreme because here one has a maximum visibility of the divine presence in humanity that is nonetheless destroyed. This can provoke a kind of death of God nihilism which affirms that we glimpse the truth in and through destruction. However, such nihilism is qualified in the Christian gospel because it offers, even in the extreme of the death of the divine, an image of something trustworthy. The death of Christ becomes a sign of promise since in the resurrection, the shedding of Christ's Blood is transformed into the gift of the Eucharist. And in every Eucharist, the extreme contrasts that one sees in the Passion are repeated, and repeated in their reconciliation. Every Eucharist is a representation, a reactualization of the sacrifice of Christ, therefore it is a continuation of His loss and destruction. However, since this loss *feeds* us, this ultimate dereliction is also revealed as the pure essential food that is substantive passage. And this death as food can therefore act as the ultimate trustworthy sign—the passage of the Eucharistic food is also the unique Christian passage of sacrifice to sign which constitutes the very nature of a sacrament.

One can sum up this balancing of the Eucharist as presence with a non-elided *desire* for the Eucharist by invoking the mediaeval allegorical linking of the Eucharist with the quest for the Holy Grail. And this invocation is far from being arbitrary, because the period of emergence of grail literature (roughly 1170–1220) is contemporary with the increasing articulation of a doctrine of transubstantiation.[44] The allegory of the Grail helped to ensure that the seemingly most commonly available thing in every Church in every town and village was made the object of a difficult quest and high adventure, a quest indeed so difficult that it was almost impossible to attain, as if it were scarcely possible even to locate and receive the Eucharist. Nonetheless, the ultimate vision accorded Sir Galahad ensures that the postmodern fetishization of pure postponement is also here avoided.

In the above, we have seen how the Eucharist is situated between presence and absence. Because of this situation, it does not pretend that indeterminism of meaning can be cancelled by pure presence; on the other hand, since presence is not denied, the Eucharist remains something meaningful. But now the further question arises as to how this can possibly benefit meaning in general. In conclusion, I will try to indicate the outlines of an answer to this question.

Outside the Eucharist, it is true, as postmodern theory holds, that there is no stable signification, no anchoring reference, and no fixable meaning. This means that there is no physical thing whose nature one can ultimately trust. We have seen how the Eucharist dramatizes this condition, pushes it to an extreme, but then goes beyond it. The circumstance of the greatest dereliction of meaning is here read as the promise of the greatest plenitude of meaning.

However, if we do trust this sign, it cannot be taken simply as a discrete miraculous exception, if we are true to a high mediaeval and Thomistic construal of the Eucharist. First of all, we have seen how Aquinas sees bread and wine as the most common elements of human culture. Hence, if these become the signs of promise, they pull all of human culture along with them. Secondly, "This is my body" cannot be regarded as a phrase in isolation any more than any other linguistic phrase. Here, the Saussurean point holds true, that every phrase of language in some sense depends for its meaningfulness upon the entire set of contrasts which forms the whole repertoire of language, such that, for example, "this" only makes sense in contrast to "that", "my" in contrast to "your" and "his", "is" in contrast to "is not" and "was" and the other verbs, and so forth *ad infinitum*.

For this reason, if this phrase is guaranteed an ultimate meaningfulness, it draws all other phrases along with it.

In the third place, these words and events only occur in the Church. And we only accept real presence and transubstantiation because the giving of Body and Blood in the Eucharist gives also the Body of the Church. The Eucharist both occurs within the Church and gives rise to the Church in a circular fashion. In consequence, a trust in the Eucharistic event inevitably involves trusting also the past and the future of the Church. In receiving the Eucharist, we are in fact receiving an entire historical transmission which comprises the traditions of the Church and then those of Greece and Israel. This tradition includes the Bible in which it is declared that God is in some fashion manifest to all traditions and in the physical world as such. Thus, trust in the Eucharist draws all historical processes and then every physical thing along with it. One could even say that just as the accidents remain, so the supreme event of the Eucharist, which other things anticipate, is only present in a kind of dispersal back into those very things. One is referred back to a primitive trust in the gifts of creation. For all peoples, these things have enabled a beginning of trust in the divine, even if it is only the incarnation, the Passion and the gift of the Eucharist which ensure that this trust does not run into an ultimate nihilistic crisis.

This idea, according to which the Eucharistic fulfilment of prophecy turns one back towards the original prophecies and ennobles them (just as reception does not cancel desire; just as the accidents remain; just as the body teaches the mind) is dramatized in the mediaeval allegorical text, *The Quest of the Holy Grail*, which reflects a Cistercian spirituality focused upon desire, and which reads devotion to the Eucharist in terms of a search,[45] just as Aquinas said that we are "wayfarers" who can only discern the Body of Christ through faith.[46] On their way to the Grail castle, the knights in the story are led to a mysterious ship which has been voyaging since the time of King Solomon. This ship has a mast made of the Tree of Life from the Garden of Eden and other insignia which foreshadow Christ. It had been built by Solomon's wife who was concerned that future times should know that Solomon had prophesied Christ's coming. Her female left-handed *ingenium*, which is a crafty capacity to make things, is contrasted to Solomon's male contemplative wisdom.[47] The ostensible concern in the story is that we should recognise the prophetic power of our ancestors, but surely the deeper point is that if there were no record of the anticipation of Jesus and the Eucharist, we would not recognise them as significant at all, nor discern them, for they are only meaningful as fulfilment; without the record of Israel, there could be no manifest incarnation. It follows that Jesus and the Eucharist are in some way a ship, just as the Tree of Life was read allegorically in terms of the God-man. The ship is already the Church and the Eucharist, as a tentative human construction, whereas the fulfilled Eucharist is perfect human and yet divine art. Inversely, one can say that the Eucharist remains the ship because it persists as quest despite fulfilment. This allows us to link the notion of non-cancelled desire with the idea that trust in the Eucharist points us back towards a trust in everything, and especially the ordinary and the everyday. For if we are to go on questing, then all the things pointing towards the Eucharist retain their pregnant mystery without cancellation. We are still knights looking for the Grail, just as we are still Israel on pilgrimage. Since knowledge consists in desire, we must affirm that the aporia of learning is resolved all the time in the promise of everyday human practices. We are usually unaware of this recollection, and yet in a way we do have a certain inchoate awareness of it. Thus we can see that what the Eucharist is is desire. Although we only know via desire, or wanting to know, and this circumstance alone resolves the aporia of learning, beyond this we discover that what there is to know is desire. But not desire as absence, lack and perpetual postponement; rather, desire as the free flow of actualization, perpetually renewed and never foreclosed.

NOTES

1 Blaise Pascal, *Pensées*, trans. A. J. Krailsheimer, (London: Penguin Books, 1966), § 65.
2 Antoine Arnauld and Pierre Nicole, *Logic or the Art of Thinking*, trans. Jill Vance Buroker (Cambridge: Cambridge University Press, 1996), pp. 70–71, and p. 231 re Pascal § 72.
3 Ibid., p. 72; see also G. W. F. Hegel, *Phenomenology of Spirit*, trans. A. V. Miller (Oxford: Oxford University Press, 1977), § 109.
4 Arnauld and Nicole, op. cit., p. 231.
5 Ibid., p. 71.
6 Steven Shapin and Simon Schaffer, *Leviathan and the Air-Pump: Hobbes, Boyle, and the Experimental Life* (Princeton, NJ: Princeton University Press, 1985), pp. 36–37; Steven Shapin, *A Social History of Truth: Civility and Science in Seventeenth-Century England* (Chicago, IL: University of Chicago Press, 1995), pp. 194–195; Maurice Mandelbaum, *Philosophy, Science, and Sense Perception: Historical and Critical Studies* (Baltimore, MD: The Johns Hopkins University Press, 1964), ch. 2; B. J. Shapiro, *Probability and Certainty in Seventeenth-Century England: A Study of the Relationship between Natural Science, Religion, History, Law, and Literature* (Princeton, NJ: Princeton University Press, 1983), pp. 61–62; Albert van Helden, "'Annulo Cingitur': The Solution of the Problem of Saturn", *Journal of the History of Astronomy*, 5 (1974), pp. 155–174.

7   Pickstock, *After Writing* (Oxford: Blackwell, 1998), pp. 35–37, 116–118.
8   John D. Caputo, *The Prayers and Tears of Jacques Derrida: Religion Without Religion* (Bloomington and Indianapolis: Indiana University Press, 1997), p. 13.
9   Jacques Derrida, "Plato's Pharmacy" in *idem., Dissemination*, trans. Barbara Johnson (London: Athlone Press, 1981), pp. 63–171, pp. 95–96.
10 Pickstock, op. cit., chapter 3.
11 Henri de Lubac, *Corpus Mysticum: L'Eucharistie et L'Eglise au Moyen-Age* (Paris: Aubier-Montaigne, 1949); Michel de Certeau, *The Mystic Fable*, trans. Michael B. Smith, (Chicago, IL: University of Chicago Press, 1992); Pickstock, op. cit., pp. 158–166.
12 de Lubac, *Corpus Mysticum*, pp. 253–254, 266–267.
13 Marion, *God Without Being*, trans. Thomas A. Carlson, (Chicago, IL: University of Chicago Press, 1991), pp. 161–183.
14 Arnauld and Nicole, op. cit., p. 211; see further, Marin, in idem., "La Parole Mangée ou le corps théologico-politiques", (Quebec: Boreal, 1986), pp. 12–35.
15 *S.T.*, III. q. 75 a. 1; III. q. 76. a. 7.
16 Marin, op. cit., pp. 23–25.
17 *S.T.*, III. q. 78 a. 6.
18 *S.T.*, III. q. 78 a. 5.
19 *S.T.*, III. q. 75 a. 1; q. 76 a. 7.
20 *S.T.*, III. q. 80 a. 4.
21 *S.T.*, III. q. 83 a. 4.
22 *S.T.*, III. q. 83 a. 4 ad 8.
23 *S.T.*, III. q. 73 a. 1–a. 2; q. 74. a. 1; a. 4; a. 5; q. 75 a. 8 ad 1; q. 76 a. 2 ad 1; q. 77 a. 6; q. 79 a. 1.
24 *S.T.*, III. q. 74 a. 3 ad 1; q. 79 a. 1; q. 81 a. 1 ad 3; q. 83 a. 5 ad 2.
25 *S.T.*, III. q. 74 a. 8.
26 *S.T.*, III. q. 74 a. 6; a. 8; q. 77 a. 5.
27 *S.T.*, III. q. 74 a. 1; a. 3.
28 *S.T.*, III. q. 75 a. 8 ad 4; q. 77 a. 1 ad 4; q. 77 a. 3 ad 2; a. 5.
29 *S.T.*, III. q. 75 a. 8; III. q. 78 a. 2 ad 2; III q. 77 a. 3; a. 5.
30 *S.T.*, III. q. 77 a. 1 especially ad 2.
31 P. J. FitzPatrick, *In Breaking of Bread: The Eucharist and Ritual* (Cambridge: Cambridge University Press, 1993), pp. 12–17.
32 See further Mark Jordan, "Theology and Philosophy" in Norman Kretzmann and Eleonore Stump (eds) *The Cambridge Companion to Aquinas* (Cambridge: Cambridge University Press, 1993), pp. 232–251; A. N. Williams, "Mystical Theology Redux: The Pattern of Aquinas' *Summa Theologiae*", *Modern Theology*, 13.1 (January 1997), pp. 53–74.
33 *S.T.*, III. q. 77 a. 1, esp. ad 2.
34 *S.T.*, III. q. 77 a. 1 ad 2.
35 *S.T.*, III. q. 73 a 1; a. 2; q. 74 a. 1; a. 4; a. 5; q. 75 a. 8 ad 1; q. 76 a. 2 ad 1; q. 77 a. 6; q. 79 a. 1.
36 *S.T.*, III. q. 75 a. 8; q. 78 a. 2 ad 2.
37 *S.T.*, III. q. 73 a. 3 ad 2.
38 *S.T.*, III. q. 73 a. 3 ad 2; q. 78 a 3; q. 79 a. 3; q. 80 a. 1 ad 3; a. 2 ad 1; a. 9 ad 1.
39 *S.T.*, III. q. 80 a. 4.
40 *S.T.*, III. q. 76 a. 8; q. 78 a. 1 especially ad 4; q. 79 a. 4; a. 5; q. 80 a. 11; q. 83 a. 2; q. 83 a. 4 ad 1; ad 6; ad 7.
41 *S.T.*, III. q. 73 a. 5; q. 83 a. 2 ad 3.
42 *S.T.*, III. q. 80 a. 11 ad 1.
43 *S.T.*, III. q. 75 a. 1.
44 Ronald Hutton, *The Pagan Religions of the Ancient British Isles: Their Nature and Legacy* (Oxford: Blackwell, 1991, 1993), p. 319.
45 Sister Isabel Mary SLG, "The Knights of God: Citeaux and the Quest of the Holy Grail" in Sister Benedicta Ward SLG (ed) *The Influence of Saint Bernard* (Oxford: SLG Press, 1976), pp. 53–88; Andrew Sinclair, *The Discovery of the Grail* (London: Century, 1998) *passim*.
46 *S.T.*, III. q. 76 a. 7.
47 *The Quest of the Holy Grail*, trans. P. M. Matarasso (Harmondsworth: Penguin, 1969), especially p. 230.

THE WORLD IN A WAFER: A GEOGRAPHY OF THE EUCHARIST AS RESISTANCE TO GLOBALIZATION

WILLIAM T. CAVANAUGH

There is a great deal of confusion in Christian social thought over the phenomenon known as globalization. Many who write on the Church and politics carry on as if nothing had happened, preoccupied with the question of if and how the Church should enter "the public realm", an imaginary national space where conflicts are settled. Globalization is left for those who deal in so-called "economic ethics", either to decry transnational firms paying Salvadoran textile workers thirty-three cents an hour, or to hail the capitalist catholicity which is including those "currently excluded within the beneficent circle of fruitful practices", as Michael Novak has it.[1] Those of us who have been critical of the nation-state as such are also confused. One would think that we would be pleased—or would at least find something else to do—now that the global economy has rendered national borders increasingly irrelevant. Africans and Minnesotans commune on the Internet, and the world has shrunk to proportions measurable by the click of a mouse. A catholicity undreamed by the original *Catholica* is now dawning. Ought we, like the Donatists in Augustine's phrase, sit like frogs in our swamp croaking "We are the only Catholics",[2] when a much broader universality is now within reach?[3] Or is it a universality at all? MacIntyre and Lyotard conversely invoke images of fragmentation to characterize the situation of late capitalism. Has the possibility of true catholicity been defeated in the triumph of global capital?

William T. Cavanaugh
Department of Theology, University of St. Thomas, 2115 Summit Avenue, St. Paul, MN 55105-1078, USA

I was going to subtitle this essay "How to be a Global Village Idiot", but "A Geography of the Eucharist" better captures what I hope to accomplish, for I believe that much of the Christian confusion over globalization results from a neglect of the Eucharist as the source of a truly Catholic practice of space and time. Globalization marks a certain configuration for the discipline of space and time; I would like to juxtapose this geography with another geography, a geography of the Eucharist and its production of catholicity. In the first half of the paper, I will argue that globalization is not properly characterized by mere fragmentation, but enacts a universal mapping of space typified by detachment from any particular localities. This is not a true catholicity, however, for two reasons: first, this detachment from the particular is actually used as a discipline to reproduce divisions between rich and poor, and second, it produces fragmented subjects unable to engage a catholic imagination of space and time. Globalism is a masternarrative, the consumption of which ironically produces fragmented subjects incapable of telling a genuinely catholic story. In the second half of this paper, I show that the Eucharist produces a catholicity which does not simply prescind from the local, but contains the universal *Catholica* within each local embodiment of the body of Christ. The body of Christ is only performed in a local Eucharistic community, and yet in the body of Christ spatial and temporal divisions are collapsed. In the complex space of the body of Christ, attachment to the local is not a fascist nostalgia for *gemeinschaft* in the face of globalization. Consumption of the Eucharist consumes one into the narrative of the pilgrim City of God, whose reach extends beyond the global to embrace all times and places.

I. The Dominance of the Universal

The "giant sucking sound" that Ross Perot heard in 1992 was the sound of "American" jobs being drained into Mexico as a result of NAFTA.[4] "If he's against it, I'm for it" would be a natural reaction for someone allergic to the kind of nationalistic particularism put forth by the likes of Perot and Pat Buchanan in opposition to NAFTA. What I hope to show in this section, however, is that globalization does not signal the demise of the nation-state but is in fact a hyperextension of the nation-state's project of subsuming the local under the universal.

The rise of the modern nation-state is marked by the triumph of the universal over the local in the sovereign state's usurpation of power from the Church, the nobility, guilds, clans, and towns.[5] The universalization of law and rights would liberate the individual from the whims of local custom, thereby creating a direct relationship, or "simple space", between the sovereign and the individual. As John Milbank uses the term, simple space contrasts with the complex space of overlapping loyalties and authorities in medieval society.[6] Rights did not pertain to individuals alone; local groupings were themselves possessed of rights and freedoms which were not simply conferred by a sovereign center. These associations overlapped in the rights and duties which individual persons owed to each other and to the different associations to which they belonged. Both the person and the local association were wholes to themselves, while each also constituted part of a larger whole. Otto Gierke's now classic work in medieval law shows how this complex conception of space was based on the Pauline theology of the body of Christ.[7]

The new configuration of space that arose with modernity is helpfully illuminated by Michel de Certeau's distinction between "itineraries" and "maps". Pre-modern representations of space marked out itineraries which told "spatial stories", for example, the illustration of the route of a pilgrimage which gave instructions on where to pray, where to spend the night, and so on. Rather than surveying them as a whole, the pilgrim moves through particular spaces, tracing a narrative through space and time by his or her movements and practices. A fifteenth-century Aztec representation of the exodus of the Totomihuacas, for example, displays what amounts to a log of their travels: footprints accompanied by pictures of successive events from the journey, such as river crossings, meals, and battles.[8] By contrast, modernity gave rise to the mapping of space on a grid, a "formal ensemble of abstract places" from which the itinerant was erased. A map is defined as "a totalizing stage on which elements of diverse origin are brought together to form the tableau of a 'state' of geographical knowledge".[9] Space itself is rationalized as homogeneous and divided into identical units. Each item on the map occupies its proper place, such that things are set beside one another, and no two things can occupy the same space. The point of view of the map user is detached and universal, allowing the entire space to be seen simultaneously.[10] The type of mapping that Certeau describes is a corollary of the rise of the modern state, which depends on the ability to survey a bounded territory from a sovereign center and make uniform the relations of each particular unit of space to every other.

The flattening of complex social space by the modern state does not mean that local groups simply vanished with the rise of the state. Rather, local social groupings were recast as "intermediate associations" between state and individual, and such institutions have played an important role in mediating the state project. The universal is mediated by the local; the institutions of civil society, as Hegel saw, are educative, or as Foucault would later say, disciplinary. Parties, unions, churches, families, prisons, hospitals, and schools help to embody and produce the state project. Such institutions in modernity depend on a rational mapping of space, captured well by Foucault's famous image of the Panopticon, a prison space organized around a central surveillance tower. Space is made homogeneous and uniform; each particular unit relates directly to the center, which sees all but is not seen. Not knowing when one is being supervised, each individual becomes self-disciplining.[11]

In the political economy which precedes globalization, then, the local is subsumed under the universal, but local attachments still play an important role in mediating the universal. The Fordist economic model which reigned from World War I to the early 1970s depended on strong attachment to nation, corporation, family, community, and union. Economic historians characterize this era by reference to Henry Ford's two-fold idea of production and consumption: 1) the concentration and discipline of labor through assembly line production in large factories, and 2) the cooperation of unions, families, and local communities in prioritizing mass consumption (the assumption being that mass production depends on the workers being able and willing to buy what they produce). The state did not simply overcome civil society, but rather the state was a diffused complex of power relations produced and reproduced in the institutions of civil society through the generation of consensus.[12]

The post-Fordist global economy currently emerging, however, goes farther than Foucault envisioned in subsuming local social groupings under the universal, to the point of detachment from any particular space. Foucault still depends on a strong account of the institutions of state and civil society. Those institutions, however, are everywhere in crisis.[13] Governments have ceded or lost control over the transnational economy; through deregulation and computer transfers money has become virtually stateless. The disciplinary mechanisms of the factory and the factory town are no longer necessary for the extraction of surplus labor, and have given way to part-time labor, home labor, various forms of illegal labor, and global "outsourcing". The subcontracting operations of multinational corporations, such as Nike in Asia, no longer demand or even allow the direct oversight or disciplining of labor by the purchasing company. Labor is hidden, and the sources of production are constantly shifting location. Unions have consequently lost much of their power. With the loss of geographical stability, family, church, and local community have also given way to global monoculture and "virtual community". In sum

> "The new order eschews loyalty to workers, products, corporate structures, businesses, factories, communities, even the nation", the *New York Times* announces. Martin S. Davis, chair of Gulf and Western, declares, "All such allegiances are viewed as expendable under the new rules. You cannot be emotionally bound to any particular asset."[14]

As is often remarked, the nation-state itself is apparently giving way before the free flow of global capital. The geographical flexibility of the transnational corporation under post-Fordism produces competition among nations and localities to sacrifice their own control over wages, working conditions, and environmental standards in order to attract business. Under the conditions of the Uruguay Round of GATT, nation-states have surrendered their sovereignty over trade to the World Trade Organization, which is empowered to judge which laws enacted in any community of the signatory nations constitute a barrier to free trade. National or local laws governing such activities as pesticide use, clear cutting of forests, and hormones in meat are subject to revocation by the WTO, from which there is no appeal.[15]

And yet the nation-state perdures as an important factor in the neutralization of opposition to globalization and its acceptance as natural and inevitable. While the Commerce Department and USAID have spent hundreds of millions to encourage US businesses to move jobs overseas,[16] the US congressional debate over NAFTA was conducted in such a way that nationalism wholly occluded the issue of class. The terms of the debate became "Is NAFTA good or bad for America?" Absent was the possibility that the agreement eliminating the last trade barriers between North American nations might be good for *some* Americans (or Mexicans)—namely shareholders and consumers with purchasing power—and bad for *some* Americans—namely workers.

GATT and NAFTA represent a voluntary loss of sovereignty for the nation-state. This apparent act of self-sacrifice is incomprehensible unless we see that these changes do not mean the end of the state project, but rather its generalization across space. If the state project is characterized by the subsumption of the local under the universal, then globalization hyperextends this project. Just as the nation-state freed the market from the "interventions" of local custom, and freed the individual to relate to other individuals on the basis of standardized legal and monetary systems,[17] so globalization frees commerce from the nation-state, which, as it turns out, is now seen as one more localization impeding the universal flow of capital.

Advances in the management of time have made possible the extension of the universal mapping of space to a global level. The speed with which information and people can travel across space has overcome spatial barriers and shrunk the dimensions of the world. The metaphor of the "global village" is often invoked to elicit catholic sentiments of the world's peoples coming into communion with each other, overcoming the ethnic, tribal, and traditional barriers which have produced so much bloodshed over the centuries. Global mapping appears to make all the people on earth contemporaries, sharing the same space and time. And indeed, a universal corporate culture increasingly penetrates local cultures worldwide. If one were parachuted into a shopping mall, it would take some investigation to discover whether one had touched down in Cambridge or Fort Worth, Memphis or Medicine Hat, Dar es Salaam or Minsk.

Examples of the dominance of the universal—the "McDonaldization of Society", to quote the title of George Ritzer's study[18]—are too common to belabor. In corporate language, the vision is often presented as a beneficent catholicity which produces peace through the overcoming of division. Utopia, says the president of Nabisco Corporation, is "One world of homogeneous consumption … [I am] looking forward to the day when Arabs and Americans,

Latins and Scandinavians will be munching Ritz crackers as enthusiastically as they already drink Coke or brush their teeth with Colgate."[19] As I will suggest in the next section, however, the triumph of the universal does not simply overcome spatial barriers. Indeed, the attempt to map space as homogeneous and catholic, overcoming spatial divisions, is often itself a ruse to divert attention from the new forms of division that are being produced.

II. The Discipline of Detachment

The post-Fordist economy is marked by geographical flexibility and the overcoming of Fordist segmentation of space. Nevertheless, all this apparent decentralization and despatialization masks a different discipline of space which is in some ways "ever more tightly organized *through* dispersal".[20] Workers in one location will be much more compliant to the demands of management if the company has the capability to close the plant and move operations somewhere else where wages and other standards are lower. The domination of space becomes detached from any particular localities and becomes a matter of the abstract and universal potentiality of *any* space to produce profit. Domination of space relies less on direct supervision and more on information, an accurate and up-to-the-minute mapping of labor markets and exchange rates worldwide which gives the corporation mobility.[21] Now the Panopticon does not simply characterize the discipline of space within a particular location, such as a factory. It characterizes the gaze spread over the entire map of the globe.

Gilles Deleuze's concept of the "line of flight" is often invoked as an image of resistance to highly segmented and disciplined spaces. One creates "nomad spaces" of flight from territorialization, the surveillance and control of space. The irony here is that in the globalized economy direct discipline over a particular locality has given way to the discipline of sheer mobility, the ability to flee. The transnational corporation's flight to another location on the map is based on the mapping itself, and only serves to increase control over the workers. Deleuze and Guattari do acknowledge the inevitable reterritorialization of flight; they ask rhetorically "Do not even lines of flight, due to their eventual divergence, reproduce the very formations their function it was to dismantle and outflank?"[22] In the post-Fordist economy, however, reproduction of these formations is not a divergence; the whole *point* of flight is to reproduce these formations. Globalization has complicated any dichotomy between the oppressive mapping of a fixed space, and a nomadic resistance to that mapping. In globalization, flight is facilitated by the universal mapping itself, and flight reproduces the segmentation of space.

Far from yielding peaceful flight, the compression of space in the "global village" has not only exacerbated but produced insecurity and conflict in the late twentieth century, since global mapping brings diverse localities into competition with one another.[23] Globalization increases potentially deadly competition among nation-states, since free trade is paradoxically put forth as a competitive development strategy for particular countries. Through transcending spatial barriers, capital is able to map and exploit even minute spatial differentiations, unleashing an economic war of all against all.[24]

Competition produces an apparent attachment to the local, for in an effort to lure capital, diverse places must emphasize what is unique and advantageous to their location (cheap wages, weak unions, good resources and infrastructure, lax regulation, attractive environment for management, etc.). Yet at the same time, competition paradoxically increases detachment from the local, as for localities compete for capital, the supposed uniqueness of each local place is increasingly tailored to attract development, modeled on those localities that have previously been successful. David Harvey puts the paradox in these terms: "the less important the spatial barriers, the greater the sensitivity of capital to the variations of place within space, and the greater the incentive for places to be differentiated in ways attractive to capital."[25]

An ephemeral particularity is therefore merely the flipside of a dominant universality. Mexican food is popularized in places like Minnesota, but its dominant form is the fast-food chain Taco Bell, which serves up a hot sauce that a native Minnesotan could mistake for ketchup. Nevertheless, just as the food must be universalized and made bland enough to appeal potentially to the taste of *anyone anywhere*, to compete there must be a simultaneous emphasis on its unique qualities; advertised images must be rooted in a particular location, for example, the traditional Mexican culture of the *abuelita* before the clay oven, sipping *pulque* and shaping tortillas in the palm of her hand. Anyone who has stood at a Taco Bell counter and watched a surly white teenager inject burritos with a sour cream gun knows how absurd these images are, not just because Taco Bell does not conform to the Mexican reality, but because the *abuelita* herself is a manufactured image. Today's Mexican woman is more likely to wash down her tortillas with a can of Diet Coke, while sitting before dubbed reruns of "Dynasty". The more "muy auténtico" a place claims to be, the more it exposes itself as a simulacrum, a copy of a copy for which there exists no original.[26]

Global mapping produces the illusion of diversity by the juxtaposition of all the varied products of the world's traditions and cultures in one space and time in the marketplace. Mexican food and tuna hotdish, mangoes and mayonnaise all meet the gaze of the consumer. For the consumer with money, the illusion is created that all the world's peoples are contemporaries occupying the same space-time. It is important that the other be "different", but it is equally important, as Ken Surin puts it, that the other be *"merely different"*.[27] The production of the simulacrum, difference at the surface only, precludes engagement with the genuinely other. So the conceit is advanced that my consumption contributes to your well-being through mutually beneficial global trade; my eating slakes your hunger.[28] The consumption of others' particularity absorbs them into a simulated catholicity while it simultaneously hides the way that space remains rigidly segmented between the Minnesotans who enjoy mangoes in the dead of winter and the Brazilian Indians who earn forty cents an hour picking them.

While globalization markets the traditions of the local culture, the people who inhabit the latter space are often losing their own traditions to the universal culture of Coke and Colgate. Historical continuity is difficult to maintain in the whirlwind of flexible accumulation. Local attachments are loosed by the centrifuge of ephemeral desire, which is fueled by global capitalism's ever accelerated need for growth. The post-Fordist economy has pursued ever increasing rates of turnover, most significantly by developing markets addicted to quickly changing fashion, and by shifting emphasis from goods to services, which have a much shorter "shelf-life". Short-term planning is endemic. Disposability, not simply of goods, but of relationships and particular attachments of any kind, is the hallmark of consumption in the new economy.[29] The result is not merely the dominance of a few name brands; the search for demand mandates a proliferation of specialized and exotic products (for example, bottled water for dogs or gourmet coffee beans recovered from Sumatran luwak dung[30]). The local and particular are prized precisely because of their novelty. The ideal consumer, however, is detached from all particulars. Novelty wears off, and particulars become interchangeable; what is desired is desire itself. The global economy is characterized by the production of desire as its own object, or as Fredric Jameson says, "the consumption of sheer commodification as a process".[31]

In this economy images themselves have become commodities, and are prized as commodities precisely because of their ephemerality. Images are not only subject to a very rapid turnover, but they also easily transcend spatial barriers in a way that goods cannot. The depthlessness of these images obeys the logic of the simulacrum. The logic of exchange value has almost entirely extinguished the memory of use value.[32]

As a result, the subject is radically decentered, cast adrift in a sea of disjointed and unrelated images. If identity is forged by unifying the past, present, and future into a coherent narrative sequence, the ephemerality and rapid change of images deconstructs this ability. The late capitalist subject becomes "schizophrenic", in Lacan's terms, and experiences only "a series of pure and unrelated presents in time".[33] But this new construction or deconstruction of subjectivity is inaccurately described as pure heterogeneity, the triumph of the particular. For the subject created is the Nabisco executive's universal homogeneous consumer, whose "catholic" tastes preclude it from attachment to any particular narratives. Yet this by no means signals simply "the end of masternarratives", as Lyotard would have it. It is instead a new catholicity, or, to quote Jameson, "the return of narrative as the narrative of the end of narratives".[34]

III. The World in a Wafer

Does the Eucharist offer a counter-narrative of global proportions? Surely the Eucharist is to be done so that *from east to west* a perfect offering might be made to the glory of his name. Aquinas defines the catholicity of the Church in the broadest possible terms, as transcending all boundaries of space and time, as well as natural and social divisions among people.

> The Church is Catholic, i.e., universal, first with respect to place, because it is everywhere in the world, against the Donatists ... This Church, moreover, has three parts. One is on earth, another is in heaven, and the third is in purgatory. Secondly, the Church is universal with respect to the state of humanity, because no one is rejected, whether master or slave, male or female ... Thirdly, it is universal with respect to time ... because this Church began from the time of Abel and will last to the end of the world.[35]

The true catholicity produced by the Eucharist, however, does not depend on the mapping of global space. The church gathered in the catacombs, after all, was as catholic as the church that would ride Constantine's chariots to the ends of the known world.[36] I will argue in the second half of this essay that the Eucharist overcomes the dichotomy of universal and local. The action of the Eucharist collapses spatial divisions not by sheer mobility but by gathering in the local assembly. The *Catholica* is not a place, however, but a "spatial story" about the origin and destiny of the whole world, a story enacted in the Eucharist.

The Greek adjective *katholikos*—derived from *kath' holou*, "on the whole"— in antiquity was commonly used as an equivalent of "universal" or "general". The earliest patristic application of the term to the Church, however, is not univocal; by "catholic" some imply "universal" or "total", but others imply "authentic". By the middle of the fourth century, the term had taken on more precise meaning as that which distinguishes the great Church as a whole from dissident or heretical Christian groups.[37] Although we continue to use the word "catholic" in English as an equivalent of universal, as Henri de Lubac points out, the terms in some senses diverge. "Universal" suggests spreading out; "catholic" suggests gathering together. In modern English "universal" indicates a reality prevalent everywhere. According to de Lubac,

> "Catholic" says something more and different: it suggests the idea of an organic whole, of a cohesion, of a firm synthesis, of a reality which is not scattered but, on the contrary, turned toward a center which assures its unity, whatever the expanse in area or the internal differentiation might be.[38]

The center toward which the true *Catholica* is turned is the Eucharist which, in de Lubac's famous phrase, makes the Church. However, the Eucharist is a decentered center; it is celebrated in the multitude of local churches scattered throughout the world, with a great diversity of rites, music, and liturgical spaces. It is precisely this fact that complexifies the calculus of particular and universal within the Church catholic. As Hans Urs von Balthasar puts it,

> The *Catholica* is in fact a region whose middle point is everywhere (where the Eucharist is celebrated); and (structurally) she can theoretically be everywhere: geographically, her periphery extends to "the very ends of the earth" (Rev. 1:8), a periphery that in any case can never be far from the midpoint.[39]

As Balthasar goes on to say, however, the normal condition of the *Catholica* is not Christendom—a permanent place with borders defensible by force—but diaspora. Although the Church is catholic in its missionary imperative to spread the gospel to the ends of the earth, catholicity is not dependent on extension through space.

The Eucharist celebrated in the scattered local communities is, nevertheless, gathered up into one. From the early Church, this principle was expressed by the participation of at least two bishops, as heads of local eucharistic communities, in the ordination of another bishop.[40] In the ancient Roman liturgy, at the papal Mass, a particle of the host was set aside for the following Mass. Other particles were sent out to priests celebrating Mass in the various localities.[41] In such practices the Body of Christ is not partitioned, for the whole Body of Christ is present in each fraction of the elements: the world in a wafer.

By the same liturgical action, not *part* but the *whole* Body of Christ is present in each local Eucharistic assembly. In Romans 16:23 Paul refers to the local community as *hole he ekklesia*, the whole Church. Indeed, in the first three centuries the term "catholic Church" is most commonly used to identify the local Church gathered around the Eucharist.[42] Each particular church is not an administrative division of a larger whole, but is in itself a "concentration" of the whole. The whole Catholic Church is qualitatively present in the local assembly, because the whole Body of Christ is present there.[43] Catholic space, therefore, is not a simple, universal space uniting individuals directly to a whole; the Eucharist refracts space in such a way that one becomes more united to the whole the more tied one becomes to the local. The true global village is not simply a village writ large, but rather "where two or three are gathered in my name" (Mt. 18:20).

The transcendence of spatial and temporal barriers does not depend on a global mapping, therefore, but rather on a collapsing of the world into the local assembly. It is crucial to note that, for the early Church, the Eucharistic assembly would be the only one in a particular city. The Eucharist would therefore unite all the members of the Church in a particular location, regardless of age, race, sex, language, or social class. As John Zizioulas notes, gathering in solidarity and love was not a Christian innovation. Members of Roman *collegia* addressed each other as brethren and often held goods in common. What distinguished the Christian eucharistic community was the way that it transcended natural and social divisions. In Christ there is no Jew or Greek, slave or free, male or female (Gal. 3:28).[44] This remarkable collapsing of spatial barriers is what makes the local community truly catholic.

IV. The Eucharist as Spatial Story

I have tried to show how the Eucharist breaks down the dichotomy of universal and local, but the suspicion may arise that Eucharist as antidote to globalism is simply a retreat into a place-bound theocracy or sect. Certainly the Eucharist—as in some medieval Corpus Christi rites—can be used to reinforce a fixed social hierarchy within a certain location, and to exclude others, especially the Jews, from that space.[45] Are not all Christian attempts to privilege the local similarly subject to the fascist temptation, or the temptation of "sectarianism", the very antithesis of a catholicity which seeks to unify rather than divide?

In this final section of my paper, I will argue that the *Catholica* enacted by the Eucharist is not a place as such, but a story which performs certain spatial operations on places. I will draw once again on Certeau's discussion of spatial stories, and his useful distinction between maps and itineraries. Stories organize and link spaces in a narrative sequence. They not only move from one space to another, but more accurately construct spaces through the practices of characters who trace an itinerary through the story. In contrast to the global and abstract mapping of space, medieval representations of space measured distance in hours or days, the time it would take to arrive at a destination on foot. These itineraries told stories about the way which was made by the pilgrims themselves as they walked towards their destinations.[46]

The itinerary implies not seeing but going; the subject does not survey the space detached as from above but as immersed in the movements indicated by the story. A story is not simply told but performed; space is organized by a body in movement, its gestures and practices. As such, the spatial story is not simply descriptive, but prescriptive. Stories give us a way to walk; "They make the journey, before or during the time the feet perform it."[47] As Certeau says, the story "opens a legitimate *theater* for practical *actions*".[48]

The spatial story is an act of resistance to the dominant overcoding of the map. And yet it does not depend on establishing its own place, its own territory to defend. Instead it moves on pilgrimage through the places defined by the map and transforms them into alternative spaces through its practices. The City of God makes use of this world as it moves through it on pilgrimage to its heavenly home. But this pilgrimage is not the detachment from any and all spaces, the sheer mobility of globalism. The Eucharist journeys by telling a story of cosmic proportions within the particular face to face encounter of neighbors and strangers in the local Eucharistic gathering. In an economy of hypermobility, we resist not by fleeing, but by abiding.[49] The community may journey without leaving its particular location, because the entire world and more comes to it in the Eucharist. The Letter to the Hebrews informs the humble community that they are not alone at their Eucharist.

> You have come to Mount Zion and to the city of the living God, the heavenly Jerusalem, and to innumerable angels in festal gathering, and to the assembly of the firstborn who are enrolled in heaven, and to God the judge of all, and to the spirits of the righteous made perfect, and to Jesus, the mediator of a new covenant, and to the sprinkled blood that speaks a better word than the blood of Abel (Heb. 12:22–24).

Though the eschatological dimension of the Eucharist is only recently being reemphasized, the patristic writings and ancient liturgies are replete with the vivid transgression of spatial and temporal barriers at the Eucharist to unite the whole Church on earth with the Church of all times and places in eternity.[50] The Eucharist not only tells but *performs* a narrative of cosmic proportions, from the death and resurrection of Christ, to the new covenant formed in his blood, to the future destiny of all creation. The consumer of the Eucharist is no longer the schizophrenic subject of global capitalism, awash in a sea of unrelated presents, but walks into a story with a past, present, and future.

In the detached hypermobility of global capitalism, signs and locations become interchangeable, for what is desired is desire itself. Augustine's lament "I was in love with love"[51] captures this condition. Augustine saw that one's true identity is only found in desire for God, who is beyond the fleeting things of this world. We might add that it is precisely God's transcendence of the world that allows liturgical difference, for where God cannot be fully grasped, a diversity of locations and practices is necessary to imply the transcendent.[52] Nevertheless, liturgical difference is possible not because all particular signs are interchangeable. On the contrary, in the Eucharist the particular is of the utmost importance, for this particular piece of bread at this particular place and time *is* the body of Christ, and is not merely a pointer to some abstract transcendent standing behind the sign. In the Eucharist there is a hypostatic union between reality and sign, *res et sacramentum*. Christ saturates the sign, such that consumption of the Eucharist identifies the consumer with God.[53]

In the Eucharist, the consumer does not stand detached from the consumed. Through consuming the Eucharistic bread we are in fact consumed by the body of Christ. Augustine reports Christ's words to him: "I am the food of the fully grown; grow and you will feed on me. And you will not change me into you like the food your flesh eats, but you will be changed into me."[54] It should be clear that calling the Eucharist a "story" by no means denies the reality of transubstantiation. It is the very body and blood of

Christ that organize the spaces into which we walk. It is Christ, not we, who tells the story. Each consumer of the Eucharist receives the whole body of Christ, though the body remains one throughout the whole world. This is only possible because the consumer is absorbed into the body. The consumer of the Eucharist begins to walk in the strange landscape of the body of Christ, while still inhabiting a particular earthly place. Now the worldly landscape is transformed by the intrusions of the universal body of Christ in the particular interstices of local space. Turn the corner, and the cosmic Christ appears in the homeless person asking for a cup of coffee. Space is constantly "interrupted" by Christ himself, who appears in the person of the weakest, those who are hungry or thirsty, strangers or naked, sick or imprisoned (Mt. 25:31–46).

Practicing the narrative of the body of Christ collapses spatial barriers, but in a way very different from globalizing capitalism. Globalization depends on a mapping which juxtaposes people from all over the world in the same space-time. This juxtaposition situates diverse localities in competition with one another. At the same time, the illusion is fostered that the world's people are contemporaries, different from each other, but *merely* different. In Eucharistic space, by contrast, we are not juxtaposed but identified. In the body of Christ, as Paul says, "If one member suffers, all suffer together with it; if one member is honored, all rejoice together with it" (1 Cor. 12:26).[55] This radical collapsing of spatial barriers accomplishes not competition, but says Paul, greater honor and care for the weakest member, who is identified with oneself. At the same time the other is not merely different but wholly other, for the suffering are identified with Christ himself (Col. 1:24), who nevertheless remains other to the Church.

In organization of space, therefore, the Eucharist does not simply tell the story of a united human race, but brings to light barriers where they actually exist. When Paul discovers that the Corinthians are unworthily partaking of the Lord's Supper because of the humiliation of the poor by the rich, Paul tells them, "Indeed, there have to be factions among you, for only so will it become clear who among you are genuine" (1 Cor. 11:19). This verse is puzzling unless we consider that the Eucharist can be falsely told as that which unites Christians around the globe while in fact some live off the hunger of others. Theologians of the southern hemisphere remind us that the imperative of "Church unity" is often a cover for exploitation of the worst kind. In the North American context, many of our Eucharistic celebrations too have been colonized by a banal consumerism and global sentimentality. The logic of globalization infects the liturgical life of the Church itself; Christ is betrayed again at every Eucharist. Where the body is not properly discerned, Paul reminds the Corinthians, consumption of the Eucharist can make you sick or kill you (1 Cor. 11:30). This might explain the condition of some of our churches.

I will close with an illustration of how the Eucharist can operate as a spatial discipline which suggests resistance to the pretense of one united world advanced by globalizing capital. On February 13, 1977, Fr. Rutilio Grande of El Salvador gave a homily during Mass in the village of Apopa.

> The Lord God gave us ... a material world for all, without borders ... "I'll buy half of El Salvador. Look at all my money. That'll give me the right to it." ... No! That's denying God! There *is* no "right" against the masses of the people! A material world for all, then, without borders, without frontiers. A common table, with broad linens, a table for every-body, like this Eucharist. A chair for everybody. And a table setting for everybody. Christ has good reason to talk about his kingdom as a meal. He talked about meals a lot. And he celebrated one the night before his supreme sacrifice ... And he said that this was the great memorial of the redemption: a table shared in brotherhood, where all have their position and place ... This is the love of a communion of sisters and brothers that smashes and casts to the earth every sort of barrier and prejudice and that one day will overcome hatred itself.[56]

Less than a month later, Rutilio Grande was gunned down by a government-sponsored death squad. In response, Archbishop Oscar Romero took the extraordinary measure of declaring that only one Mass, the funeral Mass, would be celebrated in the Archdiocese that Sunday. All the faithful, rich and poor, would be forced into a single space around the celebration of the Eucharist. The elite reacted with outrage, but Romero stood firm.[57] He was drawing on the power of the Eucharist to collapse the spatial barriers separating the rich and the poor, not by surveying the expanse of the Church and declaring it universal and united, but by gathering the faithful in one particular location around the altar, and realizing the heavenly universal *Catholica* in one place, at one moment, on earth.[58]

NOTES

1   Michael Novak, *The Catholic Ethic and the Spirit of Capitalism* (New York, NY: Free Press, 1993), p. 153.
2   See Peter Brown, *Augustine of Hippo* (Berkeley, CA: University of California Press, 1967), p. 221.
3   Robert H. Nelson argues that global capitalism has replaced Christianity with a far more effective means of universal salvation. For his exposition of global capitalism as theology, see *Reaching for Heaven on Earth: The Theological Meaning of Economics* (Savage, MD: Rowman and Littlefield, 1991).
4   The North American Free Trade Agreement, signed into law by President Clinton in 1993, eliminates all trade barriers among the US, Mexico, and Canada.
5   Robert Nisbet details this process in his *The Quest for Community* (London: Oxford University Press, 1953), pp. 75–152.
6   John Milbank, "On Complex Space" in *The World Made Strange: Theology, Language, Culture* (Oxford: Basil Blackwell, 1997), pp. 268–292.
7   Otto Gierke, *Associations and Law: The Classical and Early Christian Stages*, trans. George Heiman, (Toronto, Ont.: University of Toronto Press, 1977), pp. 143–160.
8   Michel de Certeau, *The Practice of Everyday Life* (Berkeley, CA: University of California Press, 1984), p. 120.

9   Ibid., p. 121.
10 Ibid., pp. 115–130.
11 G. W. F. Hegel, *The Philosophy of Right*, trans. T. M. Knox, (Oxford: Clarendon Press, 1952), §§ 256–257; Michel Foucault, *Discipline and Punish: The Birth of the Prison*, trans. Alan Sheridan, (New York, NY: Vintage Books, 1977), pp. 293–308.
12 On Foucault's relationship to Hegel, see Michael Hardt, "The Withering of Civil Society", *Social Text* 45, vol. 14, no. 4 (Winter 1995), pp. 31–34.
13 On the disappearance of the conditions of possibility of civil society, see Hardt, pp. 34–40; Kenneth Surin, "Marxism(s) and 'The Withering Away of the State'", *Social Text* no. 27 (1990), pp. 42–46; and Antonio Negri, *The Politics of Subversion: A Manifesto for the Twenty-First Century* (Cambridge: Polity Press, 1989), pp. 169–199.
14 David Morris, "Free Trade: The Great Destroyer" in Jerry Mander and Edward Goldsmith, eds., *The Case Against the Global Economy* (San Francisco, CA: Sierra Club Books, 1996), p. 221.
15 Ralph Nader and Lori Wallach, "GATT, NAFTA, and the Subversion of the Democratic Process" in Mander and Goldsmith, eds., pp. 92–107.
16 The article "Losing our Shirts" in *The Independent* (Durham, NC), April 6, 1994, documents how, for example, USAID has spent over a billion dollars since 1980 on grants, loans, and advertising encouraging US companies to seek cheap labor in the Caribbean and Central America. US tax dollars have paid for USAID advertisements in trade journals, such as one that reads "Rosa Martinez produces apparel for US markets on her sewing machine in El Salvador. *You* can hire her for 33 cents an hour."
17 Anthony Giddens, *The Nation-State and Violence* (Berkeley, CA: University of California Press, 1987), pp. 148–171.
18 George Ritzer, *The McDonaldization of Society* (Thousand Oaks, CA: Pine Forge Press, 1993).
19 Quoted in Jerry Mander, "The Rules of Corporate Behavior", in Mander and Goldsmith, eds., p. 321.
20 David Harvey, *The Condition of Postmodernity* (Oxford: Basil Blackwell, 1989), p. 159.
21 Ibid., 159–160, 233–239.
22 Gilles Deleuze and Félix Guattari, *A Thousand Plateaus*, trans. Brian Massumi, (Minneapolis, MN: University of Minnesota Press, 1987), p. 13. There is a difficulty in terminology here because Deleuze and Guattari use the term "map" in almost the exact opposite way that Certeau uses it. For Deleuze and Guattari, a "tracing" is a "competence" which homogenizes and captures space. A "map", on the other hand, is "rhizomatic" and productive of lines of flight; Ibid., pp. 12–20.
23 See, for example, Helena Norberg-Hodge, "The Pressure to Modernize and Globalize" in Mander and Goldsmith, eds., pp. 33–46. Norberg-Hodge traces the destructive influence of globalization on the traditional culture of the Ladakhi people of northern India. She argues that ethnic conflicts in India are produced largely by the competition, artificial scarcity, and unrealizable desires created by globalization.
24 Harvey, pp. 271; 293–296.
25 Ibid., pp. 295–296.
26 I have in my possession an illustration of a young man, arms spread wide, standing on a beautiful desert highway. Superimposed around him are the slogans, "discover difference", "seek the unusual", "take another road", "forget typical", "nothing ordinary about it", "leave ordinary behind". The illustration is printed on a paper tray liner from Taco Bell.
27 Kenneth Surin, "A Certain 'Politics of Speech': 'Religious Pluralism' in the Age of the McDonald's Hamburger", *Modern Theology* 7/1 (October 1990), p. 74.
28 The latter phrase is taken from Catherine Pickstock's brilliant exposition of the logic of the Eucharist in medieval Europe in her *After Writing: On the Liturgical Consummation of Philosophy* (Oxford: Basil Blackwell, 1998), pp. 121–166. Pickstock adopts the phrase from a Reformation controversy over the Eucharist.
29 Harvey, pp. 284–286.
30 Unfortunately, I'm not making these up.
31 Fredric Jameson, *Postmodernism, or, the Cultural Logic of Late Capitalism* (Durham, NC: Duke University Press, 1991), p. x.
32 Ibid., p. 18.
33 Ibid., p. 27.

34   Ibid., p. xii.
35   Thomas Aquinas, *Oposculum VII*, "In Symbolum Apostulorum, scil., *Credo in Deum*, Expositio", quoted in Avery Dulles, *The Catholicity of the Church* (Oxford: Clarendon Press, 1985), p. 181.
36   See Oliver O'Donovan's comments on the charge of "sectarianism" in *The Desire of the Nations: Rediscovering the Roots of Political Theology* (Cambridge: Cambridge University Press, 1996), p. 216.
37   Dulles, p. 14.
38   Henri de Lubac, *The Motherhood of the Church*, trans. Sr. Sergia Englund (San Francisco, CA: Ignatius Press, 1982), p. 174.
39   Hans Urs von Balthasar, *Explorations in Theology IV: Spirit and Institution*, trans. Edward Oakes, S.J. (San Francisco, CA: Ignatius Press, 1995), pp. 65–66.
40   John Zizioulas, *Being as Communion: Studies in Personhood and the Church* (Crestwood, NY: St. Vladimir's Seminary Press, 1985), p. 155.
41   de Lubac, p. 206.
42   de Lubac comments in a footnote that, while Zizioulas' claim that during the first three centuries the term "catholic Church" was used *only* for the local Church is a bit exaggerated, "it was nevertheless enough for the difference from 'universal' to become apparent"; de Lubac, p. 177, n. 23.
43   Ibid., pp. 199–202. de Lubac uses "local Church" to designate bodies such as the Uniate Churches which possess their own liturgical usage and disciplines. For the purposes of this essay, I use "local" and "particular" interchangeably to refer to the community gathered around the Eucharist in a particular place.
44   Zizioulas, pp. 150–152.
45   See Miri Rubin, *Corpus Christi: The Eucharist in Late Medieval Culture* (Cambridge: Cambridge University Press, 1991), and Sarah Beckwith, *Christ's Body: Identity, Culture, and Society in Late Medieval Writings* (London: Routledge, 1993).
46   Certeau, pp. 115–130.
47   Ibid., p. 116.
48   Ibid., p. 125.
49   Frederick Bauerschmidt suggests that Certeau did not fully appreciate the way that resistance to certain practices often necessitates institutions such as monasteries and soup kitchens which, although appearing quite stationary, are a way of walking; see "Walking in the Pilgrim City", *New Blackfriars* 77, no. 909 (November 1996), pp. 504–517.
50   See Geoffrey Wainwright, *Eucharist and Eschatology* (New York, NY: Oxford University Press, 1981).
51   Augustine, *Confessions* III, 1, trans. Henry Chadwick (Oxford: Oxford University Press, 1991), p. 35.
52   Catherine Pickstock makes this point in her "Liturgy, Art and Politics", forthcoming in *Modern Theology*.
53   Jean-Luc Marion, *God without Being*, trans. Thomas A. Carlson (Chicago, IL: University of Chicago Press, 1991), p. 156; also Frederick Bauerschmidt, "Aesthetics: The Theological Sublime" in *Radical Orthodoxy: A New Theology*, John Milbank, Catherine Pickstock, Graham Ward, eds. (London: Routledge, 1999), pp. 201–219.
54   Augustine, (VII, 10), p. 124.
55   Jerome Murphy-O'Connor stresses that Paul had in mind much more than "fellowship", but a real "co-existence" in the body of Christ, that is, a common source of life. The community is one, and the community is Christ; "Eucharist and Community in First Corinthians" in *Living Bread, Saving Cup: Readings on the Eucharist*, ed. R. Kevin Seasoltz (Collegeville, MN: The Liturgical Press, 1982), pp. 1–30.
56   Rutilio Grande, S.J., quoted in Jon Sobrino, *Jesus in Latin America* (Maryknoll, NY: Orbis Books, 1987), pp. 96–97.
57   An account of the debate over the single Mass can be found in James R. Brockman, *Romero: A Life* (Maryknoll, NY: Orbis Books, 1989), pp. 9–18.
58   Thanks are due to Fritz Bauerschmidt, Mike Baxter, Mike Hollerich, Steve Long, and Paul Wojda for helpful comments on an earlier draft of this essay.

WHOSE EUCHARIST?
EUCHARISTIC IDENTITY
AS HISTORICAL SUBJECT

MIRI RUBIN

In the interview for my current job, as a History Tutor at Pembroke College Oxford, one of the questions posed to me, towards the end, was, "What are *you* doing studying the Eucharist?" As the interview had gone rather well up to then, I decided that this was a friendly question, one which would allow me to explain an intellectual autobiography, rather than a trick, or hostile one. I thus unfolded a truncated version of the following story, and that version must have satisfied my interviewers, a panel of eleven men, since they elected me unanimously to the post.

The story related to the intellectual aspirations which prevailed and still prevail in the Hebrew University in Jerusalem, my *alma mater*.[1] There the teaching of history is contained within frames defined by the presence or absence of Jews: there was the department of Jewish History which covered all periods and places, and then the department of General History, which excluded Jews from the history of Europe and the rest of the West. Asian and African histories were studied in separate departments. It was thus possible to reach the fifth year of the study of History, in my case 1980, without ever having come across Jews: I had studied Ottoman history, the Crusades, medieval trade, Roman citizenship, and the Jews had been absent from all of these themes and pedagogic programmes. In 1979 I embarked on a methodological course for MA students the theme of which was "Popular religion and popular culture in early modern Europe". Here we encountered the then new and fresh ideas of Keith Thomas, Natalie Davis, Robert Muchembled, Jean-Claude Schmitt, and were each charged with the task of writing an extended research essay on a source for the study of popular religion. Being a medievalist, I chose to look at medieval drama for my

Miri Rubin
Pembroke College, Oxford OX1 1DW, UK

paper. I dutifully went to the English department, acquainted myself with the hundreds of brown volumes of EETS, and began to read the plays known as Corpus Christi drama.

What is the Corpus Christi drama? What indeed is Corpus Christi? These are questions to which later work, indeed some twelve years later, would aim to provide some answers. But the beginning of a search for an answer was my task back then. And it began with an unravelling of the feast of the Eucharist—Corpus Christi—and then the Eucharist itself. I did so without the stirring of personal memory or snippets of childhood rhymes, without smells and sounds that still flow from the many public and private manifestations of the Eucharist for those who grow up in Europe or the Americas. As opposed to those who studied Jews alone, and who felt equivocal about investigating the Christian mysteries too closely, I did not even feel that: not revulsion, not fascination, just the dutiful curiosity that well-trained and hard-working historians entertain *vis-à-vis* their subjects as a matter of course.

Yet despite the attempt to define two separate historical projects: the General, scientific, largely German-inspired history of the Department of General History, or the providential and pious Jewish History, when I began to do research for my PhD in Cambridge, I found that my chosen theme, hospital formation and charity in England in the Middle Ages, nonetheless brought me in touch with Jews again and again: sermons which encouraged Christians to give to the poor often cited the example of Jews, famed for the care which they offered to their own: ending with the hortative question "Have you ever seen a Jew begging in the streets?"[2] When I explored the endowment of hospitals such as St John's Oxford, it became clear that hospital-founders often benefited from deals struck with Jews who were able to amass properties pawned and sometimes lost to them, since they could not undertake land tenure in fee. Jewish businessmen were thus keen to sell the lands, and enterprising founders of charitable institutions—hospitals and academic colleges—accumulated the lands needed to found: charitable creation enabled by Jewish legal incapacity. I noted these cases, this confluence, but engaged little with the realities of life behind them.[3]

It was in the years of research for *Corpus Christi*, in the attempt to explore as a sort of historical ethnographer the practices and meanings which came to be related to the Eucharist in the later Middle Ages, that I came to the closest and most arresting realisation of the impossibility of excising Jews from the history of Europe. It was then that I came to appreciate the deadly intimacy of the relationship between Christians and Jews. Never before had an historical environment been more telling and rich in such messages than the terrains of Eucharistic practices: from the meal at the Eucharist's inception, the Last Supper, to the many ways in which the Jews came to be the central endorsers and guarantors of the Eucharistic moment of Christian culture after around 1200. The Eucharist developed out of the discussions of theologians and the reasoning of canonists, the political aspirations of papal officials, and the pastoral dilemmas raised by bishops and preachers; it was endorsed by the formulations of the Fourth Lateran Council (1215), was made of the immediacy of materiality, which was nonetheless always qualified: the Eucharist as Christ's body was not to be seen like other objects, nor was its materiality amenable to the changes which operate on other ingested foods. Periodically, it miraculously revealed its qualities for all to see. Increasingly, it became something of a touchstone. Ever truthful it distinguished between the real and the false, ever correct it could delve into intentions beyond appearances and ritual form. It was a prime marker which people wore with pride, rejected with passion, and claimed with invention and even audacity. It alone could tell true claims from delusions: the Eucharist alone in its many-formed self-fashioning.

It is the century which saw the pastoral dissemination and parochial absorption of all the dictates and the promises of the Eucharist, the thirteenth century, which also saw the making of the powerful tale of its abuse in the hands of Jews. In this narrative were imputed to Jews inventive stratagems for the acquisition of the host and its desecration and shaming, stratagems worthy of those keen Eucharistic purveyors, the holy women of the Low Countries described so lovingly by medieval writers such as Jacques de Vitry and Thomas of Cantimpré and by contemporaries such as Caroline Bynum and André Vauchez.[4] The questions which Jews were said to have posed to the Eucharist—"If he is God let him show himself to us"—echoed those which were attributed to doubting layfolk, weak priests and all manner of Eucharistic players in the dramas of *exempla* and inquisition. Yet the narrative which attached such questions to Jews differed, inasmuch as its end was violent and finite: the Jew/perpetrator was destroyed, as were his kin and neighbours and often tens of communities in the neighbourhood of his town. The Eucharist's most deliberate foe called forth the most excellent manifestation, and brought forth greater violence than any other doubter or questioner could elicit. A great intimacy thus developed between the Eucharist and the Jew: the Jew came to be told through his Eucharistic doubts, and the Eucharist through the Jew's rejection.

The powerful signification of the Eucharist, that which lent to it the charisma that bestowed identity and dignity on so many, was located in its many and rich associations. It was food, it was God, it was small and mundane, it was lofty and impenetrable. It was white, it was red. It was man-made, it was made for humanity. Its quality as food brought it home, into the intimacy of hearth, into spheres of women, and thus, imaginably, of doubt and error, into the nurture and protection of children. Claudine Fabre-Vassas has recently unfolded the rich ethnography which related Jews, Christians and the pig in her *The Singular Beast*, based on the historically situated observation of pig-rearing, killing and eating in the south of France.[5] She shows how the intricate processes of bleeding and baking still resonate with

Eucharistic meanings, how pig and child enjoy still a symbolic equivalence which renders the Jew the enemy of both. Current practices may possess echoes of the medieval apocryphal treatment of Christ's childhood, wherein Christ is said to have been shunned by the parents of Jewish children. When he appeared to seek his playmates their parents hid them in the oven, and when they opened the oven they found pigs, not children, therein.[6]

The image of baking similarly linked Jews to the most intimate space of the female, and even the Marian, body. Images of the female body in the Middle Ages likened the womb to an oven, to a secret and dark but nurturing space; they also named Mary the oven of the Eucharist, portraying her as the baker of the Eucharist. Inasmuch as Jews rejected the Virgin Birth, they also rejected the hallowed space in which Christ was born, as enemies of the bread baked therein.[7] A famous early medieval tale has presaged the meaning of these images. The tale of the Jewish Boy ended with the Jewish father throwing his son, who had come to appreciate Eucharistic truth when he received communion with Christian school-friends, into an oven, only to be saved by the Virgin and to convert to Christianity.

The association of the inner, the private, the whole and the unsullied, with Christianity through the mediation of the image of the Virgin further served to enhance the difference of those who did not accept the underpinnings of the whole salvific system, and within it Mary's special niche. Such were not only Jews but those dualists who abhorred the notion of God's birth of a woman, like those to whom the words of the Dominican preacher Moneta of Cremona were directed in the mid-thirteenth-century: "Why do you say that a pregnant woman is like a devil, when Luke attests that she is full of the Holy Spirit?"[8] It was that fertility of the inner *sanctum* which was the essence of femininity, full of secrets and of potential fecundity, which Jews were accused of defiling and abusing: in the desecration of women and in the magic allegedly operated on pregnant women in the working of maleficent abortions.[9] The trail which connected femininity with incipient sanctity was clearly threatened by the *maleficium* which Jews and Jewish doctors were seen to work.

The multivalent imaginings which the Eucharist inspired further expressed in their twists and turns the many possibilities of appropriation which it offered. In the niceties of their fine theological-philosophical distinctions as they discussed the fortune of the Eucharist during digestion by the Christian's body, Franciscan and Dominican theologians found an occasion to mark their difference from each other.[10] Franciscans, who cleaved to the humanity of Christ, were particularly wedded to the notions of continued corporality which became one with the body of the recipients. Dominicans insisted rather on the strict meaning of accidents, so that once the Eucharist no longer resembled itself, it could no longer pose a serious intellectual theological dilemma, and was not to be discussed in pastoral exchange. If Franciscans were willing to dwell at least awhile upon the possibility that something

meaningful occurred when a mouse or a cat occasioned to receive the consecrated host, Dominicans were able to establish their intellectual identities
and priorities by finding *prima facie* reasons for stopping short of discussing
the problem. Intellectual identities, not only styles, were forged in debates
about the Eucharist. And yet even the friars with their sophisticated, subtle
preaching and single-minded devotion to pastoral and ecclesiastical causes,
could never compete with the simple privilege of the priest in orders, perhaps that is why so many were ordained in the later medieval centuries. To
St Francis the respect due to the person who handled his Lord in his hand
every day, and upon whom even he, Francis, depended for access to Christ's
Body, was awe-inspiring, possessing a mystique and power which no amount
of preaching and exemplary living could rival.

The image offered by the Eucharist could be widely inclusive or insistently
obscure and exclusive. Think of late medieval images of the mill of the host
or the mystic wine-press, those images for contemplation and decoration
of psalter and bibles of monastic houses of southern Germany. Possessing
the habit of allegorical reading of scripture, and with access to the glosses,
one could, just as art historians can today, unravel the images and their
many layers of meaning, binding the Old and New Testaments through
the promise, and then the fulfilment of a Eucharistic Christian history. The
images circulated in these exclusive circles, in monastic houses which in the
later Middle Ages also consumed quite avidly a diet of tales and protocols
of a quite gory nature, the confessions of Jews in the course of well-known
trials for ritual-murder such as the famous case of Trent in 1475,[11] host-
desecration such as that of Passau in 1477.[12] The details of confessions dragged
out of accused persons with torture, and possessing truth value as vindica-
tions of Eucharistic claims, were copied and re-copied for no administrative
or legal purpose but for the reading and edification, the exemplary and
titillating value, of the transgressive and the dangerous.

The Eucharist's enormous power and promise and the centrality of its
location within a system at once liturgical and pastoral, allowed for such
appropriations, claims and uses to be made around and about it: what is it
about the Eucharist that particularly promoted such incessant creativity? By
being so centrally positioned, by occupying the centre stage of discussion
and emphasis, the Eucharist denuded other symbols and symbolisers of what
Lacan called "a second life", of anything beyond the brute existence, where
nothing is really at stake, and of which nothing lasts.[13] The Eucharist's promise
was of that second life of meaning, such as Antigone wished to bestow upon
her brother; it is that capacity to bear meaning, to transcend, that is denied
the Eucharist's perceived enemies.[14] Its foes were the enemies of signification,
and thus fell short, were crude, passing and lonely. This qualitative difference was a crucial one for those who embraced campaigns of moral revival
and invigoration, those who hoped exactly to animate and imbue Christian
European polities with the challenges of renewal and reform. Such voices

were heard repeatedly and strongly between 1350 and 1450 and were ultimately engaged in the processes of refiguration encompassed within the two Reformations.

These movements against corruption, loss of direction and decline—institutional, political, environmental, civic and economic—were mightily involved in the offering of Eucharistic purity as a rallying cry and discipline for their adherents.

In these calls for change made by late medieval reformers ranging from Jean Gerson to Nicholas of Cusa, from Henry of Langenstein to Giovanni da Capistrano—Eucharistic renewal, remodelling of liturgical practice, re-drawing of the boundaries between lay-person and priest—coincided with a resounding call against usury, and often against those rulers whose needs allowed usury to flourish. The type of moral cleansing envisaged was often accompanied by various types of expulsions—of Jews, of beggars, of prostitutes, of Lombards. It is interesting to note the operation of town councils within these politics of moral hygiene. Overbearing and interventionist town-councils after the Black Death and in the ensuing decades of endemic plague, led the way in attempting to provide clean water and clear air. Theirs was the language of good stewardship, good house-keeping, that intersected so fruitfully with the language of moral cleansing, as programmes related to sumptuary legislation and against usury took root. The triumphant Eucharist offered a symbol for the type of political and moral order they desired. If usury and begging were the product of ill-value and the vicissitudes of laziness, of moral turpitude, then the Eucharist was pristine and clean, unchanging in value, utterly reliable. A sub-section of tales about the Eucharist associated it with coinage, as it turned miraculously into coins, or was mistaken for coins. It was after all inscribed like coins and deep thought could develop about the nature of its perimeter, its edges. Probably the greatest exponent of the tension between the Eucharist's properties and the finitude of its geometrical, spherical shape was exploited by St Bernardino of Sienna, a leading reformer, preacher against usury and Jews: in his devotional mind the Eucharist became an emblem, an external sign of great force and coherence, as the Eucharistic host, that sphere came to burn in the colours of blood and flesh, blood surrounded with the circumference of flesh, yet still embossed with the anagram of Christ.

The host desecration narrative and populist vindication of anti-usuary campaigns were clearly intertwined, as the case of Prague in 1389 demonstrates. There *Judenpolitik* stood as a contentious issue between clergy and King, between clergy and the King's men. The synodal statutes of October 1381 railed against usury:

since the sin of usury is a horrible and detestable crime and it occurs frequently nowadays not only among common folk but also among men of high status, in many ways both under the guise of profit and through counterfeit, which we report with sorrow, because of the things done by the same Jews and by other infidels to taunt us, and this creates great scandal in the hearts of the faithful of God's church.[15]

One of the bearers of these complaints in eloquent homiletics and devotional poetry was the Archbishop of Prague, John of Jenstein (*c*. 1348–1400). In a Christmas sermon delivered some time in the 1380s, he argued that the property which they accumulated and the privileges Jews enjoyed favoured them over clergy; their influence in high places rendered Jews more powerful than magnates and churchmen.[16] The subject of usury immediately followed, and Jews were accused of pauperising prince and magnate alike, and then using their riches in the service of Antichrist their Lord.[17] Another vehement critic of the Jews and their protector was the Augustinian abbot Ludolf of Sagan (d. 1422; abbot from 1394), who saw the king, in a period of grave lapses in justice, rejected by clergy and people, by nobles, townsmen and peasants, and accepted by Jews alone.[18] Thus the treatment of the Jews was seen as leading to pride which resulted in offences against Christians and their Saviour, as expressed in Prague in 1389:

> since the Christian people could no longer pretend and bear, in just revenge of the blasphemy (committed) against the Eucharist ... on the feast of Easter, moved by zeal, it burnt those very Jews and their houses by fire.[19]

The political context and the anti-Jewish discourse are emphasised in these reports of the city's actions in 1389. Because of the King's absence, the crowd was drawn by the leadership of John (Gesco); the city elders supervised the collection of Jewish property, on expectation of a heavy fine. Moreover, the King placed armed men around the Jewish houses to reclaim them. As mentioned in the "Passion of the Jews", the bodies of the Jews were dug up and burnt, removing evidence and cleansing the city of their "usurious fats". In the face of the loot offered by the Jewish houses, some claimed that this should not be touched as it was the product of usurious gain. The rhetoric of the report on Prague, within the context of clerical complaints which we have already noted, allows the offence of host desecration to reverberate as only one instance of a greater evil, that which was preached regularly and insidiously, Jewish usury.[20]

It is this anti-usury discourse which structured some of the memories of the massacre. This peculiar association with usury, which intersected with the accusation of host desecration, was carried over into another type of writing, that of the physician and homiletic writer John Lange of Wetzlar (1365–*c*. 1427). A scholar of the University of Prague and Doctor of Medicine, who wrote texts on the management of epidemics, John also composed didactic and devotional works, the most famous of which is the *Dialogus super Magnificat* ("Dialogue on the Magnificat"), a work of 2668 hexameters dedicated to the Archbishop of Worms.[21] John Lange turned the telling of the events of Prague 1389 into a polemic against King Wenzel and his servants, especially Minister Sigmund Huber. The King is cast as a supporter of Jews, while the crowd take just revenge. The King protected his Jews for nefarious reasons:

> O kings, kings! Be shamed for such a crime! The usurious gain on the capital which is earned by the accursed people, in which you yourselves are proven to be accursed usurers.

> You have done this not on account of them, or because of their virtues, in which they are experts, nor for reason of justice, which attaches to them, rather on account of their vile silver and other gifts of gold. You know that they frequently enact nefarious acts against Christ's faithful, and you have consumed gifts but have worn down the justice of the law again and again.[22]

John Lange is confident of the moral opposition which the case of Prague demonstrated—between protectors of Christ's body and protectors of Jews. He accuses the royal councillors of having "sharpened" the king against the citizens of Prague, thus allowing for the all too real possibility that Christ's body be abused again.[23]

***

We see here a local instantiation of the power of the Eucharist to crystallise fear about value, identity and authentic rule. True piety, that of the people, was vindicated against a miscreant ruler. The Eucharist was thus inserted by the power of its unassailable truth into moments of authentication. Its proximity with coins—in shape, in countervailing the character of usury and Jewishness, in its emblematic value—recurs interestingly throughout late medieval culture. Paul Strohm's *England's Empty Throne* contains breathtaking pages about late medieval desire to associate Eucharistic error, such as was preached and practised by Lollards, with counterfeiting, fraud, treason and particularly that of passing bad coins.[24] An elaborate metaphor developed around the socially disruptive and inherently evil effect of fraudulent tampering with a country's currency, which received very severe punishment at the hand of the state; it came to express the error of those who tampered with the Eucharist and its value. If coinage and currency was a tangible and communicable token of a real power and majesty, possessive of intrinsic value validated by its symbolic appearance, the Eucharist was similarly both itself valuable and representative of powers and promise extending from it. Yet both were vulnerable: almost anyone could handle each, and repay that generosity of circulation with abuse—clipping, deriding, devaluing. These perpetrators were the mis-guided, and divisive. They could only see immediate profit, short-term gain—usurers,

Jews, coin-clippers, fraudsters, Lollards—oblivious to the system of value and community which their actions eroded. Both deserved swift response action, exemplary punishment, and the images of both interacted and interpenetrated in specific political contexts such as late fourteenth-century Prague, early Lancastrian England, late fifteenth-century Bavaria.

***

The Eucharist offered not only a mystery to engage minds for life-times, a vocation and badge of difference for priests, the comforting companion for female religious, the focus for anti-clerical sentiment and religious discontent, the banner for reformers and populist leaders of crusades against Jews. It has also offered interesting trails for contemporary scholars in their investigations and explorations of self and vocation. I have already shared with you some of my own experiences leading up to my standing here among you. This conference's organiser, Sarah Beckwith, has combined disciplinary approaches —theology, social theory, literary theory—to produce *Christ's Body*.[25] For Sarah Beckwith, the Eucharist crystallises some central dialectics within late medieval social and cultural organisation: that which values the material— work, the body—and yet attempts to transcend their prescriptive contours. She has turned sacramentality into more than an aspect of liturgical practice and into an epistemological category, which characterises, among others, displays of power and the very action of drama. Among us is Eamon Duffy, the author of *The Stripping of the Altars*, in which tens of pages situate the mass within a system of traditional religion, in a sensitive rendering of an ideal type of mass, with an emphasis on aspects of both individual and collective participation.[26] For Duffy the Eucharist enabled vast creativity and extension from a set of official versions of liturgy and practice into the many instances of localities and temporalities. David Aers has responded rather vigorously to Duffy's book, seeing in it an interpretation of late medieval religion which pays insufficient attention to inequality of access to symbols, and to the entrenched conformity in social and inter-personal matters which conventional religion forced upon people. According to Aers, Duffy also fails to appreciate the currents of anti-clerical and anti-sacramental sentiment which characterised late medieval communities.[27] Although I feel that Aers' and Duffy's positions and sympathies are probably closer than the surface exchange might suggest, we have here the Eucharist and sacramentality used as touchstones, as keys to a whole set of interpretations: for Duffy, to a world alleviated, enriched and informed by the routines which parishioners created around and with conventional sacramental religion; for Aers, to a community expressed through a shared stream of critical engagements with hegemonic religion, one which fundamentally strives for corrective operation of justice, perhaps in keeping with a pre-sacramental Christianity, and which helps bind communities around such creations.

The lamented Bob Scribner, who created the social history of the Reformation, was an adept reader of the lingering sacramentalities of Lutheran culture and practice. He too used the Eucharist as a window upon the social, political and communal worlds of sixteenth-century German people.[28]

Recently Stephen Greenblatt used the Eucharist as cypher for the understanding of *Hamlet* and for a number of canonical texts of early modern England. The Eucharist's dialectics of presence and absence, authority and power, of faith and betrayal, make it a lingering riddle in a "disenchanted" world obsessed with Protestant identity and authority and in constant polemical tension with Catholicism.[29] At the same time, Greenblatt has been writing about his Jewish childhood, just as David Mamet has written about his memories of childhood Passovers.[30] I suggest that there is something attractive, both pristine and infinitely inscribable, utterly incomprehensible as a literal entity and thus utterly demanding of other types of interpretation, to those who have not consumed the Eucharist. I suggest further that while those aspects of transubstantiation that have always moved some Christians and many non-Christians to reflection on the cannibalistic, improbable, unsavoury associations with the notion of ingesting a God who was human, remain somewhat repellent, it is the breadth of symbolic possibilities, the simplicity and accessibility of the Eucharist which nonetheless draws to it scholars who are clearly not Christian, or ambivalent Christians. The Eucharist today offers scope for the most fervent intellectual interdisciplinarity, it requires constant association and sharing of associations. Working on it creates communities and demonstrates those aspects of cultural production which are meaningful to many of us engaged in the historicist unravelling of religious cultures.

The Eucharist's plurality of appeal and openness to use—both when a high price had to be paid for expressing one's ideas about it, and nowadays in the relative freedom of intellectual inquiry—offers the pristine slate of representation, total innocence, total power, vulnerability as the potential victim at the hands even of its most fervent adherents. Its utter inscrutability has disconcerted Jews then and now; its malleability has challenged projects of historical ethnographic inquiry; its ability to be regenerated, and endlessly shared, marks a place in our historical subjectivities that, as these collected essays doubtless show, has much to reveal to us about the pluralities of the past as well as those which we inhabit.

NOTES

1   For the development of departmental demarcations see A. Rein, "History and Jewish History, Together or Separate: the Definition of Historical Studies at the Hebrew University, 1925–1935", *The History of the Hebrew University in Jerusalem: Origins and Beginnings* [in Hebrew], eds. M. Heyd and S. Katz (Jerusalem: Magnes Press 1997), pp. 516–540.

2   *The Sermons of Thomas Brinton, Bishop of Rochester (1373–1389)*, ed. M. A. Devlin, Camden series 85–86 (London, 1954); I, sermon 35, pp. 148–149, sermon 44, pp. 196–197; II, sermon 90, p. 411.

3 Miri Rubin, *Charity and Community in Medieval Cambridge* (Cambridge: Cambridge University Press, 1987), pp. 273–275.

4 C. W. Bynum, *Holy Feast and Holy Fast: the Religious Significance of Food to Medieval Women* (Berkeley, CA: University of California Press, 1987); André Vauchez, *Sainthood in the Later Middle Ages* (Cambridge: Cambridge University Press, 1997).

5 C. Fabre-Vassas, *The Singular Beast: Jews, Christians and the Pig*, trans. C. Volk (New York, NY: Columbia University Press, 1997).

6 Miri Rubin, *Gentile Tales: The Narrative Assault on Late Medieval Jews* (New Haven and London: Yale University Press, 1999), pp. 24–25.

7 M. Rubin, *Corpus Christi: the Eucharist in Late Medieval Culture* (Cambridge: Cambridge University Press, 1991), p. 145.

8 Moneta de Cremona, *Adversus catharos et valdenses libri quinque*, ed. T. A. Ricchini (Rome: Palladi, 1743), col. 335b.

9 For some of the accusations which might arise around accidents or malpractice see M. P. Lillich, *Rainbow like and Emerald: Stained Glass in Lorraine in the Thirteenth and Fourteenth Centuries* (University Park and London: Pennsylvania State University Press, 1991), pp. 78–81, 111–112 and pl. IV, 4; J. Shatzmiller, *Jews, Medicine, and Medieval Society* (Berkeley, CA: University of California Press, 1994), p. 84.

10 D. Burr, *Eucharistic Presence and Conversion in Late Thirteenth-Century Franciscan Thought*, Transactions of the American Philosophical Society 74/3 (Philadelphia, PA: American Philosophical Society, 1984).

11 R. Po-chia Hsia, *Trent 1475: Stories of a Ritual Murder* (New Haven, CT: Yale University Press, 1992).

12 R. Po-chia Hsia, *The Myth of Ritual Murder: Jews and Magic in Reformation Germany* (New Haven, CT: Yale University Press, 1988), pp. 50–56, 81–90.

13 J. Lacan, *Le Séminaire. VII: L'Ethique de la psychanalyse*, ed. J.-A. Miller (Paris: Seuil, 1986), pp. 285–348, esp. pp. 337–348; P. Guyomard, *La Jouissance du tragigue: Antigone, Lacan et le désir de l'analyste* (Paris: Aubier, 1992).

14 I am grateful to Louise Fradenburg for her iluminating introduction to this discussion.

15 "quia tamen hujusmodi usurarii nephas horrendum et detestabile ... hodie nedum per populares verum etiam per magni status homines multimodis et quaesitis et fucatis coloribus, quod dolenter referimus, frequentatur, propter quod ab ipsis Iudaeis et aliis infidelibus in improperium nobis objicitur et fidelium cordibus in Dei ecclesia scandala gravantur", 16 October 1381, *Concilia pragensia, 1353–1413*, ed. C. Höfler (Prague: Gerzabek, 1862), p. 30.

16 "... Nam bene videtis clerum et Christofideles cottidie in suis iuribus et libertatibus supplantari et subici multasque iniurias perpeti et magis synagogam quam Christi proficere ecclesia et inter principes plus unum posse Judeum quam procerem vel prelatum", in R. E. Weltsch, *Archbishop John of Jenstein, 1348–1400: Papalism, Humanism and Reform in Pre-Hussite Prague*, Studies in European History 8 (The Hague and Paris: Mouton, 1968), p. 62, n. 89.

17 "Ymmo per usurias inauditas principes et magnates adeo depauperantur, ac si cum thesauris illis suum dominum Antichristum ditare et adiuvare queant", Ibid.

18 "Non fuit temproibus illis qui vic regia justiciam faceret pupillis et viduis, ymmo nec baronibus, nobilibus et vassalis, quorum pars non modica, querelas emisit, de illata sibi regali violencia. Exosus igitur erat clero et populo, nobilibus, civibus et rusticis, solis erat acceptus Iudeis", in "Catalogus abbatum Saganensium", *Scriptores rerum silesiacarum* I, ed. G. A. Stenzel (Wroclaw: Josef Max, 1835), p. 214.

19 "quia christiana gens dissimilare et ferre non potuit, in vindictam blasphemiam illius, quadam die ... in sollempnitate paschali ... zelo mota Judeos ipsos et domus eorum igne cremavit", Ibid.

20 Rubin, *Gentile Tales*, pp. 135–140.

21 See entry by E.-S. Bauer and G. Baeder in *Die deutsche Literatur des Mittelalters. Verfasser-lexikon* (Berlin and New York: de Gruyter, 1985), cols. 584–590; on the *Dialogus*, cols. 585–586.

22 "O reges, reges pudeat vos criminis huius!
Usuras capitis, quas gens maledicta lucratur,
in quo vos ipsos maledictos esse probatis usuratores.

... Non propter eos, non propter eorum
virtutes, quibus expertes sunt, nec racione
iusticie, qui subdit eos, sed propter eorum
argentum vile vel cetera dona vel aurum
istud fecisti. Tu scis, quod facta nephanda
sepius intulerant hii Christi fidelibus, et tu
munera sumpsisti, sed legis preteristi iusticiam crebro",
E.-S. Bauer, *Frömmigkeit, Gelehrsamkeit und Zeitkritik an der Schwelle der grossen Konzilien. Johannes von Wetzlar und sein Dialogus super Magnificat* Quellen und Abhandlungen zur mittelrheinsichen Kirchegeschichte 39 (Mainz: Selbstverlag der Gesellschaft für mittelrheinische Kirchengeschichte, 1981), pp. 274–276, lines 2084–2087, 2103–2110.

23 "... Sed consilliarie nequam
qui contra cives Pragenses exacuisti
regem, peniteas nec ultra tam malefidam
gentem promoveas, ne contra corpus amandum
Christi tale quid accidat amplius, esurientes
quo saciat Dominus", Ibid., p. 280, lines 2177–2182.

24 P. Strohm, *England's Empty Throne: Usurpation and the Language of Legitimation, 1399–1422* (New Haven, CT: Yale University Press, 1998), pp. 128–152.

25 S. Beckwith, *Christ's Body: Identity, Culture, and Society in Late Medieval Writings* (London: Routledge, 1993).

26 Eamon Duffy, *The Stripping of the Altars: Traditional Religion in England, c. 1400–c. 1580* (New Haven, CT: Yale University Press, 1992), esp. pp. 91–130.

27 D. Aers, "Altars of Power: Reflections on Eamon Duffy's *The Stripping of the Altars*", *Literature and History* third ser. 3 (Autumn, 1994), pp. 90–105; and the following exchange in *Literature and History* third ser. 4 (Spring, 1995), pp. 86–88 (Duffy), p. 89 (Aers).

28 R. W. Scribner, *Popular Culture and Popular Movements in Reformation Germany* (London: Hambledon Press, 1987).

29 This work is yet to be published; he has also written some reminiscences in S. Greenblatt, "Miracles", *The Threepenny Review* Vol. 69 (Spring, 1997), p. 34.

30 D. Mamet, *Passover* (London: HarperCollins, 1995).

THE EUCHARIST: ITS CONTINUITY WITH THE BREAD SACRIFICE OF LEVITICUS

MARY DOUGLAS

For Christians a loaf of bread and a cup of wine would substitute for the flesh and blood of animals. Jesus' death was to be the offering that would replace the offerings required in the old law. The institution of the Eucharist was understood to be a new covenant, the foundation of a new relation to God, the basis for the Christian theology of redemption. Jesus is recorded as having said it clearly enough on that occasion (Matthew 25:26; Mark 14:22; Luke 22:20). It was a radical break, but at the same time no one could argue that the Christian Eucharist was a brand new institution. It clearly has continuity with the Bible. The Last Supper was the paschal meal. The bread sacrifice of Melchizedek (Gen. 14:18; Ps. 110:4) is honoured in Christian teaching (Heb. 5:6, 10; 6:20; 7:1). But neither of these points allow a parallel to be drawn between the Eucharist and the regular sacrificial system of the temple. Melchizedek, king of Salem, was not a descendant of Abraham; he is mentioned in Genesis and not in the law book, Leviticus. Here I wish to argue that the doctrine of the Eucharist was actually continuous with Bible teaching on sacrifice and that there was a solid basis for bread sacrifice laid down in Leviticus itself.

Apart from the switch from animal to bread sacrifice, some have claimed that another innovation of the Eucharist was to open the communion feast to non-Jews.[1] This might seem to make it a new covenant in the sense that it was to include people not descended from the heirs of Abraham, Isaac or Jacob. Jesus celebrated this family festival, the Passover, without his family, only his disciples sharing communion with him and each other. This would

Mary Douglas C.B.E., F.B.A.
22 Hillway, London N6 6QA, UK

constitute a major break with the past if it be assumed that the message of the Bible was destined for an exclusive, hereditary group. But according to the texts, to open the Eucharist communion feast to all believers would not be very radical. The priestly teaching in Numbers (9:14) expects the stranger or sojourner to celebrate the passover.

To make the case convincing I have to combat the tendency to dismiss the priestly books. There is a mistaken but widespread idea that the sacrifice of the old law was materialist, and that the religion as taught by the priestly editors was exclusionary and focused on old-maidish rules of physical purity. On the contrary, the evidence of the text of the priestly books shows that they did not teach a narrowly sectarian doctrine, and even that it would have been compatible with their teaching to open up the promises of God to all mankind.

I admit that when I first read Leviticus for enlightenment on African dietary laws[2] I accepted the anti-priestly bias that I now reject, but that was thirty-plus years ago. Since then I have been reading Leviticus, Numbers and Deuteronomy, more carefully. The case for the continuity of the Eucharistic doctrine with the sacrifice of the Old Testament develops through three supporting arguments. The first concerns the place of animals in the divine plan.[3] The priestly editors, unlike the other Bible sources, put animal life on the same plane as human life, and demanded accountability to God for shedding animal blood as well as for shedding human blood (Lev. 17:4, 14).

Second, there always was a cereal offering in the biblical system of sacrifices, and so far from being subsidiary to the animal sacrifice, it was recognized as a separate, autonomous and very holy offering, with covenantal implications as strong as those implied in animal sacrifice.

Lastly, a fair reading of Leviticus emphasises the spiritual dimension of the act of sacrifice. The word for "body" has multiple references as microcosm for the temple and for God's universe. We have also to take into account the interchangeability in the Bible of words for spiritual and material food, bread and flesh, wine, blood, life and soul. Even the reference to the covenant is the same, as when Jesus said,

"This is my body which is given for you. Do this in remembrance of me … This cup which is poured out for you is the new covenant in my blood" (Luke 22:17, 20, and see Matthew 26:26 and Mark 14:22).

Compare the wording for the altar of show bread:

Every sabbath day Aaron shall set it in order before the Lord continually on behalf of the people of Israel as a covenant for ever (Lev. 24:8).

The mention of the covenant by Jesus would have keyed in the relevant associations for the strong reading given by the apostle who was not present (Paul, 1 Cor. 11:23–29).

Animals under God's Protection

The first argument starts with the treatment of animals in the food rules of Leviticus and then moves on to the rules about animals fit for sacrifice. We tend to read the Bible as if there were no other peoples around or as if what these other peoples were saying or doing in the sixth and fifth centuries has no bearing on our reading of the book. But Judah was not an island. The theme of animal rights was being widely canvassed in the eastern Mediterranean and hinterland, and further east, in the centuries before the final editing, seventh, sixth, fifth. There were conspicuous philosophical and literary debates about whether humans should not eat animals because of their common descent and kinship. There were passionate controversies about whether animals are inferior to humans because they cannot reason, whether they can really feel pain, and whether it is right to take animal life at all. The priestly editors could not have failed to know about these debates, as they had been in Babylon while and before the work of editing. Some practical issues were at stake, concerning the rules for eating animal flesh, as these times were replete with vegetarian movements, (Parmenides, the Pythagorean school, Zoroastrianism, Orphism, and in India, Buddhism and Jainism). We do not know when these movements started. It is quite implausible that they all burst into life at the point at which they were reported, in the sixth or fifth century. They had surely started with the first ascetic traditions. It goes without saying that people who adopted vegetarian food rules did not practice animal sacrifice, since sacrifice usually involved doctrines about eating together with the god. Sacrifice was a communion rite.

The priestly editors, after having been in exile in Babylonia, must have known of the ferment of new religions from the east. Their own claims to spirituality would be under challenge. They had accepted a charge to edit the ancient texts recording their people's relation to God, the creator. In these texts the series of covenants with God were always ratified by animal sacrifice. The vegetable offering of Cain had been rejected. The texts took the form of a pastoral history, a people who lived as shepherds and herders, and who were beloved by a God who was kind and merciful as well as just. All around them, in these foreign dissident religions, God's kindness and mercy were being interpreted as applying to animals as well as to humans. In the Bible the prophets and psalms give plenty of reason for taking God's mercy to extend to all his creation. At the same time, the priestly editors would have had no wish to impose a vegetarian regime on the congregation. It would have been unthinkable to turn their back on Moses and the forefathers whom he led across the desert with their flocks and herds. But the editors did impose a very strict care in the matter of animal life.

In effect, the detailed rules about impure animals brought the meat diet of the Israelites into correspondence with the sacrificial regime. What was impure for the altar was impure for the body of the Israelite, the meat that defiled the one defiled the other. We can call this correspondence a microcosm effect. A parallel was drawn between body and altar by the law of food impurity. The only animals which were allowed for sacrifice were the flocks and herds which the people of Israel reared for their livelihood, and these were the only land animals which the people were allowed to eat. Every other kind of land animal was excluded from the diet. As to the birds of the air and the fish in the water, they could eat any of them except the teeming things (which are often translated as crawling or creeping). The teeming things are recognized and blessed by God in Genesis for their abounding fertility, and whether they teem on the land, the water or the air, Leviticus forbids the people of Israel to eat them or to touch their carcases. In effect, this was like a game law or a rule for protecting endangered species. It protected every living thing from the knife of the Israelite. I keep repeating this word, Israelite, because the laws were not expected to apply to the rest of humankind. They were part of what the people of Israel accepted when they accepted the covenant with God. Not only were the covenanted people not allowed to eat furry animals with claws, or crawling animals, or swarming birds and shrimps, or slithering animals like snakes and eels, they were not allowed to touch their carcases. This would be really disabling if you wanted to set up as a furrier, or a taxidermist, or to make snakeskin bags or ornament of bone or tusks. It meant no mink coats, no beads or dice of ivory, no containers made of animal stomachs, no musical instruments stringed with gut. And so on.

The religion required that an account be made to God of the life of every animal (Lev. 17:2–4). By implication, of those that they were allowed to eat, or dismember and use, that is, the livestock they reared, each one that was killed had first to be consecrated at the altar and killed for sacrifice (Lev. 17: 8–9). Their livestock were treated in parallel with themselves, as covenanted creatures. If they were work animals they had to observe the sabbath (Exod. 20:10) and the first born of cattle were consecrated as were the first born of the people of Israel (Exod. 13:2; Lev. 27:26). The domestic flocks and herds came under the same covenant as the people of God and their servants. If you want to protest that these animal rights only led to slaughter, you can try to defend the ignominious and hidden deaths of our cattle in modern slaughterhouses in contrast with the dignity of the consecrated deaths of the livestock of Israel. For if you are going to eat animal meat at all, this is what it comes to, only the vegetarian has the right to protest.

In sum, this reading of Leviticus reduces the gulf between the priestly teaching and the prophets and psalms about God's compassion for all that he has made and his love for all living things. It also rescues the priestly reputation from the quest for purity for its own sake. It puts the religion more than halfway between a practical religion that everyone can observe without undue suffering, and an ascetic religion that calls for heroic asceticism. In this reading Leviticus is seen to place strong emphasis on the covenant, it also places strong emphasis on animal sacrifice for redemption, but there is also a cereal offering. So we come to the second part of our argument.

The Cereal Offering

Now read Leviticus again with an open mind to understand what it says about the cereal offering. The first chapter is on how to make a burnt offering, the second is on how to make a cereal offering, they are strictly "how-to-do-it" chapters. Then follow chapters 3–6:14, about which animals to give as peace or sin offerings. Notice that if a person cannot afford the full rate, he can bring two birds, and if he cannot afford birds he can bring flour to be burnt on the altar as a sin offering. But this default use of flour in absence of an animal is strictly discriminated from the "cereal offering" in which oil has to be incorporated and on which incense is laid (Lev. 5:11).

The word (*minhah*) used for the cereal offering in Leviticus has a secular connotation in the rest of the Bible. It means tribute, offerings in kind brought by subjects to their king, a gesture of submission by the vanquished to the conqueror. It means homage, recognition from one monarch to another. It may include food, but not necessarily, and the richest gifts can be very varied and sumptuous. The queen of Sheba's (*minhah*) homage to Solomon took the form of gold, spices and precious stones (1 Kings 10:2, 10). When the king of Syria was sick he sent a present (*minhah*) to Elisha, forty camel loads of all kinds of goods from Damascus (2 Kings 8:9). When the idea is extended to the religious context, the tribute takes the form of a meal: as for example, cooked meat, with its gravy and bread presented by Gideon to the angel of God (Judg. 6:11–24).

Throughout the Bible there are scattered and fragmentary references to the cereal offering. When we come to examine the priestly teaching we find that it has been developed very systematically. Alfred Marx's review of the cereal offering[4] argues that the priests have made it not minor, nor even equal in importance to animal offerings, but the prime sacrificial form. It is a solemn requirement; it must accompany all the daily sacrifices and sabbaths; it is prescribed for the new moon sacrifices and all public feasts. It is required for consecration of persons, from consecration of a priest to the reintegration of a healed leper. It is required for private sacrifices and it can also be offered as a solemn sacrifice in its own right. The cereal offering is destined to be shared between God and the priests, only by them; it is called "sacrosanct", and it is declared to be "the most holy portion out of the offerings by fire to the Lord" (Lev. 24:9). God's part is burnt on the altar to give the sweet savour, in the same words used of Noah's sacrifice. It is never assimilated into the performance of animal sacrifice, but remains always distinctively subject to its own rules. This reverses the common idea that it is a mere accompaniment.

Alfred Marx gathers evidence from Leviticus and Numbers, the two priestly books, to show that the priestly editors have taken immense pains to create a separate system for the cereal sacrifice, separate from but alongside the system of animal sacrifice. This is specially apparent in the repeated requirement for the cereal sacrifice for the feasts around the seventh month, the great feast of Atonement, and around the feast of Tabernacles, which is the culmination of all the sacrifices of the calendar. Everyone who has read in the Book of Numbers the laws pertaining to the number of animals which must be sacrificed in the third week after the Day of Atonement is struck by the strong patterning of the rules for the number of bulls to be sacrificed. From thirteen bulls on the fifteenth day, which counts as the first day of the week, it decreases by one each day, so twelve on the second day, eleven on the third day, through ten, nine, eight, matching the seventh day with seven bulls, and finally closing the pattern and coming back to normal on the next day with one bull. What is going on? What is the numerical patterning all about? With each day on which the number of bulls is reduced, the number of rams and lambs is invariant, two rams, fourteen lambs. All the commentators note how the pattern of sacrifices in Number 28–29 makes use of the number seven and multiples thereof, thus honouring the Sabbath, the six days of creation and the day of rest. Milgrom's commentary remarks:

> In addition to the frequency of the number seven (and its multiple fourteen) in the above table there are other occurrences of seven: the seven festivals (including the paschal observance, 28:16, and excluding Sabbaths and New Moons); the seven-day Unleavened Bread and Sukkot festivals; the preponderance of festivals in the seventh month (New Year, Yom-Kippur, Sukkot, ʿatseret); the seven festival days, in addition to the Sabbath, on which work is prohibited, listed in 28:18, 25, 26; 29:1, 7, 12, 35; the bulls required for Sukkot add up to seventy; the total number of animals offered on this seven-day festival is $7 \times 7 \times 2$ lambs, 7×10 bulls, and 7 goats.[5]

There seems to be no pattern, just an abundance of sevens in honour of the sabbath.

Alfred Marx's argument about the importance of the cereal offering suggests that we should also calculate the changes through the week of Sukkot for the amounts of flour for the cereal offerings. The amounts are precisely prescribed at the same rate throughout the calendar: for a bull, the cereal offering shall consist of three-tenths of an ephah of flour, for a ram, two-tenths, for a lamb one-tenth, no cereal offering to accompany the goat for the sin offering.

This is what the text of Numbers 28 and 29 requires:

Table 1. Animals for sacrifices through the calendar.

Day	Animal				Complement of Flour
	Bull	Ram	Lamb	Goat	Total in tenths
Daily Burnt offering		–	–	2	2
Sabbath	–	–	2		2 + 2*
New Moon	2	1	7	1	15 + 2*
(Passover)					
15th day of 1st month	2	1	7	1	15 + 2*
First Fruits	2	1	7	1	15 + 2*
Seventh Month					
1st day	1	1	7	1	12 + 2*
15th day	1	1	7	1	12 + 2*
16th day	13	2	14	1	57 + 2*
17th day	12	2	14	1	54 + 2*
18th day	11	2	14	1	51 + 2*
19th day	10	2	14	1	48 + 2*
20th day	9	2	14	1	45 + 2*
21st day	8	2	14	1	42 + 2*
22nd day	7	2	14	1	39 + 2*
23rd day	1	1	7	1	12 + 2*

*The total amount of flour for each feastday is augmented by the two-tenths of an ephah to correspond to the two lambs sacrificed for the daily burnt offering.

In effect, the priestly master of ceremonies has produced a rule for the animal offerings of the mid-week of the seventh month which successfully brings the daily declining number of bulls from thirteen to seven on the seventh day of the week, and it ends up with a multiple of seven, a total of seventy bulls. He has choreographed a dance or made a poem in honour of the sabbath, a kind of rhyming with numbers, obviously very deliberate and no mean mathematical feat. But we still only have a plethora of sevens.

Alfred Marx observes: "Fourteen bulls, seven rams, 49 (7 × 7) lambs are brought for burnt offerings in the feast of unleavened bread, with a cereal accompaniment of 105 (15 × 7) tenths of flour. At the end of the harvest seven times the amount of lambs and of cereal prescribed at its opening phase are required. In the first 7 days of the feast of Booths, 70 bulls are sacrificed, of which seven on the seventh day. In the course of this same festival 105 (15 × 7) lambs were offered as a burnt offering." So, still lots of sevens. But

Table 2. Animals for Sukkot

The seven days of Sukkot, plus the inaugurating and closing days, in the seventh month:

15th day	1	1	7	1	12 + 2*
16th day	13	2	14	1	57 + 2*
17th day	12	2	14	1	54 + 2*
18th day	11	2	14	1	51 + 2*
19th day	10	2	14	1	48 + 2*
20th day	9	2	14	1	45 + 2*
21st day	8	2	14	1	42 + 2*
22nd day	7	2	14	1	39 + 2*
23rd day	1	1	7	1	12 + 2*
Totals	71	14	49	7	364

then he goes on to calculate the cereals for the festival as a whole: "Three hundred and sixty four (7×52) tenths of flour are offered, in all, between the 15th and the 22nd day ..."[6]

He actually gets this result by counting in the fifteenth day inaugurating the week and the twenty third day closing it, each with only one bull. The result is extraordinary, it could not have happened by accident. The Jews had a lunar calendar, so 7×52 does not refer to the days of the year. There are, however, approximately fifty-two sabbaths in the year, and when a year of sabbaths is multiplied by seven we have the seven years of the jubilee cycle. The sum of the units of flour for the nine days comes to the number of sabbatical weeks in the year, fifty-two, multiplied by seven, which can only refer to the seventh year sabbath of rest for the land which produces the cereals. (Chapter 25 of Leviticus expounds this very fully.) So apart from the reference to the seventh day, this particular multiple of seven carries a more complex reference to the sacred calendar.

If it makes sense to ask why the number of bulls declines each day by one there are three possible answers. One could be that it is calculated to arrive at the sum of seven bulls on the seventh day. Another could be to arrive at a multiple of seven, seventy bulls by the end. A more interesting one comes from the fact that each bull calls for three-tenths of an ephah of flour, so that the changing amount of flour, three-tenths of an ephah of flour less for each decrease in bull numbers, combined with the invariant amounts of flour to be given along with each ram and lamb and the lambs of the daily offering, could come out to the sum of sabbaths in a calendar year!

When attention shifts from the animals to the cereals it suddenly appears that it is the cereal offerings which are calling the shots, not the other way round; the bulls are only dancing (as it were) to the tune of the tenths of ephahs of flour. The column for cereals declines in proportion to the declining numbers of bulls, until when the list is complete the apparently haphazardly repeated celebration of the sabbatical seven has produced in the column for cereals a result to achieve which requires a perversely brilliant talent for numeral acrostics. But the argument for the autonomy and dignity of the cereal offering in the priestly books does not depend on this curious calculation. It has been worth quoting because it illustrates how completely the precedence of the animal sacrifices has been taken for granted, and the cereal offering played down.

The main case is convincing because of scrupulous examination of the texts. At the end the author asks what the obscuring of this independent series of cereal offerings means. To explain how it has been so well-forgotten, he delves into the controversies surrounding the offerings of Cain and Abel in Genesis. Why did God reject the vegetable offering of Cain? Was it because vegetables are the product of the earth and of human hands, whereas the herd animals are his own creation? This suggestion refers to the curse which God placed on the earth when he discovered the disobedience of Adam and Eve: "Cursed is the ground, because of you!" (Gen. 3:17). Or was it a reflection of the general rejection of everything to do with the Canaanite religion, which prominently featured horticultural products in offerings to Baal? Was it an ideological bias in favour of nomadic pastoralism, the open country, the free life of wandering shepherds, as against the bourgeois materialism of farmers and immorality of cities? Marx reviews but does not choose between these possibilities.

His own conviction is that the teaching of the priests in Leviticus and Numbers was at variance with subsequent readings of the Bible. The members of any religious community may all read the same books, but most certainly they do not read them in the same way. It is not only a matter of reading, it is to miss their message not to see that the priestly books are taking a different line on many points. They accept the earth and all of God's creation, they believe in the forgiveness of God after the sacrifice of Noah, they remember that when God swore never again to destroy the earth he also blessed the descendants of Noah, telling them to be fruitful and multiply, and he established an everlasting covenant with them, with the sign of the rainbow. The words of Genesis for describing the pleasing odour of Noah's sacrifice, which occasioned God's change of heart, are used again repeatedly in Leviticus for the pleasing odour of the cereal offering, thus giving the latter convenantal status, as well as referring to the first covenant which was with all humankind.

This chimes perfectly with my own findings in trying to read Numbers and Leviticus with an anthropologist's eye. To show that Leviticus is not besotted about impurity, I have had to establish different meanings for key words, such as unclean, teeming and abominable. On other counts I find that Numbers favours friendship with the sons of Joseph in Samaria.[7] Leviticus has no rules about marriage partners, it makes no laws for marrying inside the community, or against marrying foreigners. Both Leviticus and Numbers are solicitous that persons who are living among them but not related by birth to the people of Israel shall be included in the cult. For an Old Testament source for Mark, 12:28–34, (also John 13:34; 15:12), "the great commandment, greater than them all, first you shall love the Lord your God", see Deut. 10:12; 11:13. Deuteronomy also tells the people to love their neighbours, the strangers who live among them (Deut. 10:19); and Leviticus actually gives the words of the second great commandment, "You shall love your neighbour as yourself" (Lev. 19:34).

The gesture of Jesus in celebrating the Passover supper with his disciples instead of with his family, and they with theirs, would hardly have been censured in that tradition, any more than would his talking to the Samaritan woman and her people (John 4:1–43). When Jesus taught in the temple and astonished the sages by his knowledge of the law and the prophets, I surmise that he was explaining to them this more benign reading of the law inscribed in the priestly books, a reading which had been brushed aside in favour of nationalist exclusiveness in Deuteronomy and ritual cleanness in the rabbinical traditions. Somewhere along the line, the continuity of writing and reading Leviticus was broken.

That this was a serious break is shown by the many paradoxes and complications which arise, and apparently insoluble puzzles that follow from reading Leviticus through the eyes of Deuteronomy.[8] The latter is a very different book, the editor is more of a nationalist politician, brilliant at rousing the emotions of the congregation, a tugger at heart strings, not very interested in the cult nor in metaphysics. With such a different training and outlook he would be sure to miss a subtle and complex literary structure. I put it this way because in the absence of information it is safer simply to state the gap between the two books without speculating on historical causes. But it is possible that some principle that the priests stood for was an underlying political stumbling block, perhaps even the inclusionary principle that would have given non-Jews a right to join the cult might have given offence in later times. We do not know, but it certainly seems that Leviticus has been misread and half the teaching lost. We are able to say this because the book is there to read, and to be set beside the standard interpretations of different generations.

Microcosmic Models

This brings me to the third plank in my argument. I have discussed the attitude to animals as being consistent with high regard for a cereal offering. I have discussed the esteemed place of the cereal offering in the sacrificial system. Finally I must try to suggest what it could have meant for a master solemnly to tell his followers: "This is my body", while holding a loaf of bread. The first thing is to disabuse modern readers that the simple fishermen of Galilee would not have enough education to understand microcosmic models when they see them. My argument will be that they could have been absolutely familiar with microcosmic modelling from Leviticus and used to a concept of the body that has multiple meanings. You do not have to be literate to understand a series of graphic analogies given in a well-known context. It is much harder to understand a sermon made of verbal abstractions.

The anthropological record is stacked with religions in which temples and bodies are presented as if built on the same principles, and these, the very principles of the universe. The projection of the cosmos can start with the roof as a cover, or with the alignment of the front and back of the body with the entrance and rear of the building; in the vertical plane, foot to head corresponds in an obvious way with floor and roof; in the horizontal plane the right and left of the body can be projected on to the internal space by taking the entry as a fixed point of reference. When this fixed point is the front, if the entry corresponds to the sunrise the whole space is aligned with the cardinal points. Hindu temples are explicitly built on the model of the human body.[9]

When bodies are assimilated with the cosmos the abstractions that are being made from the body and from space can be so closely assimilated to each other it makes little sense to say which generated which, or which is projected upon the other. The biblical system of reference to cardinal points is no exception.[10] The Hebrew language uses the same word for the conventional alignments, for example, the words for south and north are the words for right and left respectively, with the tacit assumption that the body is fronting east in alignment with the tabernacle. We can safely assume that the apostles assembled in the upper room for the Last Supper were perfectly familiar with microcosmic ranges of meaning for the word "body".

The priestly writer is a hierarchist much preoccupied with due times and spaces. He invents analogies and plays them against each other, to make harmonies in time and space. The idea of a body is replete with possibilities for the metaphysician. The body of an animal and the body of a human, and the body of the temple, he speaks the word and makes each one resonate with the meanings of the others. The idea that "a rose is a rose" has no sense in this kind of writing. By analogies of right ordering he teaches the people of Israel to honour in their lives the order of God's creation, and by doing so to share in his work. The living body is his paradigm. In the space of the animal's body he finds analogies with the tabernacle and the history of God's revelation to Israel. When he talks about abstractions such as honesty and justice, he uses simple measuring examples: "You shall do no wrong in judgement, in measures of length or weight or quantity, you shall have just balances, just weights ..." (Lev. 19:35). The body is also treated as a measure of justice. Only the perfect body is fit to be consecrated, no animal with a blemish may be sacrificed, no priest with a blemished body shall approach the altar, "a man blind or lame, or one who has a mutilated face or a limb too long, or a man who has an injured foot or an injured hand, or a hunchback, or a dwarf ..." (Lev. 21:16–20). Leviticus makes physical blemish correspond to blemished judgement, the scales that judge weight, length, or quantity in the market invoke the scales of divine judgement. We can take it that readers of Leviticus were quite used to the cosmologizing of the body and to micro-cosmic models of many dimensions and kinds.

The Three-fold Body Logic

To be brief about a long and complicated topic, Leviticus turns out to have made use of a threefold analogy, in which the first two models are the desert tabernacle and Mount Sinai. Each is constructed upon the proportions of the other, and third is the body of the animal to be sacrificed, constructed upon the same proportions. This is a very unexpected thing to have found. For me the discovery started when I read that the mystic philosopher and revered medieval interpreter, Rambam, established this parallel from the Book of Exodus. If he was right about Exodus, it is not surprising that Leviticus should have adopted the scheme and extended it.

Remember that the same priestly hand that edited Leviticus is credited in source criticism with the chapters in Exodus in which God gave Moses the plan of the tabernacle, and fenced off Mount Sinai. God forbade the people to go up into it or even to touch it until permission was given by the sounding of a horn (Exod. 19:12–25). Rambam's parallel between mountain and tabernacle was based on the triple zoning of each and the graduated holiness coming to a climax at the top of the mountain and in the inner recesses of the tabernacle. Nahum Sarna explains that,

> Both Sinai and the Tabernacle evidence a tripartite division. The summit corresponds to the inner sanctum, or Holy of Holies. The second zone, partway up the mountain, is the equivalent of the Tabernacle's outer sanctum, or Holy Place. The third zone, at the foot of the mountain, is analogous to the outer court. As with the Tabernacle, the three distinct zones of Sinai feature three gradations of holiness in descending order. Just as Moses alone may ascend to the peak of the mountain, so all but one are barred from the Holy of Holies in the Tabernacle. Just as the Holy Place is the exclusive reserve of the priesthood, so only priests and elders are allowed to ascend to a specific point on the mountain. The confinement of the laity to the outer court of the Tabernacle, where the altar of the burnt offering was located, evokes the parallel with Sinai in the restriction of the laity to the foot of the mountain, where the altar was built.[11]

Table 3. Two Paradigms of the Tabernacle Aligned

Mt. Sinai	*Tabernacle*
Summit or head of the mountain, cloud like smoke Exod. 19:18, God came down to top, access for Moses only, Exod. 19:20–22	Holy of Holies, cherubim, ark and testimony of covenant, clouds of incense.
Perimeter of dense cloud, access restricted to Moses, Aaron, two sons and 70 elders Exod. 24:1–9	*Sanctuary*, table of show bread, lampstand; incense altar and smoke of incense; restricted to priests.
Lower slopes, open access.	Outer court, open access.
Mt. Sinai consecrated Exod. 19:23.	Tabernacle consecrated Lev. 16.

The model makes great play with parallels between fire of God's presence, smoke of fire, smoke of incense, and the cloud of God's presence. It might well be objected that this is a medieval fantasy without application to Leviticus. Jacob Milgrom, Bible scholar and Leviticus commentator, supports the idea that it was an ancient tradition because of the survival of the term, "Tent of Meeting", which name for the tabernacle commemorated the connection between it and the place where the initial meeting between God and Moses took place.[12] The cloud is the sign of God's presence. At Sinai when all the work of the tabernacle was finished, "Moses was not able to enter the tent of meeting because the cloud abode upon it and the glory of the Lord filled the tabernacle" (Exod. 40:35). In Genesis the sweet smoke of sacrifice attracted God's attention after the flood. In Exodus the incense altar was used for the priest to send up clouds of fragrant smoke in the tabernacle (Exod. 30:7–8, 34–38; 40:26). Smoke impedes visibility, like a cloud.

The Sacrificial Meat

Sacrifice invokes the whole cosmos, life and death. Normally throughout the world wherever sacrifice is practised, an elaborate symbolism governs the selection of animal victims, each gesture for the sacrifice is minutely prescribed, the animal parts cut and coded, and every detail loaded with meaning. The first few times that I read Leviticus on sacrifice I saw only a bald account of an animal led to the altar, a hand placed upon its head, nothing said about the manner of its death, a lot about disposing of its blood, and dividing the meat between the altar, the priests and the people. But no sign of the symbolic load that is put upon the sacrificial victim in other religions. Then I decided to read it again very carefully, paying close attention to the rules about what must never be eaten, the blood and the suet, a part of the liver called the long lobe, and the kidneys, and paying close attention to the placing of the pieces of meat upon the altar.

The result was to find that the animal's body was seen as divided at the midriff by a block of hard suet fat which covered the liver and kidneys and which divided the upper part, the rib cage, from the lower abdomen, intestines and genital organs. The middle part, that is, the suet and what it covered, was forbidden. Nothing was said about the head, the tongue, the neck, the lungs, or the heart, or the gall bladder, or about any other anatomical items that figure in other sacrificial lists. So I felt I had to assume that the only thing that was important was this three part division of the carcase, with a middle zone forbidden or reserved to God. When I thought of checking this against Rambam's model of the tabernacle, the proportions looked right. Furthermore, the occluding suet in the middle zone of the animal matched with the dense smoke of incense in the tabernacle and the thick clouds in the middle of the holy mountain. Rules of access to each zone also matched to some degree, (not perfectly).

Table 4. Three Paradigms of the Place of Meeting

Mt. Sinai	*Carcass of peace offering*	*Tabernacles*
Summit or head. Cloud like smoke Exod. 19:18, God came down to top, access for Moses only, Exod. 19:20–22.	Entrails, intestines, sexual organs (washed) at the summit of the pile.	Holy of Holies, cherubim, ark and testimony of covenant.
Perimeter of dense cloud, access restricted to Moses, Aaron, two sons and 70 elders Exod. 24:1–9.	Midriff area, dense fat covering, kidneys, liver lobe, burnt on altar.	Sanctuary, dense incense, symmetrical table and lampstand; access restricted to priests.
Lower slopes, open access.	Head and meat sections, access to body, food for people and priest.	Outer Court, main altar, access for people.
Mountain consecrated Exod. 19:23.	Animal consecrated, Lev. 1–7.	Tabernacle consecrated Lev. 16.

What bearing has the system of analogies with the tabernacle on the institution of the Eucharist? First as to the cereal offering: to be convincing I should have said a lot more on how priests had made the two systems run in parallel. In summary, what goes for the animal goes for the loaf of bread. Second, as to the animal sacrifice, I surmise that the congregation knew Leviticus' teaching on the triple-zoned bodies, and were sufficiently used to microcosmic modelling for the mutual projection of the holy mountain and the house of God, each upon the other, and the sacrificial animal on both. So many of the rules for eating have drawn parallels between the body and the temple or altar. Cleansing for one benefits both. These people would have been going around always conscious that their bodies were paradigms of the tabernacle, always enacting its defilement and purification. Eating the sacrificial meat the members of such a congregation would each have had the sense that in his own body he was renewing the banquet of the seventy elders who were allowed up to the middle zone of Mount Sinai (Exodus). If the analogy were to be further pursued, they themselves each became, in the act of communion, the holy meeting place. That in itself is very suggestive for a readiness to hear the words, "This is my body", in an eschatological context.

Here I rest my case. The shift to cereal offerings would have been easy. First, the attitude of Leviticus to animal life is protective and respectful. Second, in Leviticus animal sacrifice is already matched by a well-developed system of cereal offerings. These two points suggest that it would be no great problem to institute vegetable sacrifice. Third, the habit of analogical thinking was deeply ingrained in the language of religion, metaphors of cosmos and body were highly developed. The Christian doctrine of the Eucharist would have grown very naturally from the teachings of Leviticus, without necessarily requiring a violent break with the old religious forms or importing ideas from other religious traditions.

NOTES

1 The idea that it was a systematic break with the traditional celebration of the Passover is the main theme of Feeley-Harnik's fascinating study of the institution of the Eucharist. Gillian Feeley-Harnik, *The Lord's Table: Eucharist and Passover in Early Christianity* (University of Pennsylvania Press, 1981).

2 M. Douglas, *Purity and Danger: An Analysis of the Concepts of Pollution and Taboo*, second edition (London: Routledge, 1984).

3 M. Douglas, "The Forbidden Animals in Leviticus", 59 *JSOT* (September 1993), pp. 3–23.

4 Alfred Marx, *Les Offrandes Vegetales dans l'Ancien Testament: du tribut au repas eschatologique* (Leiden: E. J. Brill, 1994).

5 J. Milgrom, *Numbers, the JPS Commentary* (Philadelphia, PA: Jewish Publication Society, 1990), p. 238.

6 Marx, p. 100.

7 This is a central argument of my study of Numbers. *In the Wilderness: The Doctrine of Defilement in the Book of Numbers* (Sheffield: JSOTS Press, 1993).

8 M. Douglas, *Leviticus as Literature*, in press (Oxford University Press).

9   George Michell, *The Hindu Temple: An Introduction to its Meaning and Function* (London: Paul Elek, 1977).

10 M. O'Connor, "Cardinal Direction Terms in Biblical Hebrew", *Semitic Studies*, 2 (1991), pp. 1140–1157.

11 N. M. Sarna, *The JPS Torah Commentary, Exodus* (Philadelphia, PA: Jewish Publication Society, 1991).

12 J. Milgrom, *Leviticus 1–16* (Philadelphia, PA: Jewish Publication Society, 1991), pp. 142–143.

"SPIRIT IN THE BREAD; FIRE IN THE WINE": THE EUCHARIST AS "LIVING MEDICINE" IN THE THOUGHT OF EPHRAEM THE SYRIAN

SIDNEY H. GRIFFITH

To the east of Byzantium in the fourth century, the era in which the faith of Nicea came to its classical expression and the life of the church took on its familiar liturgical forms, Ephraem the Syrian (c. 306–373) was undoubtedly the thinker whose ideas would have the most powerful influence on later generations. He wrote in Syriac, a dialect of the Aramaic language, which carried with it a family relationship to the Jewish world in which Christianity first appeared in the synagogue communities of Mesopotamia and Syria/ Palestine. It was this language which eventually carried the Christian faith across the trade routes of Central Asia, eastward into China and southward into India. But in Ephraem's day, Syriac-speaking people living where he lived, in the cities of Nisibis and Edessa, on the Roman Empire's frontier with Persia, were also intellectually and politically very much attuned to the Greek-speaking culture of Asia Minor, and of the major ecclesiastical centers in Antioch and Constantinople. Ephraem himself was the major literary promoter of Roman imperial ideology in the region; in ecclesiology he followed the line of Eusebius of Caesarea Maritima (c. 260–c. 340); in theology he adhered to the teaching of the council of Nicea, strenuously combating what he perceived to be the inquisitive rationalism of those he called "Arians" and "Aetians"; in the east he was the relentless opponent of the teachings of Marcion, Bar Dayṣān, and Mani.[1]

Sidney H. Griffith
Institute of Christian Oriental Research, The Catholic University of America, 18 Mullen Library, Washington, DC 20064, USA

Ephraem served the church in Nisibis for most of his life, beginning in the time of his patron, Bishop Jacob of Nisibis (d. 338), one of the signatories to the decisions of the council of Nicea.[2] He left Nisibis as a refugee in the year 363, when the city was handed over to the Persians as part of the price of peace after the death of the emperor Julian on 26 June 363, while on campaign against the Persians deep in Mesopotamia. Ephraem, along with many other refugees from Nisibis, then took up residence in Edessa, where he served the local bishop until his death on 9 June 373. All his life Ephraem was a bishop's man, possibly a deacon, definitely a teacher (*malpānâ*) and commentator on the scriptures, an apologist/polemicist and a liturgical poet.[3] One modern scholar has written enthusiastically that Ephraem was "the greatest poet of the patristic age and, perhaps, the only theologian-poet to rank beside Dante".[4]

After his death, Ephraem gained a wide reputation as a holy man, not only in his own Syriac-speaking community but throughout the Byzantine world, and later in the medieval west and Russia. Many Greek-speaking admirers, particularly in the monastic communities of late antique and early medieval times, both translated his spiritual counsels and themselves composed treatises in Greek in his name.[5] In this guise Ephraem has often been listed among the fathers of monasticism and icons of him often portray him in a monk's garb. Even the standard *Vita* of Ephraem in Syriac reflects this development.[6] But Ephraem was never in fact a recluse or a hermit, or even a monk in any conventional sense of the term.[7] He was all his life long a busy pastoral minister, whose main business was the composition of "teaching songs" (*madrāshê*) in Syriac, often to be presented at the divine liturgy. This was the portrait that Ephraem himself penned in the final stanzas of one of his memorable "teaching songs" at the end of his *Hymns against Heresies*. He wrote prayerfully,

> O Lord, may the works of your pastoral minister (*ʿallānâ*) not be
>   discounted.
> I will not then have troubled your sheep,
>   but as far as I was able,
> I will have kept the wolves away from them,
>   and I will have built, as far as I was able,
> enclosures of "teaching songs" (*madrāshê*)
>   for the lambs of your flock.
>
> I will have made a disciple
>   of the simple and unlearned man.
> And I will have made him hold
>   onto the pastoral ministers' (*ʿallānê*) staff,
> the healers' medicine,
>   and the disputants' arsenal.[8]

II

Although Ephraem wrote biblical commentary, prose refutations of the teachings of those whose views he regarded as false, prose meditations, dialogue poems and metrical homilies (*mêmrê*), there can be no doubt that his preferred genre was the "teaching song" (*madrāshâ*).[9] Translators have often called these songs "hymns", but since they are not primarily songs of praise, the term is not really apt.[10] Rather, they are "teaching songs", as Andrew Palmer has happily styled them; they were to be chanted to the accompaniment of the lyre (*kennārâ*), on the model of David, the Psalmist.[11] Perhaps their closest analogues are the Hebrew *Piyyûṭîm*, synagogue songs which enjoyed great popularity in Palestine from the eighth century on, and which feature biblical themes and literary devices very similar to those regularly used by Ephraem.[12] They are also comparable to the Byzantine *Kontakion*. In fact, a good case can be made for the suggestion that the most famous composer of *Kontakia*, Romanos the Melode (d. after 555), who was a native of Emesa in Syria, was actively influenced by Ephraem's compositions.[13]

Ephraem composed his "teaching songs" (*madrāshê*) for the liturgy. St. Jerome says that in some churches they were recited after the scripture lessons in the divine liturgy.[14] And they have had a place in the liturgy of the hours in the Syriac-speaking churches from the earliest periods for which textual witnesses remain.[15] In his lifetime, Ephraem himself reportedly spent time and energy rehearsing the groups who would perform the "teaching songs" in church. What is more, according to one early witness, he insisted that women take their rightful place in the church's choirs. For this reason Jacob of Sarug (d. 521) called Ephraem the "second Moses for women".[16] What he meant was that because of their role in the public performance of Ephraem's "teaching songs", women effectively became teachers in the churches. Jacob of Sarug made the point explicitly. Rhetorically addressing Ephraem, he said,

> Your teaching opened the closed mouth of the daughters of Eve, and now the congregations of the glorious [church] resound with their voices.
> It is a new sight that women would proclaim the Gospel, and now be called teachers in the churches.[17]

The point not to be missed here is that the "teaching songs", which the women teachers were reciting, were the effective instruments of catechesis in the Syriac-speaking congregations. And this catechesis consisted in poetic meditations on the symbols and types which God distributed in nature and scripture to lead people across the chasm separating creatures from their Creator. For Ephraem's theology is not propositional but typological and symbolic. The symbols and types are not esoteric but commonplace. While they come from both nature and the scriptures, it is the Bible that provides the horizon for their interpretation. And within the Bible, the Gospel is the exegetical focal point; all the figures ultimately point to Christ. For Ephraem, the symbols and types are so many verbal icons, and his thought is really not so much theology as it is a sacramental iconology. Indeed, the image of the image maker is one of Ephraem's favorite figures of speech to refer to the ways in which God has communicated with people in the Bible.[18] In this way Ephraem's thought is Semitic rather than Hellenic, flowing almost directly from the discourse of the scriptures rather than commenting on them.[19]

III

In the divine revelation, what one most often finds, according to Ephraem, even in the names and titles of God, are manifest symbols, which he most often calls *râzê* (sing. *râzâ*) in Syriac, which in turn, by God's grace, disclose to the human mind those aspects of the hidden reality or truth which are within the range of the capacities of human intelligence. Ephraem and other Syriac writers use the word *râzâ* more in the sense of a "mystery-symbol", which is not so much mysterious in its function as it is indicative, disclosing to human minds according to their capacities what is hidden from human knowledge in its essence, such as the being of God and the course of the economy of salvation. While *râzâ* is often synonymous with "type" in Ephraem's works, his use of the term goes well beyond what one normally thinks of as the typological sense of the scriptures, i.e., words, actions, facts, and narratives in the Old Testament that foreshadow their models in the New Testament. For Ephraem, biblical typologies are indeed *râzê*, but so are many things in nature, and also in the apostolic kerygma and the life of the church, like sacraments. For him, the *râzê* all point to the incarnate Christ, who is "the Lord of the *râzê*, who fulfills all *râzê* in his crucifixion".[20] So they may point forward from nature and scripture to Christ, who in turn reveals his Father to the eye of faith, or they point from the church's life and liturgy back to Christ, who in turn reveals to the faithful believer the events of the eschaton, the ultimate fulfillment of all creation in the economy of salvation. They may be biblical characters and their actions, facts about nature or scripture, concrete objects heard, seen or used in scripture or liturgy, or narratives almost cinematically imagined and poetically presented from Bible or life. They take their significance from the role they play in highlighting Christ for the believer, or even embodying him for the eyes of faith. Within this kaleidoscope of images a coherent figure of church and faith emerges, sufficient to ground a solid sense of Christian identity, which comes to view most resolutely in liturgy and song.[21] The Eucharist is in many ways the ideal place from which to observe this uniquely Syriac program in action, as it is presented in the inimitable works of Ephraem the Syrian.

IV

Ephraem never used the Greek word "Eucharist". But he had much to say about the Body and the Blood of the Lord in the bread and wine of the church's daily sacrificial offering to God. Ephraem himself may have even composed an *Anaphora* that was in use in the Church of the East as late as the eleventh century, but if so, only traces of it have survived.[22] For his thoughts on the Body and Blood of the Lord, and their place in the life of the church, one must survey the wide range of his "teaching songs", searching for the verses in which he instructs the faith of the Christians in attendance at the sacred mysteries.

Qûrbānâ is the Syriac word Ephraem and his contemporaries used for the liturgical action westerners call the Eucharist. It has the sense of "sacrificial offering", and as it occurs in the "teaching songs" it refers both to the sacrificial offering associated with the Jewish Passover, and to the sacrifice of Christ on the cross, commemorated at the Last Supper, and in its sacramental representation in the daily liturgies of the churches. Since Ephraem was in constant controversy with the Jews of his milieu, whose religious services many Christians frequented, especially at Passover time,[23] one sees best how he uses this term (*qûrbānâ*) in the "teaching songs" associated with the liturgy of Maundy Thursday, where he speaks in a polemical tone to those likely to frequent the synagogue at *Pesaḥ*. He says,

> My brothers, do not eat,
>   along with the medicine of life,
> the unleavened bread of the People,
>   as it were, the medicine of death.

> For Christ's blood
>   is mingled, spilt,
> in the unleavened bread of the People,[24]
>   and in our Eucharist (*qûrbānan*).

> Whoever takes it in the Eucharist (*bqûrbānâ*)
>   takes the medicine of life.
> Whoever eats it with the People,
>   takes the medicine of death.[25]

In Ephraem's world Christians offered the holy *qûrbānâ* not only at Eastertime, and not only on Sundays and major feastdays, but every day. This is the clear implication of a stanza in one of Ephraem's "teaching songs" *On Paradise*. He says,

> The assembly of the saints
>   is on the type of Paradise.
> In it the fruit of the Enlivener of All
>   is plucked each day.
> In it, my brothers, are squeezed
>   the grapes of the Enlivener of All.[26]

Ephraem not infrequently refers to the daily *qûrbānâ* as "the breaking of the bread and the cup of salvation",[27] often speaking as well of our Lord's "breaking his own body",[28] at the Passover supper, in an obvious evocation of the close connection in his mind between Calvary and the Last Supper. Ephraem put it this way in one of the "teaching songs". He says of our Lord at the Last Supper,

> He broke the bread with his own hands
> in token of the sacrifice of his body.
> He mixed the cup with his own hands,
> in token of the sacrifice of his blood.
> He offered up himself in sacrifice,
> the priest of our atonement.[29]

For Ephraem, as Edmund Beck has well said, "the Last Supper and its table is the first church and the first altar, and thus the representative of all churches and all altars".[30] Therefore, in his "teaching songs" Ephraem often calls attention to the prefigurations of the Eucharist in the New Testament, and the numerous types and symbols of it in the narratives of the Old Testament.[31] In his estimation, they all find their ultimate focus in the Last Supper and in its consummation on the cross, when blood and water flowed from the pierced side of Christ (John 19:34), representing the sacraments of the Eucharist and Baptism respectively, and thereby inaugurating the era of the church. Ephraem's thought on this subject is particularly rich in symbology, involving a typological connection between the Cherubim's sword that guarded the way to the tree of life in paradise after Adam's sin (Genesis 3:24), and the lance which opened Christ's side on the tree of the cross, thus providing a new entry to glory for the new Adam's progeny. Robert Murray, who has studied this motif in detail, provides the following brief summary:

> Ephrem's symbolic interpretation of the piercing of Christ's side is particularly complicated. Christ is the second Adam, from whose side is born the second Eve, the Church; yet through that opening we enter paradise, to come again to the Tree of Life, which is sometimes the Cross but also sometimes Christ himself.[32]

V

According to Ephraem, it is in the reception of the Body and the Blood of the Lord that Christians are united to Christ in his church. He says,

> In a novel way, his body is kneaded into our bodies.
> Even his pure blood is poured into our arteries.
> His voice is in our ears, his appearance in our eyes.
> By reason of his compassion, all of him is kneaded into all of us.

And since he loved his church very much,
he did not give her the Manna of her rival—
he became himself the living bread for her to eat.[33]

And so it is for Ephraem that the sacrament of the Eucharist, as Tanios Bou Mansour has well put it, "is not reduced to a simple system of reference, but it is the medium of a presence, which is first of all that of the body of Christ".[34] The sacramental body of Christ is continuous with the historical body of Christ, as Ephraem conceives of it. For him, the bread and the wine become the Body and Blood of Christ by the action of the Holy Spirit, just as it was by the Spirit that Christ was in the womb of Mary, and in the water of Baptism. Addressing Christ, Ephraem wrote,

See, Fire and Spirit were in the womb of her who bore you,
see, Fire and Spirit were in the river in which you were baptized.
Fire and Spirit are in our baptismal font;
in the Bread and Cup are Fire and Holy Spirit.[35]

By invocation, Fire and Spirit are for Ephraem the agents of Christ's presence in the church and in the sacraments, just as at the Annunciation, by Mary's invitation, they were the agents of the divine son's presence in her womb. In the holy *Qûrbānâ*, the church, in the words of the priest, invites Fire and Spirit to come into the bread and wine, transforming them for the eyes of faith into the Body and Blood of Christ. For Ephraem, and the Syrian tradition after him, the presence of Christ in the bread and the wine of the Eucharist is, therefore, a continuation of the presence of the Word of God incarnate in Christ. Dionysius bar Ṣalîbî (d. 1171) put the matter clearly in his *Commentary on the Liturgy*.

The Body and Blood are called "mysteries" (*râzê*) because they are not what they appear to the physical eye to be; for to look at, they are just bread and wine, but properly understood, they are the Body and Blood of God. Just as Jesus was seen by the physical eye as man, yet he is also God; similarly the mysteries are seen outwardly to be bread and wine, but they are in fact the Body and Blood. And although the Spirit makes the mysteries the Body and Blood, they are nevertheless [the Body and Blood] of the Son. It is like what was done in the virgin; although the Spirit embodied the Son, it was nevertheless the Son who was embodied.[36]

As for the connection between Fire and Spirit in the Eucharistic bread and cup, as Ephraem described it in the "teaching song" quoted above, the fire is "a symbol of the consecratory role of the Holy Spirit".[37] In this connection there is a striking passage, illustrative of the sacramental thinking in Syriac-speaking, Christian communities, included in a biography of Jacob Baradaeus

(c. 500–578). It describes what happened one day when Jacob visited a certain monastery. The text says,

> One day, when he was offering the *Qûrbānâ*, a certain Arab who had recently been baptized was present there; and he saw that fire came down from heaven, and he saw tongues of flame hovering over the *Qûrbānâ*, and hosts of angels with bowed heads before the divine sacrifice.[38]

The association of fire with the Holy Spirit as a powerful symbol of divine presence in the sacraments of Baptism and the Eucharist, and even in Mary's conception of the Word of God, is widespread in Syriac liturgical texts. It owes its prominence to the eastern Christians' observance of the role of fire and fire imagery in numerous passages in the Old Testament which describe the signs of God's acceptance of sacrifices from his faithful servants, and thereby for Syrian Christians also signifying the action of the Holy Spirit.[39] Ephraem himself makes the point explicitly in what he says about fire in one of his "teaching songs" *On Faith*. He says,

> The mystery symbol (*râzâ*) of the Spirit is in it (i.e., in fire),
>   and the type of the Holy Spirit,
> who is blended with water,
>   so it yields forgiveness,
> and is kneaded into bread,
>   so it becomes the *Qûrbānâ*.[40]

Even the priest's role in praying the *epiclesis* in the Syrian liturgy is reported by the poet Balai (d. after 432) in fire imagery. He says of the officiant at the holy *Qûrbānâ* on the occasion of the consecration of a church,

> The priest stands, he kindles the fire, he takes bread,
> but gives forth the Body; he receives wine, but
> distributes the Blood.[41]

Similarly, fire imagery figures in a number of other expressions not infrequently used in reference to the Eucharist in Syriac texts. For example, particles of the Eucharistic bread are often called "embers" or "burning coals" (*gmûrāthâ*), usually with at least an implicit reference to the passage in Isaiah 6:6–7, where the prophet speaks of the Seraph who touched his mouth with a burning coal from the altar of the temple. Ephraem makes this connection in the following stanzas from his "teaching songs" *de Fide*. He says,

> The Seraph could not touch the fire's coal with his fingers,
> the coal only just touched Isaiah's mouth:
> the Seraph did not hold it, Isaiah did not consume it,
> but us our Lord has allowed to do both!

To the angels who are spiritual Abraham brought
food for the body and they ate. The new miracle
is that our mighty Lord has given to bodily man
Fire and Spirit to eat and to drink.[42]

In the following prayer of thanksgiving after communion, found in the ancient *anaphora* called *Sharar*, the text similarly likens the Eucharist to a burning ember. The celebrant prays:

Consuming Fire which our hands have held, Live Ember
which our lips have kissed, the seraphim do not dare take
it in their hands. The prophet held it and was purified
by it.[43] Lord, purify our mouths and lips and hands which
hold your body. Sanctify the bodies, souls, and spirits
which have received your victorious blood.[44]

Finally, there is a fire-related image to be seen in the practice of Ephraem and Jacob of Sarug to speak of the Eucharistic elements as "pearls". For in the Syrian conception, the pearl is born when lightning strikes the mussel that produces it in the sea.[45] Similarly, according to the Syrian fathers, Christ was conceived in the womb of Mary, when Fire and Spirit came within her, and bread and wine regularly become the Body and Blood of Christ due to the action of Fire and the Spirit. Accordingly, it is not surprising to find Ephraem and others in the Syrian tradition often using the popular symbol of the pearl for Christ himself and for the Eucharistic elements. In one place Ephraem says, "Christ gave us pearls, his Body and Blood".[46] And Jacob of Sarug, in a striking passage referring to the holy *Qûrbānâ*, says,

It is not the priest who is authorized to sacrifice the Only-Begotten or to
raise up that sacrifice for sinners to the Father's presence: rather, the
Holy Spirit goes forth from the Father and descends, overshadows and
resides in the bread, making it the Body, and making it treasured pearls
to adorn the souls that are betrothed by him.[47]

Finally, in another homily, after an extended comparison of the Eucharistic elements to expensive pearls, Jacob of Sarug gives this advice to would-be communicants in attendance at the holy liturgy:

The Body and the Blood are living pearls;
let them not be demeaned in soul and body that are unclean
    vessels.
Heaven and earth are in the incomparable pearl;
do not receive your Lord's holiness in an unclean vessel.[48]

VI

According to Ephraem, the Eucharist makes Christ visible and accessible to people in the church comparable to the way that his birth from his mother Mary made him physically visible and accessible to the people of his time on earth. In one of his "teaching songs" *On the Nativity*, Ephraem compares the two images (*salmê*) of God's incarnate Son to which human beings have access. There is the visible (*galyâ*) one, born of Mary, whom Mary herself and all their contemporaries could see in the flesh, like Adam, and the invisible (*kasyâ*) one, portrayed in the mind of the beholder. In the song, Mary says,

> When I see your image,
>   the created one,
> which is before my eyes,
>   your invisible one
> is depicted (*sîr*) in my mind.
>   In your visible image
> I see Adam;
>   in the invisible one
> I see your Father
>   who is kneaded into you.[49]

As the song continues, Mary ponders the fact that it is not to her alone, or only to those who saw him in the flesh, that her Son has revealed himself in two images, one visible and one invisible. She recalls that to the eyes of faith he is visible also in the Eucharistic bread. And so, in Ephraem's song, she says to her Son:

> Let bread depict you,
> the mind too.
>   Dwell in the bread
> and in those who eat it.
>   In the visible and the invisible
> your church will see you,
>   just as your mother does.[50]

The marvel of it all for Ephraem, and for Mary in whose voice he speaks in this song, is that whether one loves or hates Christ in the flesh or Christ in the bread, both visible, he will nevertheless, as Mary says to her son, "have seen you"[51] in the flesh or in the bread. This realization then leads Mary to ask,

> Is then, O child, your bread
>   more momentous
> by far than your body?
>   For even infidels
> saw your body,

but they do not see
your living bread.
   Those remote in time rejoice;
their lot surpasses
   that of the nearly contemporary![52]

In Ephraem's view then, the perception of Christ in the living bread of the Eucharist is more momentous because it requires the eyes of faith to perceive it. As he goes on to say to Christ in the next stanza,

See—your image is depicted
   in the blood of grapes
on the top of the bread,
   and it is depicted on the heart
by the finger of love,
   with all the pigments
of faith.
   Blessed is he who made
the sculpted images pass away
   in favor of his true image.[53]

Ephraem here uses the liturgical image of the priest at the holy *Qûrbānâ*, in the liturgy of St. James, anointing the Eucharistic bread with a few drops of the precious blood, to highlight the eye of faith's active perception of the Son of God in the visible Eucharistic bread. That perception then leads to the mind's recognition of the invisible Father, "kneaded", as Ephraem likes to say, into the very bread and flesh of his eternal Son. The role of the "eye of faith" in lovingly recognizing Christ in the visible bread of his Eucharistic presence, as Ephraem conceives of it, highlights the intentional dimension of this "sacramental" or "mysterious" presence. He emphasizes the point in the following lines from one of the "teaching songs" *On the Nativity*. He says,

The bread is spiritual
   like its giver;
it enlivens spiritual people
   spiritually.

Whoever takes it
   in a bodily way,
takes it obtusely,
   without any profit.

It is distinctly
   the bread of compassion;
the mind takes it in
   as living medicine.[54]

As Dom Edmund Beck has pointed out, this intentional, spiritual dimension of Christ's presence in the Eucharistic bread, visible to the "eye of faith", portrays Ephraem's conception of "the temporal and local universality of the Eucharist, which, along with the church itself, extends over all peoples and times, but always remains the one bread, which Christ broke, and the one cup, which Christ gave".[55] Beck then reminds the reader that the basis of this temporal and local universality of the one bread and the one cup is the "unconditioned power of the Spirit",[56] which, as we have seen above, is, in Ephraem's view, the power by means of which Christ is in the bread and in the wine sacramentally. Accordingly, the implication is that when the mind fails to connect with the hidden Spirit within the Eucharistic elements, because of the willful perversion of sin or heresy, Christ's own presence there is missed. Ephraem's reflection on Judas' role in the Gospel account of the Last Supper calls attention to this aspect of his thought.

In the "teaching songs" *de Azymis*, Ephraem evokes the scene of the Last Supper as recounted in John 13:21–30, where Jesus broaches the issue of the one who will betray him. John leans close to him to ask the identity of the betrayer. The text says, "Jesus answered, 'It is he to whom I shall give this morsel when I have dipped it'. So when he had dipped the morsel, he gave it to Judas, the son of Simon Iscariot" (John 13:26). Commenting on this passage, Ephraem wrote:

He dipped the bread,[57] he gave it to him,
    to the concealed dead man,
bread washed of
    the medicine of life.

The Enlivener of All had put a blessing
    on that food,
and it became the medicine of life,
    right in front of its eaters.

Bread washed
    of blessings,
that accursed man took,
    the second serpent.

He took the bread and withdrew
    from the disciples;
he removed himself,
    they did not put him out.

Our Lord did not remove him,
    so no one could utter the blasphemy
that coercion forced him,
    and not [his own] will.

...

> When he withdrew and left,
>   the concealed wolf
> from within the flock
>   of the twelve,
>
> the true Lamb rose
>   and broke his own body
> for the sheep who had eaten
>   the Paschal lamb.[58]

On the face of it, these lines seem to support the allegation that it was Ephraem's interpretation of John 13:23 that by dipping the morsel of bread he had earlier blessed, Jesus in effect washed away his "real presence" from it before he offered it to Judas, because of the latter's willful sin. When Judas subsequently left the room, Jesus then broke the bread of his body and distributed it to the remaining disciples. However, in another passage from the same collection of songs, Ephraem again speaks of a "washing" of the morsel of bread in John 13:26. Beginning with a mention of the unleavened bread of the Jewish Passover, he says:

> Moses had hidden
>   the mystery-symbol (*râzâ*) of the Son
> in that unleavened bread (*paṭîrâ*),
>   as the medicine of life.
>
> He (i.e., Jesus) washed the unleavened bread
>   of the medicine of life;
> He gave it to Judas as the medicine of death.
>
> Therefore, a man gets
>   Iscariot's
> medicine of death
>   from that unleavened bread.[59]

This passage identifies the bread that Jesus "washed" as the unleavened bread of the Jewish Passover, which heretofore, as Ephraem conceived of it, had served as a type for the Christian Eucharist.[60] In the context of John 13:23, Judas' betrayal seems to stand in Ephraem's mind for what he perceived as the general Jewish rejection of Jesus as Messiah and Son of God. Therefore, in his "teaching songs" he strongly contrasted the unleavened bread of the Jews (*paṭîrâ*) with the leavened bread (*ḥmîrâ*) of the Christian Eucharist.[61] But the problem remains about whether or not it was Ephraem's view that John 13:26 must be interpreted to mean that Jesus washed the "real presence" out of the morsel of bread he dipped and offered to Judas.

Scholars are divided on the issue. Dom Edmund Beck, following the hint in the song *De Azymis* XVIII:16, just quoted, thought that the bread in question was not the Eucharistic bread as such, but simply the unleavened bread of the Passover meal Jesus was sharing with his disciples.[62] After the meal, according to Beck, Jesus broke and distributed the Eucharistic bread.[63] Therefore, in his view, there is no substance to the idea that according to Ephraem Jesus "washed" the "real presence" out of the bread he gave to Judas at the Last Supper. G. A. M. Rouwhorst, on the other hand, relying on an earlier study he had done,[64] showing that the prayer of blessing in the Syrian liturgy is the Eucharistic *epiclesis*, by which the celebrant calls the Spirit and the Fire into the bread of the Eucharist, making it the Body of Christ, points out that the language of *de Azymis* XIV:16 fits this prescription. Therefore, in his view, Ephraem meant precisely that Jesus did "wash" away, or remove, the consecratory blessing he had put on the bread he offered to Judas.[65]

This certainly seems to have been the view of those in what one might call Ephraem's "school", who after his death passed on his teachings in works attributed to him. In the *mêmrê* on Holy Week, for example, texts which are attributed to Ephraem in the manuscript tradition, but which seem in fact to come from a sixth century writer,[66] one finds the following account of the Judas scene at the Last Supper. The text says:

> When Jesus gave his Bread
> to the eleven, without any discrimination,
>   Judas came forward to receive,
> just like his companions who had come up to take it.
>   Jesus dipped the bread
> in water and gave it to Judas.
>   He washed the blessing out of it
> and by this he distinguished the wretched man,
>   and then the disciples knew
> it was Judas would betray Him.
>   Jesus dipped the Bread he gave him,
> so the blessing would be released from the Bread.
>   He did not eat blessed bread,
> nor did he drink from the Cup of life.[67]

Clearly the writer of this *mêmrâ* interpreted Ephraem's exegesis of John 13:26 to mean that Jesus did remove the Eucharistic consecration from the Bread offered to Judas, but one notices that while he seems to be following the account of the Last Supper in Luke 22:14–22, Ephraem himself was following the account in John.[68] What is more, the writer of the *mêmrâ* had already expressed the view that Christian faith was a prerequisite for the perception of the Body of Christ in the Eucharistic bread.

Just a few verses earlier, recounting the institution of the Eucharist, he has Jesus say:

> Take, eat in faith,
> and do not doubt that this is my body.
>   Whoever eats it in faith,
> eats the Fire and Spirit in it.
>   Whoever doubts and eats it,
> for him it is plain bread.[69]

Here is not the place to try to settle the difference of opinion over the proper interpretation of Ephraem's meaning when he said that Jesus gave Judas "bread washed of the medicine of life" at the Last Supper. Whether he had the Eucharistic bread in mind, as Rouwhorst maintains, or only the unleavened bread of the Jewish Passover supper, conceived as a *râzâ* for the true "medicine of life", as Beck came to hold, it is clear that for Ephraem the "real presence" of the Body and Blood of the Lord in the Bread and Wine of the holy *Qûrbânâ* was something physical, which affected its recipients physically, albeit perceived only through the eyes of faith. In one of his "teaching songs" *On Virginity*, he wrote of the moment of communion:

> In a new way his body
>   has been fused with our bodies,
> and his pure blood
>   has been poured into our veins.
> His voice, too, is in [our] ears
>   and his splendour in [our] eyes.
> The whole of him with the whole of us
>   is fused by his mercy.
> And because he loved his church greatly,
>   he did not give her the manna of her rival;
> He became the Bread of Life
>   for her to eat him.[70]

VII

In Ephraem's writings the constant epithet for the Eucharist is the phrase "living medicine" or "medicine of life" (*sam ḥayyê*). The Body and the Blood of the Lord are thought to bring healing, forgiveness of sin, and preservation from eternal death to the faithful Christian. Addressing Christ himself, Ephraem put it this way in one of his "teaching songs" *On Faith*. He says,

> Your Bread slays the greedy one who has made us his bread,
> your Cup destroys death who had swallowed us up;
> we have eaten you, Lord, we have drunken you—
> not that we will consume you up, but through you we shall have life.[71]

As for the forgiveness of sins, in Ephraem's view it flows directly from the Eucharist. He makes this point in a striking way in the following stanza from one of his "teaching songs" *On the Church*, where he contrasts the willfulness of the sinner with the gratuity of God's forgiveness. He says,

> I am amazed at our will:
> while it is strong, see it brought low;
> while it is a lord, see it enslaved;
> while it is a victor, it wills to succumb;
> free, it surrenders its mouth like a slave,
> and sets its own hand on the bill of sale.
> See the foolish scribe, who is the one
> setting his own hand to the statement of his debts!
> Blessed is the one who has given us emancipation in his Bread,
> and in his Cup has erased the statement of our debts.[72]

There are many other statements about the Eucharist in the works of Ephraem the Syrian. But enough has been quoted to give one a fair idea of how he customarily spoke about it. His ideas and his words about this central Christian institution have instructed the faith of the Syriac-speaking communities for centuries, and they are still held to be authoritative. It is noteworthy that while his thoughts on the subject lack the theoretical elaboration Eucharistic theology has enjoyed in other churches, with different patristic and liturgical heritages, his language is concrete and almost entirely biblical in its inspiration. It became the classic idiom of Eucharistic thought in the Syriac-speaking world, echoed in the writings of later figures such as Jacob of Sarug (*c.* 451–521), Narsai (d. c. 503), Babai the Great (*c.* 550–628), and Jacob of Edessa (*c.* 640–708).

There were no great controversies within the Syriac-speaking churches over the nature of the Eucharist, which may explain why there were no elaborate developments of doctrine in this area, particularly in the realm of theory. Most of the adversaries were outside the Christian community, groups such as the Manichaeans, who denied that matter could be holy at all; the Jews, whose unleavened bread of the Passover was a constant temptation for Christians in Ephraem's day; and later the Muslims, who were always puzzled about the Christian Eucharist. Syriac-speaking Christians responded to them all in the traditional terms of their biblical faith, arguing that in the matter of the Eucharist, they simply followed the prescriptions of the scriptures, and particularly the Gospel. Meanwhile, within their own communities they developed an incredibly rich tradition of symbolic theology of the Eucharist, almost an iconology, the fruit of meditating on the Word of God in song and prayer, in the context of the liturgy, not so much in the mode of *fides quaerens intellectum*, but very much in the exercise of *fides adorans mysterium*, to borrow the felicitous expression of Robert Murray.[73]

The final words on the subject belong by right to St. Ephraem himself, who uttered the following prayer:

In your Bread there is hidden the Spirit who is not consumed,
in your Wine there dwells the Fire that is not drunk;
the Spirit is in your Bread, the Fire in your Wine—
a manifest wonder, that our lips have received.[74]

NOTES

1 On these matters see Sidney H. Griffith, "Ephraem, the Deacon of Edessa, and the Church of the Empire", in Thomas Halton & Joseph P. Williman (eds), *Diakonia: Studies in Honor of Robert T. Meyer* (Washington, D.C.: Catholic University of America Press, 1986), pp. 22–52; *idem*, "Ephraem the Syrian's Hymns 'Against Julian': Meditations on History and Imperial Power", *Vigiliae Christianae* 41 (1987), pp. 238–266; *idem*, "'Faith Seeking Understanding' in the Thought of St. Ephraem the Syrian", in George C. Berthold (ed), *Faith Seeking Understanding: Learning and the Catholic Tradition. Selected Papers from the Symposium and Convocation Celebrating the Saint Anselm College Centennial* (Manchester, N.H.: Saint Anselm College Press, 1991), pp. 35–55; *idem*, "Setting Right the Church of Syria: Saint Ephraem's Hymns against Heresies", to appear in a forthcoming Festschrift for Robert A. Markus. See also Peter Bruns, "Arius Hellenizans? ... Ephrem der Syrer und die neoarianischen Kontroversen seiner Zeit", *Zeitschrift für Kirchengeschichte* 101 (1990), pp. 21–57; Paul S. Russell, *St. Ephraem the Syrian and St. Gregory the Theologian Confront the Arians* (Kottayam, Kerala: St. Ephrem Ecumenical Research Institute, 1994).

2 See Paulus Peeters, "La Légende de saint Jacques de Nisibe", *Analecta Bollandiana* 38 (1920), pp. 285–373; P. Krüger, "Jakob von Nisibis in syrischer und armenischer Überlieferung", *Le Muséon* 81 (1968), pp. 161–179; David Bundy, "Jacob of Nisibis as a Model for the Episcopacy", *Le Muséon* 104 (1991), pp. 235–249.

3 On the life of Ephraem see Edward G. Mathews, Jr., "The Vita Tradition of Ephrem the Syrian, the Deacon of Edessa", *Diakonia* 22 (1988–1989), pp. 15–42; Sidney H. Griffith, "Images of Ephraem: the Syrian Holy Man and his Church", *Traditio* (1989–1990), pp. 7–33.

4 Robert Murray, "Ephrem Syrus", in *A Catholic Dictionary of Theology* (vol. II; London: Thomas Nelson and Sons Ltd., 1967), pp. 220–223. Murray reaffirmed this opinion in his landmark book, Robert J. Murray, *Symbols of Church and Kingdom: A Study in Early Syriac Tradition* (Cambridge: Cambridge University Press, 1975), p. 31.

5 The long list of them, with further bibliography, can be found in M. Geerard, *Clavis Patrum Graecorum* (vol. II; Turnhout: Brepols, 1974), pp. 366–468. A reprinting of the Greek works, together with a translation into modern Greek, is available in Konstantinou G. Phrantzolas (ed. & trans.), *Osiou Ephraim tou Surou Erga* (6 vols. to date; Thessaloniki: Ekdoseis "To Periboli tes Panagias", 1988–). See also the Web site of Archimandrite Ephrem Lash, "Saint Ephrem the Syrian; Ascetical and Other Writings Extant Only in Greek", http://www.orthodox.org.uk/Ephr-Int.htm.

6 See Joseph P. Amar, "Byzantine Ascetic Monachism and Greek Bias in the Vita Tradition of Ephrem the Syrian", *Orientalia Christiana Periodica* 58 (1992), pp. 123–156.

7 On the relevant terminology in Syriac see Sidney H. Griffith, "Asceticism in the Church of Syria: the Hermeneutics of Early Syrian Monasticism", in Vincent L. Wimbush & Richard Valantasis (eds) *Asceticism* (New York: Oxford University Press, 1995), pp. 220–245.

8 Edmund Beck, *Des heiligen Ephraem des Syrers Hymnen contra Haereses* (CSCO, vols. 169 & 170; Louvain: Secrétariat du CorpusSCO, 1957), vol. 169, LVI:10&11, pp. 211–212.

9 See the convenient representation of the titles of Ephraem's Syriac works by genre, their editions, and notice of the available translations into English in Sebastian P. Brock, "A Brief Guide to the Main Editions and Translations of the Works of Ephrem", *The Harp* 3 (1990), pp. 7–29. See also Joseph Melki, "S. Ephrem le Syrien, un bilan de l'édition critique", *Parole de l'Orient* 11 (1983), pp. 3–88.

10 See Michael Lattke, "Sind Ephraems Madrāšē Hymnen?" *Oriens Christianus* 73 (1989), pp. 38–43.

11   See Andrew Palmer, "A Lyre without a Voice, the Poetics and the Politics of Ephrem the Syrian", *ARAM* 5 (1993), pp. 371–399. For more on Ephraem's poetics, see also Andrew Palmer, "The Merchant of Nisibis; Saint Ephrem and his Faithful Quest for Union in Numbers", in J. Den Boeft & A. Hilhorst (eds), *Early Christian Poetry: A Collection of Essays* (Leiden: E. J. Brill, 1993), pp. 167–233; idem, "Words, Silences, and the Silent Word: Acrostics and Empty Columns in Saint Ephraem's *Hymns on Faith*", *Parole de l'Orient* 20 (1995), pp. 129–200; idem, "St Ephrem of Syria's Hymn on Faith 7: An Ode on his Own Name", *Sobornost* 17 (1995), pp. 28–40.

12   See J. Schirmann, "Hebrew Liturgical Poetry and Christian Hymnology", *The Jewish Quarterly Review* n.s. 44 (1953–1954), pp. 123–161; J. Yahalom, "*Piyyuṭ* as Poetry", in L. I. Levine (ed), *The Synagogue in Late Antiquity* (Philadelphia, PA: American Schools of Oriental Research, 1987), pp. 123–134; W. Jac. Bekkum, "Anti-Christian Polemics in Hebrew Liturgical Poetry (*Piyyuṭ*) of the Sixth and Seventh Centuries", in J. Den Boeft & A. Hilhorst (eds), *Early Christian Poetry: A Collection of Essays*, Supplements to *Vigiliae Christianae*, vol. 22 (Leiden: E. J. Brill, 1993), pp. 297–308.

13   See J. Grosdidier de Matons, *Romanos le Mélode et les origines de la poésie religieuse à Byzance* (Paris: Beauchesne, 1977); William L. Petersen, "The Dependence of Romanos the Melodist upon the Syriac Ephrem; its Importance for the Origin of the Kontakion", *Vigiliae Christianae* 39 (1985), pp. 171–187; idem, *The Diatessaron and Ephrem Syrus as Sources of Romanos the Melodist* (CSCO, vol. 475; Louvain, Peeters, 1985); idem, "The Dependence of Romanos the Melodist upon the Syriac Ephraem", in E. A. Livingstone (ed), *Studia Patristica* (vol. XVIII, 4; Kalamazoo, MI: Cistercian Publications & Leuven: Peeters, 1990), pp. 274–281; S. P. Brock, "From Ephrem to Romanos", in E. A. Livingstone (ed), *Studia Patristica* (vol. XX; Leuven: Peeters, 1989), pp. 139–151.

14   See E. C. Richardson, *Hieronymus, Liber de Viris Inlustribus* (Leipzig, 1896), p. 51.

15   See Robert Taft, *The Liturgy of the Hours in East and West: The Origins of the Divine Office and its Meaning for Today* (Collegeville, MN: The Liturgical Press, 1986), pp. 225–247.

16   Joseph P. Amar, "A Metrical Homily on Holy Mar Ephrem by Mar Jacob of Sarug; Critical Edition of the Syriac Text, Translation and Introduction", *Patrologia Orientalis* (tome, 47, fasc. 1, no. 209; Turnhout: Brepols, 1995), # 48, p. 37.

17   Amar, "A Metrical Homily on Holy Mar Ephrem", ## 40–44, pp. 34–35.

18   See Sidney H. Griffith, "The Image of the Image Maker in the Poetry of St. Ephraem the Syrian", in E. A. Livingstone (ed), *Studia Patristica* (vol. XXV; Leuven: Peeters, 1993), pp. 258–269.

19   See Sidney H. Griffith, *"Faith Adoring the Mystery": Reading the Bible with St. Ephraem the Syrian* (The Père Marquette Lecture in Theology, 1997; Milwaukee, WI: Marquette University Press, 1997).

20   Edmund Beck, *Des heiligen Ephraem des Syrers Paschahymnen; (De Azymis, de Crucifixione, de Resurrectione)* (CSCO, vols. 248 & 249; Louvain: Peeters, 1964), De Azymis, III:1, ʿunîtâ.

21   The most comprehensive discussion of Ephraem's thought in this regard is Tanios Bou Mansour, *La Pensée symbolique de saint Ephrem le Syrien* (Bibliothèque de l'Université Saint-Esprit, 16; Kaslik, Lebanon: L'Université Saint-Esprit, 1988).

22   See Pierre Yousif, *L'Eucharistie chez saint Éphrem de Nisibe* (Orientalia Christiana Analecta, 244; Rome: Pontificium Institutum Orientale, 1984), pp. 145–156. On the development of the *Anaphora* in the east see A. Gelston, *The Eucharistic Prayer of Addai and Mari* (Oxford: Clarendon Press, 1992).

23   For Ephraem's ideas about Passover and the Paschal season, Jewish ideas and practices versus Christian thology and liturgy see G. A. M. Rouwhorst, *Les Hymnes pascales d'Ephrem de Nisibe* (2 vols.; Leiden: E. J. Brill, 1989), vol. I, pp. 128–203.

24   Ephraem, and other Syriac writers, regularly speak of the "people" versus the "peoples", or the "nation" versus the "nations" (ʿammâ versus ʿammê) to contrast the Jews and the Gentiles, the Jews, from one nation or people, and the Christians from many nations and peoples. See the discussion in Murray, *Symbols of Church and Kingdom*, pp. 41–68.

25   Beck, *Paschahymnen, de Azymis*, XIX:22–24.

26   Edmund Beck, *Des heiligen Ephraem des Syrers Hymnen de Paradiso und Contra Julianum* (CSCO, vols. 174 & 175; Louvain: Peeters, 1957), VI:8. There also seems to be a reference to the daily liturgy in a stanza of Ephraem's *Carmina Nisibena*. Speaking of the bones of the biblical patriarch, Joseph, which the Israelites carried with them during

their wanderings in the desert, Ephraem says of Moses' account of this phenomenon (Exodus 13:19),

> It was a mystery symbol he portrayed there
> for the church,
> in which every day there is proclaimed
> the death of the Enlivener of All.

Edmund Beck, *Des heiligen Ephraem des Syrers Carnima Nisibena (zweiter Teil)* (CSCO, vols. 240 & 241; Louvain: Peeters, 1963), XLVIII:6.

27 See Edmund Beck, *Des heiligen Ephraem des Syrers Hymnen contra Haereses* (CSCO, vols. 169 & 170; Louvain: Peeters, 1957), XXVII:3.

28 See Edmund Beck, *Paschahymnen, De Azymis,* XII:5.

29 Beck, *Paschahymnen, De Azymis,* II:7. The Syriac phrase translated here as "in token of" is *brāz.* The strong Syriac term *râzâ,* usually translated as "symbol" or "mystery symbol", often corresponds in sense to the Greek term μυστήριον, and thus to the term "sacrament". See the classic study by Edmund Beck, "Symbolum-Mysterium bei Aphraat und Ephräm", *Oriens Christianus* 42 (1958), pp. 19–40, and Bou Mansour, *La Pensée symbolique,* pp. 23–120.

30 Edmund Beck, "Die Eucharistie bei Ephräm", *Oriens Christianus* 38 (1954), p. 50.

31 See the lengthy discussion of these scriptural types and symbols as Ephraem employs them in Yousif, *L'Eucharistie chez saint Éphrem,* pp. 31–107.

32 Murray, *Symbols of Church and Kingdom,* p. 126. See also R. Murray, "The Lance Which Re-opened Paradise, a Mysterious Reading in the Early Syriac Fathers", *Orientalia Christiana Periodica* 39 (1973), pp. 224–234, and the important adjustment published in the same vol., "The Lance Which Re-opened Paradise: a Correction", p. 491. See also Yousif, *L'Eucharistie chez saint Éphrem,* pp. 48–56. For further typological associations see S. P. Brock, "The Mysteries Hidden in the Side of Christ", in S. P. Brock, *Studies in Syriac Spirituality* (The Syrian Churches Series, vol. 13; Poona: Anita Printers, 1988), pp. 62–72.

33 Edmund Beck, *Des heiligen Ephraem des Syrers Hymnen de Virginitate* (CSCO, vols. 223 & 224; Louvain, Peeters, 1962), XXXVII:2.

34 Bou Mansour, *La Pensée symbolique,* p. 393.

35 Edmund Beck, *Des heiligen Ephraem des Syrers Hymnen de Fide* (CSCO, vols. 154 & 155; Louvain: Peeters, 1955), X:17.

36 Hieronymus Labourt (ed. & trans.), *Dionysius bar Ṣalībī Expositio Liturgiae* (CSCO, vol. 13; Paris & Leipzig: Bibliopola & Harrassowitz, 1903), pp. 61–62. The first part of the English translation is that of S. P. Brock, "Mary and the Eucharist: An Oriental Perspective", in Brock, *Studies in Syriac Spirituality,* p. 32.

37 S. P. Brock, "Fire from Heaven: from Abel's Sacrifice to the Eucharist; a Theme in Syriac Christianity", in Elizabeth A. Livingstone (ed), *Studia Patristica* (vol. XXV; Leuven: Peeters Press, 1993), p. 229.

38 Quoted in Brock, "Fire from Heaven", p. 229, from E. W. Brooks (ed. & trans.), *John of Ephesus; "Lives of the Eastern Saints"* (Patrologia Orientalis, vol. 19, fasc. 2; Paris: Firmin-Didot, 1925), p. 265. In the passage, Brooks translates the Syriac word *Qûrbānâ* by the English term "oblation".

39 See Brock, "Fire from Heaven", and S. P. Brock, *Holy Spirit in the Syrian Baptismal Tradition* (The Syrian Churches Series, vol. 9; Poona: Anita Printers, 1979), pp. 11–14.

40 Beck, *Hymnen de Fide,* XL:10.

41 Quoted in Brock, *Holy Spirit in the Syrian Baptismal Tradition,* p. 12, from J. J. Overbeck, *S. Ephraemi Syri, Rabulae, Balaei aliorumque Opera Selecta* (Oxford, 1865), p. 252.

42 Beck, *Hymnen de Fide,* X:10–11. The English translation is from Sebastian Brock (ed. & trans.), *St Ephrem; a Hymn on the Eucharist (Hymns on Faith, no. 10)* (Lancaster: J. F. Coakley at the Department of Religious Studies, University of Lancaster, 1986).

43 See Isaiah 6:6–7.

44 Quoted in Joseph P. Amar, "Perspectives on the Eucharist in Ephrem the Syrian", *Worship* 61 (1987), p. 451, from J. -M Sauget (ed), *Anaphorae Syriacae* (2:3; Rome, 1973), p. 320.

45 See C. M. Edsman, *Le baptême de feu* (Uppsala, 1940), pp. 190–199, as cited in Brock, *Holy Spirit in the Syrian Baptismal Tradition,* p. 17, n. 7. For an extended discussion of St. Ephraem's hymns on the pearl, see Andrew Palmer, "The Merchant of Nisibis; Saint Ephrem and his Faithful Quest for Union in Numbers", in J. Den Boeft & A. Hilhorst (eds),

Early Christian Poetry: A Collection of Essays (Supplements to *Vigiliae Christianae*, vol. 22; Leiden: E. J. Brill, 1993), pp. 167–233.

46   Edmund Beck, *Des heiligen Ephraem des Syrers Sermones, II* (CSCO, vols. 311 & 312; Louvain: Peeters, 1970), IV:9–10. The English translation is by S. P. Brock, *Holy Spirit in the Syrian Baptismal Tradition*, p. 14.

47   P. Bedjan, *Homiliae Selectae Mar-Jacobi Sarugensis* (5 vols.; Paris & Leipzig: Otto Harrassowitz, 1905–1910), vol. IV, p. 597. The English translation is by S. P. Brock, *Holy Spirit in the Syrian Baptismal Tradition*, p. 14.

48   Bedjan, *Homiliae Selectae*, vol. II, p. 222. See the important study by J. Van Der Ploeg, "Une homélie de Jacques de Saroug sur la réception de la sainte communion", in *Mélanges Eugène Tisserant* (vol. III, 2, Studi e Testi, vol 233; Città del Vaticano: Biblioteca Apostolica Vaticana, 1964), pp. 395–418.

49   Edmund Beck, *Des heiligen Ephraem des Syrers Hymnen de Nativitate (Epiphania)* (CSCO, vols. 186 & 187; Louvain: Peeters, 1959), XVI:3. For another English translation of this and the following passages from this *madrāshâ* see Kathleen E. McVey (trans.), *Ephrem the Syrian; Hymns* (The Classics of Western Spirituality; Mahwah, NJ: Paulist Press, 1989), pp. 149–150. This passage evokes the role of the *râzâ* and of the *salmâ*, the "image", the Ephraem's thought, which, like a line of Scripture, engage the mind through the eye. In the *Hymns on Paradise* he described his reading of the book of Genesis as follows:
>   The eye and the mind
>   traveled over the lines
>   as over a bridge, and entered together
>   the story of Paradise.
>   The eye as it read
>   transported the mind;
>   in return the mind, too,
>   gave the eye rest
>   from its reading,
>   for when the book had been read
>   the eye had rest
>   but the mind was engaged.
>
>   Both the bridge and the gate
>   of Paradise
>   did I find in this book.
>   I crossed over and entered;
>   my eye remained outside
>   but my mind entered within.

Beck, *Hymnen de Paradiso*, V:4–5.

50   Beck, *Hymnen de Nativitate*, XVI:4.
51   Beck, *Hymnen de Nativitate*, XVI:5.
52   Beck, *Hymnen de Nativitate*, XVI:6.
53   Beck, *Hymnen de Nativitate*, XVI:7. For the imagery used here see Sidney H. Griffith, "The Image of the Image Maker in the Poetry of St. Ephraem the Syrian", in E. A. Livingstone (ed), *Studia Patristica* (vol. XXV; Leuven: Peeters, 1993), pp. 258–269.
54   Beck, *Hymnen de Nativitate*, IV:97–99.
55   Beck, "Die Eucharistie bei Ephräm", p. 59.
59   Ibid.
57   For the Greek word τὸ ψωμίον in John 13:26 the Syriac Peshitta uses simply the Syriac word ܠܚܡܐ i.e., *lahmâ* "bread".
58   Beck, *Paschahymnen, De Azymis*, XIV:15–23.
59   Beck, *Paschahymnen, De Azymis*, XVIII:15–17.
60   See Yousif, *L'Eucharistie chez saint Éphrem*, pp. 82–84.
61   See especially "teaching songs" XVII & XVIII *De Azymis* in Beck, *Paschahymnen*, where the responsory verses are, respectively, "Blessed is he who cast away the People of the un-leavened bread, whose hands were defiled with his precious blood", and "Thank the Son who gave us his body instead of that unleavened bread which he had given to the People."

62 See Edmund Beck, *Ephraem Syrus; Sermones in Hebdomadam Sanctam* (CSCO, vols. 412 & 413; Louvain: Peeters, 1979), vol. 413, pp. 4–7. In particular Beck wrote, "Hier aber müssen sie auf Grund der herausgestellten Situation mit dem ungesäuerten Brot des jüdischen Paschamahles verbunden werden, das der Eucharistie voranging und and dem Judas noch teilgenommen hatte" (p. 5). While he does not say it in so many words, Beck leaves the impression that in Ephraem's view Jesus gave Judas a morsel of unleavened bread used in the Jewish Passover, while the bread of the Eucharist which he later gave to the disciples could have been leavened bread. Actually, Ephraem nowhere suggests that he thought that the bread of the Eucharist at the Last Supper was leavened bread, in spite of the fact that in songs XVII and XVIII *De Azymis* he makes much of the contrast between the unleavened bread of the Jews and the leavened bread of the Christians. In his works generally he makes considerable use of the image of "leaven". See Edmund Beck, "Das Bild vom Sauerteig bei Ephräm", *Oriens Christianus* 63 (1979), pp. 1–19. But when he comes to the Eucharist no mention of leaven is to be found. Pierre Yousif says, "De ces considérations générales, on ne peut pas voir à quel pain pense Ephrem lorsqu'il se réfère à la liturgie … On peut donc penser que l'Eglise de Nisibe, pour mieux se distinguer des juifs, a adopté le pain fermenté pour l'Eucharistie qui, malgré le ferment, revouvelle l'esprit." Yousif, *L'Eucharistie chez saint Éphrem*, p. 85. Yousif goes on to say that in spite of the polemics to the contrary, he does not think that Ephraem would have objected to the use of unleavened bread in the Eucharist!

63 This view is in contrast to the interpretation Beck offered twenty years earlier, when he wrote that Ephraem's interpretation of John 13:26 offered a biblical warrant for his conviction "das für den Sünder (Ungläubigen) das eucharistiische Brot der Segensgabe des Geistes beraubt ist. Er deutet nämlich den Bissen, den Jesus nach Joh 13,27 dem Verräter gab, auf das eucharistische Brot; seine Ausdrucksweise lässt darüber keinen Zweifel, obwohl dann auch bei ihm die Erwähnung der Kommunion der Apostel in Strophe 23 sehr aus dem Zusammenhang fällt. Das Eintauchen des eucharistischen Brotes in das Wasser deutet er somit in seiner konkreten Denkweise als ein Auslöschen des Geistesfeuers." Beck, "Die Eucharistie bei Ephräm", pp. 61–62.

64 See G. Rouwhorst, "Bénédiction, action de grâces, supplication; les oraisons de la table dans le Judaïsme et les célébrations eucharistiques de chrétiens syriaques", *Questions Liturgiques* 61 (1980), pp. 211–240.

65 See Rouwhorst, *Les Hymnes pascales*, vol. I, pp. 88–89. See also Yousif, *L'Eucharistie chez saint Éphrem*, p. 216.

66 See Beck, *Sermones in Hebdomadam Sanctam*, vol. 413, p. 12. It is important in the present context to notice that in 1954 Beck accepted the authenticity of these texts and quoted from them in support of his earlier view of Ephraem's interpretation of the John passage in question. See Beck, "Die Eucharistie bei Ephräm", p. 62.

67 Beck, *Sermones in Hebdomadam Sanctam*, IV:174–187.

68 Similarly, the *Commentary on Tatian's Diatessaron* attributed to Ephraem seems to agree with the author of the *mêmrâ*. In reference to John 13:26 the text says: "*He dipped it*, to render [evident] the total participation [of Judas] in his death, for his body was destined to be dipped in his blood. Or [alternatively], he dipped it so as not to give the testament with him. He moistened it and then gave it to him; moistened first because it had been prepared for [the testament] which was to follow." Carmel McCarthy, *Saint Ephrem's Commentary on Tatian's Diatessaron: An English Translation of Chester Beatty Syriac MS 709 with Introduction and Notes* (Journal of Semitic Studies Supplement, 2; Oxford: Oxford University Press on Behalf of the University of Manchester, 1993), XIX, 3, p. 284. This awkward text, which in this part of the *Commentary* has not survived in Syriac but only in Armenian, seems to be referring to the "covenant" in Luke 22:20, "This cup which is poured out for you is the new covenant in my blood". It is worth recalling here that in the view of Edmund Beck, "Ephraem was not the author of the commentary. On the other hand, the many and large connections with Ephraem's hymns and homilies allow the supposition that the work originates from his school." Edmund Beck, "Ephräm und der Diatessaronkommentar im Abschnitt über die Wunder beim Tode Jesu am Kreuz", *Oriens Christianus* 77 (1993), p. 119.

69 Beck, *Sermones in Hebdomadam Sanctam*, IV:106–111.

70 Beck, Hymnen de Virginitate, XXXVII:2. The English translation is from Murray, *Symbols of Church and Kingdom*, p. 77.

71   Beck, *Hymnen de Fide*, X:18. The English translation is from Sebastian Brock, *St Ephrem: A Hymn on the Eucharist (Hymns on Faith, no. 10)* Lancaster, U.K.: J. F. Coakley, Dept. of Religious Studies, University of Lancaster, 1986).

72   Edmund Beck, *Des heiligen Ephraem des Syrers Hymnen de Ecclesia* (CSCO, vols. 198 & 199; Louvain: Peeters, 1960), XXXII:2.

73   See Murray, *Symbols in Church and Kingdom*, p. 89.

74   Beck, *Hymnen de Fide*, X:8. The English translation is by Sebastian Brock, *St Ephrem: A Hymn on the Eucharist*.

THE STRIPPING OF THE WORDS: CONFLICT OVER THE EUCHARIST IN THE EPISCOPAL CHURCH

DAVID MARTIN

Initially I planned to give an account of controversy in England from the mid-seventies over the deposition of the Book of Common Prayer, in particular its Eucharistic rite, whether in the form stabilised in 1662 or as revised in 1928. However, events overtook me and I became briefly caught up in a later out-crop of that controversy which concerned the imposition by fiat of the Revised Common Lectionary.[1] The methods deployed and arguments used had much in common with the longer term national debate and stimulated many uncomfortable reflections, some of which I offered to the conference on the Eucharist at Duke University in April 1998. However, that was a pièce d'occasion which is now deprived of its occasion and intimate audience and it is a moot point whether it is proper publicly to retail in extenso this kind of material. Better for it to feed anonymously into the broad reflections which follow.

Something needs to be said about the long-term background of the national controversy. The Book of Common Prayer—leaving aside the Authorised (or King James') Version of the Bible—is the single most influential document in English culture. Even today, as George Steiner has pointed out, to speak planetary English is to speak Bible and Prayer Book, and that is true whether you are conscious of it or not.[2] Even in a contemporary news programme you can detect a persistent echoing of phrases which have been incised on collective memory and woven into the language quite apart from their original contexts. Moreover, as the Catholic historian Adrian Hastings has shown, the emergence of the modern languages of Europe and of national

David Martin
Cripplegate Cottage, 174, St. John's Road, Woking, Surrey GU21 1PQ, UK

consciousness was closely bound up with liturgy and with scripture[3] translated into the vernacular, more particularly in the northern countries. In England the influence of the vernacular liturgy and scripture among people at large was far greater than the influence of Shakespeare, which is in some ways quite recent. So the successful deposition of the Prayer Book within the Church which engendered it (and acquired an identity through it) marks a major cultural transition. It followed within a generation or so the virtual disappearance of classical culture, but whereas Latin and Greek were confined to an elite, the Bible and Prayer Book were national possessions, the former taught in any primary school. (There were, of course, transitions in the educational world parallel to those in the churches, more particularly in religious education, but consideration of the cultural sources of these would take us too far upstream.)

The first English Prayer Book dates from 1548/9 and was to a great extent an Englishing of the mass in the Sarum rite. A much more Protestant book appeared in 1552 and in the course of the later sixteenth century the Anglican Church absorbed many influences from Calvinism. However, by the 1630s a Catholic reaction had gained considerable influence and—after the Puritan revolution—this contributed to the delicate balances of the final version of the Prayer Book in 1662. Though Archbishop Cranmer was the chief author of the Book of Common Prayer, Diarmaid MacCulloch in his magisterial *Thomas Cranmer: A Life* suggests that the long-term history of the Anglican Church represents a recoil from the Protestant high water mark reached in the mid-sixteenth century.[4]

One aspect of that recoil in the inter-war period was the Parish Communion Movement, and another was the 1928 Book revised to accommodate the Catholic emphases introduced nearly a century earlier by the Oxford Movement. In the event, the 1928 Book was turned down by Parliament, which left a scar on relations between church and state capable of affecting ecclesiastical reactions to the renewal of controversy in the 1970s and 1980s. The 1928 Book was used in the United States and also in practice used quite widely in England. Thus when people complained of the loss of the Prayer Book it was not always certain just what they were referring to. They were clear enough that the familiar phrases and forms had been somehow spirited away but when they objected they found themselves challenged as to what exactly they were asking for. The query most frequently put in relation to the Eucharist was whether they wanted the 1662 rite or some familiar variants of it, including the rite of 1928. Indeed, the deployment of such technicalities as a smokescreen was one major source of irritation, as was the tactic of suddenly reverting to the 1662 service according to disused rubrics. A kind of low intensity conflict developed in which minor matters acquired symbolic salience, forcing an unwanted and unwonted self-consciousness on people accustomed to treating the Eucharist as a given of existence.

Similar irritations were engendered over the rites of passage. When it came to marriage, for example, you had to become something of an expert to ensure unanticipated novelties were not foisted on you. As to confirmation and ordination these were under complete episcopal control and there was no way of evading the imposition of the new forms. Of course, it is possible that only a minority objected all that strongly. The point was it had become increasingly difficult to know what to expect. Any Sunday you might be confronted by fresh variants in pamphlet form as well as by intrusive instructions or ad lib additions by the priest. Letter columns in newspapers began to reflect the growing momentum of change.

There was also political concern. A parliamentary measure of 1975 had granted substantial autonomy to the Church of England, and that included the ability to alter its liturgy within certain safeguards to protect and entrench the Book of Common Prayer. One architect of that measure, Lord Glenamara, a Labour peer and sometime Minister of Education, eventually concluded that the Church of England had circumvented the understandings which lay behind that legislation. As time went on there were even voices within the Church which contemplated the explicit overthrow of the Book of Common Prayer, and along with that total autonomy and disestablishment. There were seeds here of a serious conflict of church and state that most people would certainly have wished to avoid. Almost a century had passed since Gladstone as Prime Minister had warned that another controversy over issues of worship such as that over "ritualism" might finish the Church of England. At one point the Church even found its legislation held up in the ecclesiastical committee of Parliament.

However, there was another area of concern which provides the focus of this paper: the academic and literary critique of the new forms and texts. Quite early on W. H. Auden had complained that the Episcopal Church had "gone stark raving mad" and this was an opinion widely shared not only among Christian intellectuals but more generally. Yet these critical voices encountered problems finding their target. In the first place they had no locus standi within the organisation of the Church of England. In their view it was a national institution whose arrangements were open to comment, but increasingly within the Church itself a bureaucratic structure of committees and commissions had grown up with a prickly sense of corporate identity. What happened in the Church was its own affair and there was a division between insiders and those on the margin. If you wanted to be heard then you should work your way through the organisational structure. In short, the forum of debate was entirely internal, a point made clear by a prominent insider, Colin Buchanan, when he said "They are not going to change us from outside".

The most distressing decision, and one which underlined the tendency to distinguish between insider and outsider, concerned the Lord's Prayer. This was *the* common prayer, known almost universally by heart, and the attempt to change it not only illustrated the introverted pedantry of the revisers but in a stroke separated the usage of the minority of regular attenders from millions of people who attended church from time to time or for Christmas and the rites of passage. Nor was the new version clearer than the old, and if, as some held, the phrase "do not bring us to the time of trial" had an eschatological reference, it was positively arcane. Nothing showed more clearly the total lack of understanding of the role of oral transmission, collective memory, memorisation by heart, and repetition, than this incomprehensible decision.

Even for insiders it was not easy to find a platform. The Prayer Book Action Group (which in 1975 became the Prayer Book Society) set about the usual discreet lobbying only to find itself ignored. As for the Synod its principal alignments did not allow cross-bench views much opportunity for expression. By contrast the movement for change was well-organised within the structures of the Church, and had clear institutional bases, for example at St. John's College, Nottingham. Moreover, most of the theological colleges were staffed by the proponents of change and as time went on they progressively reduced the role of the Book of Common Prayer in the formation of ordinands.[5] In this way they successfully suppressed memory and cut off the older generation of Anglicans by preventing the reproduction of the culture of the Prayer Book in the next generation of priests. The same story could be told elsewhere: the organisational command posts were mostly under the control of the reformers, including those dealing with the dissemination of devotional literature. Whatever the de jure situation in practice the Prayer Book was demoted, above all in clergy gatherings and major conferences.

Thus any attempt to ensure the availability of the traditional Eucharist and other Prayer Book services had to rely on the media, above all books and newspapers. This posed no great difficulty since journalists as practising word-smiths had a strong preference for the traditional texts. The only exception was the BBC where religious broadcasting was under clerical influence and only marginally responsive to lobbying. This meant that older people were largely deprived of the chance to hear traditional services even at home.

So, in effect, another war of the ancients and moderns erupted in the print media, with relatively marginal ripples on radio and television. Those on the one side tended to be lay and often academic, those on the other were disproportionately clerical. With some exaggeration one might characterise the conflict as one between academics and clergy.

Insofar as this was a conflict within the church it created intense psychological discomfort, since the protesters felt intense affection for the Church and were very reluctant to argue about prayer. Academics might express their views in print but were unhappy about putting pressure on clergy locally. So the conflict took place on different planes with the academics intermittently active in the media and the clergy in full-time control of the local (and national) agenda. Needless to say control of the local agenda was in the end much more important and clergy showed themselves adept at manipulative devices, in particular using sacred auras and prayerful atmospheres to defuse meetings, along with timely reminders of charity and humility. Whoever writes the minutes controls the world.[6] There was hardly ever a direct confrontation, and the antagonists were probably only faintly aware of each other's activities. In a debate with Dr. Jasper in Hampstead Parish Church, I encountered a courteous scholar of liturgy who was a virtual stranger to the wider issues. Academics did not spend much time at Parochial Church Councils, and clergy did not read their arguments. It was a case "where ignorant armies clash by night".

Insofar as clergy were conscious at all they were annoyed at the intrusion into what they regarded as their professional space, above all the altar. Already defensive about status and the encroachments of secularisation, a critique coming from Christian academics was hard to bear, and from non-Christian academics it was intolerable. Clergy had devised the new rites "to serve the present age" and now they were being blamed for it. They felt damned for modernity and archaism alike. Worse, they had to bear the criticism that what they produced was not genuinely modern at all. Christian writers provided useful quotations when it came to sermons but had better stay ornamental on the question of how to compose liturgy.

Probably the period of most intense conflict occurred between 1979 and 1982, around the time of the publication of the Alternative Service Book in 1980. Obviously many people were involved in this in ways which cannot be detailed here and I can only summarise my own involvement with extreme brevity. In the autumn of 1978 it seemed to me that the only way to gain a hearing was to persuade a Christian of standing to express concern in a national newspaper. So, rather unwillingly, I wrote to the editor of *The Daily Telegraph* suggesting he approach Dame Helen Gardner. I then received a phone call asking me to visit the editor and arriving at his office I found him slightly bemused. He said he already had somebody "to deal with Marxism in the Church". However on my explaining this was Cranmer not Marx he asked me to write the articles myself. I did so and when they appeared they certainly helped ignite the controversy and produced a very large correspondence.

Thereafter, I was taken over by the momentum of the issue, which so far as I was concerned focused on three initiatives: a petition to the General Synod, presented in association with an issue of *Poetry Nation Review*, which I edited,[7] a Gallup Poll, and a Prayer Book Protection Bill, introduced into both Houses of Parliament. With regard to the first I wrote at least one thousand letters, mostly to well-known people, asking them to sign one of three petitions—literary, political and musical.

To engage in this correspondence was like engaging in dialogue with the imaginative intelligence of the nation. The "St. Cecilia" petition, for example, included such names as William Walton, Peter Pears, John Tavener, Janet Baker, Edmund Rubbra, Herbert Sumsion, Herbert Howells, Julian Bream, Ursula Vaughan Williams, Malcolm Williamson, Lennox Berkeley, David Willcocks, Andrew Lloyd-Webber, Peter Maxwell Davies, William Wordsworth, Alfred Deller, George Thalben-Ball, and most of the masters of music in the major cathedrals. (Such a petition aligned the tension between academic and cleric with a long-term tension between musician and cleric. Most musicians were liturgical conservatives and they usually preferred to compose for the traditional texts. The only gain from their viewpoint has been the opportunity to use the musical texts of the Roman Mass from Byrd to Berkeley according to the Roman sequence.)

The presentation of the petitions at the Synod was very widely reported with supporting comment and *The Guardian* carried the headline "Half the people you have ever heard of". The Gallup Poll which followed received similar publicity, including an editorial in *The Times* headed "Gallup to the Rescue".

The third initiative relating to Parliament was more problematic and was only entered upon with great unease when no response was forthcoming to the earlier efforts. The "Prayer Book Protection Bill", sponsored by the Labour M.P. Frank Field and the Conservative M.P. Lord Cranborne, was only taken to the Second Reading since the object was solely to make the kind of symbolic gesture which could not be ignored. Even so we were conscious it would once again raise the spectre of a crisis between church and state. Indeed, when I was subsequently invited in company with two colleagues, C. A. A. Kilmister and Ian Thompson, to talk to the Archbishop of Canterbury at Lambeth Palace, it was precisely this issue the Archbishop initially insisted on discussing. He feared the ignition of a further controversy over disestablishment. However, this meeting did mean that protest had been heard. Certain things followed which partly stabilised the situation, such as an article by the Archbishop in a national newspaper pointing out that people had a right to ask for traditional services, and a helpful statement by the House of Bishops.

The problem here was that institutions have poor memories: new incumbents do not remember who among their predecessors promised what. Basically the more ruthless revisers were waiting for "used up" believers to die off. On the other hand, a new generation was emerging in the episcopate, for example, Stephen Sykes at Ely and David Stancliffe at Salisbury. The appointment of the latter to chair the liturgical commission was also part of a generational shift in its composition, and there was an increasing sense of the destruction of resources involved in the first impetus of liturgical change. Indeed, both the Archbishops over the main period of change subsequently expressed their concern at the losses incurred. It was also realised that numerical decline had not been halted by these measures, while many faithful people had been needlessly alienated. In 1992 some regular meetings were instituted between the Prayer Book Society and members of the Liturgical Commission.[8]

The focus of this essay is not so much on the eventful course of this controversy as on the aspects which illustrate its peculiar character, more particularly as these aspects involved a conflict between academics active in the print media and the clergy controlling the situation and the agenda in the parishes.[9] The academics principally concerned were mostly committed Christians, with a strong representation of writers and literary critics. On the literary side were Donald Davie, Charles Sisson, Michael Schmidt (all associated with *Poetry Nation Review*) Brian Morris (later the Labour peer Lord Morris), Ian Robinson, Derek Brewer (then Master of Emmanuel College), Andor Gomme, Ronald Blythe, Rachel Trickett, Stephen Prickett, with some intermittent reinforcement or comment from people like Beryl Bainbridge, Alan Bennett, John Betjeman, Iris Murdoch, Helen Gardner, Tom Paulin and A. N. Wilson. Some idea of those concerned and the arguments used can be gleaned from the volume edited by Peter Mullen and David Martin, *No Alternative*.[10] Among non-literary people involved were the distinguished Christian philosophers Basil Mitchell, Mary Warnock, R. M. Hare and Mary Hesse. Among Americans were such well-known literary critics as Cleanth Brooks and Margaret Doody.

There was also from time to time a sociological and anthropological critique emanating mainly from Catholics such as Victor Turner and Mary Douglas. What was abundantly clear was the depth of interest among these people and also the existence of untapped intellectual resources available to the Church in its laity. As already indicated, however, the contribution of that laity was far from welcome. When an academic group asked through me to meet with members of the liturgical commission, the chairman, Professor Douglas Jones, though himself well disposed to the idea, replied that they were "not ready for that". That in itself points to one of the paradoxes of the dispute: the proclaimed desire of reformers to stimulate lay participation and their dismay when it turned out not the sort they anticipated. The paradox is worth developing.

The thrust of liturgical reform lay not only in the amendment of the text but in the spatial dispositions and pattern of the sacred action. The priest was democratically renamed the Eucharistic president and he now faced towards the "People of God". Sometimes the signs demarcating the sacred were eroded, and a vertical, eastward orientation converted into a semi-circle of gathered believers. Often this contradicted the spatial symbolism of ancient buildings as well as dismantling a great deal of devotional furniture with treasured personal associations. In such matters clergy disconcerted lay people by arguing that what they thought immemorial practice was merely Victorian liturgical reform.

Reformers sought to facilitate communal interaction and inter alia to convert the Eucharist into an exchange of gifts; the gifts of God for the people of

God. Lay people were to be winkled out of their individual space and integrated into "the body of Christ". Indeed, they *were* the body of Christ, at least in theory; and a key sentence in the new rite was "Though we are many, we are one body, because we all share in the one bread". Attractive though this might be many lay people experienced it as an orchestration of communal feeling. They also regretted the unused east end and were reluctant to take up the invitation to trespass on sacred space. They did not want to be familiar with the elements or drop practices expressing "due reverence" in receiving communion. The pressure applied to stand rather than to kneel was a particular focus of symbolic tension.

Yet the moment they spoke their concerns, they were countermanded in the name of priestly authority. Obviously the participation sought did not include critical evaluation. By promoting gestures of inclusion and facing westward priests felt they had abandoned their own perceived isolation for eye to eye contact, but there was scant welcome for serious criticism. However, when this came from anthropologists and sociologists, believed to be natural allies of innovation, the usual dismissals sounded unconvincing. Mary Douglas in particular was concerned about the way the treatment of the Friday fast in the Roman Church loosened the anchors of identity and Victor Turner with the way the orchestration of community reduced defensible space. The question, especially for "Catholics", Anglican or Roman, was how far the specific symbolism of Christianity, rooting devotion in patterns of habit and gesture and in tangible icons was giving way to a culture of free-floating notions. Peel off the successive layers of the onion and you arrive not at authentic being but nothingness. Reformers did not seem to understand that you cannot unilaterally determine the ambiguous potential of symbolic rearrangements. A semi-circle can enclose as well as open out and a row can look forward and up as well as convey authority and immobility.

The debate itself centred around three key areas, political, aesthetic and theological. As for the political issue it was bound up in two kinds of linkage, one being the residual, legal and symbolic connections of church with state, including the monarchy, and the other being those informal connections whereby the traditional elites thought of the Church of England as their natural habitat. About the former, Anglican leaders were ambivalent. They appreciated the opportunity to be heard as a right in the national forum but wanted to shed the negative aura of establishment. As to the monarchy their ambivalence increased as the royal family increasingly needed their prayers, which, in any case, the royal family was known to prefer in traditional form. In fact this was a minor issue in its own right since the Prayer for the Church Militant in the Prayer Book Holy Communion service referred very specifically to the monarch, asking that "under her we may be godly and quietly governed". In the new prayers, however, there was a loose sequence of topics in which the Church and the bishops came first followed by a perfunctory reference to the monarch. This sequence, replacing the resplendent and integrated prayer of the 1662 rite, notoriously offered opportunity for prolonged tours through world trouble spots. At any rate, it was clear that many leaders in the Church had had enough of regalism.

More important, however, than these formal links, which few Anglicans really wished to sever, were the connections between the Church and the elite, especially in the independent schools and "the county". The Church had for generations been treated as a junior partner in these circles and was literally fed up with patronage. Priests knew that their residual association with gentry culture and manners was now a journalistic superstition rather than a reality and saw it as cutting them off from people at large. It was the great disadvantage of the Book of Common Prayer to be thought of as bound up in this antique social connection, especially when the priesthood itself came increasingly from rather different social backgrounds. The problem was that the social associations of the traditional liturgy were all too traditional, and the Church of England wished to remake itself in a new image.

The aesthetic issue was, for the most part, raised by rather different people and they subjected the work of the revisers to detailed literary criticism. What then ensued was a clash of quite different kinds of scholarship. Those whose concern was linguistic in the narrow sense were irritated by those whose concern was language more widely understood. They appeared to have little interest in writing as an activity or in different genres or in what would constitute a contemporary language. They seemed unconscious of the incongruous reminiscences in their "modern" prose and had no idea why some were so infuriated by lacerated fragments of archaic phrasing in a supposedly contemporary text. Wherever possible their instinct was to substitute abstraction for metaphor and to break up integrated forms of expression into something between a list and a report. Above all they had a prejudice against "redundancy" and cumulative repetition.

The points of contention appeared endless and a meeting of minds remote. So far as the revisers were concerned, they sought intelligibility and what some of them called "the language of the market place", though that was never specified in terms of the many varieties of contemporary English. The broader issues of "Religious English" as raised by Ian Robinson or of the translation of the Hebrew Bible as raised by (say) Gerald Hammond seemed to pass them by.[11] It was as if they thought there was some extraneous extra called "beauty" or (worse) "dignity" that literary gentlemen could be asked to stick on once you had completed the real work. This was not true of Professor David Frost, but he often ploughed a lonely furrow, and indeed eventually decided to resign. (Of course, underneath all this was the issue of the aesthetic in every aspect of Christian worship, but this was rarely entered into in depth. Protagonists of the replacement services often used the word "aesthetic" in a comminatory way, but their animus seemed mostly directed at "the word" and to some extent music, not the visual arts and certainly not vestments.)

One would really like to know how much consideration was given to the way in which shared, memorable and constantly repeated texts eventually inform the inward substance of the mind until they evoke devotion in the act of recollection. What is the role of quotation in moments of crisis? Are people's minds "made up" by language rather than the other way round? Or to ask a different sort of question: how is it that a text like the Authorised Version can enter easily and naturally into the heart of African-American and Caribbean culture and yet somehow appear difficult and unavailable to people educated in England's premier universities?

The theological issue was the one where the revisers and their supporters felt they were on home ground. They had a cure of souls not the curatorship of a museum. If you could "get the theology right"—and recover the message and practices of the spring-time of the Church, then spring-time would come again. Yet it was not as easy as all that. They knew that theological revision hovered uneasily between recovery of ancient emphases and modern glosses, between the third and fifth centuries and the Zeitgeist of the sixties.[12] Any suggestion they were scrapping the classic formularies could induce a crisis of authority and suspicions of Pelagianism or Gnosticism. (That way the Romans lost a whole generation of priests.) So the Prayer Book was surreptitiously shuffled sideways with talk of "alternative" services rather than replacements and by making it *a* standard of doctrine not *the* standard. Language turned very slippery so that great emphasis was placed on "common prayer" rather than on *The* Book of Common prayer.

The objective here was to create an aura of continuity with the specific tradition while actually jettisoning it. Whereas an earlier ecumenism had celebrated the possibility of different contributions to a shared treasury the latest version depended on the products of international church bureaucracies owned and treasured by none. Of course, to some degree this meant an approximation to what was produced by Catholics, though the version of the mass produced for English-speaking countries had been particularly impoverished because aiming to cover an impossibly wide range of linguistic usages. Occasionally the politics of ecumenism appeared to produce some peculiar results as, for example, in the Revised Common Lectionary where St. Willibrord of Frisia is in but Martin Luther is out.

A persistent theme in theological criticism of the new texts was a drift to Pelagianism i.e., a stress on the potentials of human virtue and will rather than the assistance of divine grace. The new Anglican General Confession was a target here and reforming clergy declared themselves shocked at the number of closet Augustinians that "came out". Reformers wanted less stress on penitence, sin and redemption and a shift in tonality towards celebration and they were disconcerted by an intellectual counter-attack. It sometimes looked as if the problem was to reduce the influence of Paul and Augustine without being too obvious about it, and in this connection it had to be admitted the Book of Common Prayer was all too awkwardly scriptural. At any rate, the theme of human frailty had to be played down since the spirit of the sixties and seventies was not at all compatible with the notion that "miserable sinners" had "no power of themselves to help themselves". A proper balance could be introduced by admitting that one was decently sorry but amenable to improvement.

One problem in all this was that an Anglican age structure tilted to the upper ranges meant that too many people had vivid memories of an earlier generation of bishops lauding "our incomparable liturgy". This somehow made them unresponsive to the idea that it did not measure up to the four-fold pattern of Eucharistic action declared mandatory by Dom Gregory Dix. If a couple of decades later they find themselves once again told that the alternative services in their turn need to be replaced, they are apt to conclude they have been here before. Of course, some lay people have become well schooled in the idea that the Holy Spirit offers a progressive revelation, sometimes reversing an earlier reversal or reforming an earlier reformation. All the same, it needs some intellectual dexterity to know just when what the Holy Spirit "has to say for us today" cancels what the Spirit had to say the day before yesterday. A "dynamic God" tends to confuse those who suppose Him "the same yesterday, today and for ever".[13]

In conclusion something needs to be said about two issues which troubled the Church over this period and are instructive in the way they bore on controversy over the Eucharist.

The first issue, which had quite immediate bearing, concerned the ordination of women. It by no means followed, of course, that all those who were anxious to maintain the presence of the traditional liturgy were opposed to the ordination of women. Far from it. Indeed, a considerable number of those within the English Prayer Book Society, myself included, were happy to support female ordination, or else they were of the view that each issue should be pursued separately. Naturally there were those of a generally traditionalist cast of mind who did see a direct linkage.

What was interesting, however, and indicative of the crucial role of clergy in relation to matters touching on the occupation of sacred space, was the marked contrast between the arrangements carefully worked out to accommodate the largely clerical opponents of female ordination, and the very limited and ill-defined scope accorded the mainly lay critics of the new liturgical arrangements and texts. Presumably the accommodation devised for the former was necessary because there was a definable clerical pressure group able to inflict immediate costs should its members be ignored. The latter, however, were diffuse and scattered, and their views implied no course of action which might prove costly to Church organisation. That meant they had nowhere to go and so might hang on after making a protest, or at most travel some distance to find a church more to their liking. Congregations were disinclined to break off en bloc over the Prayer Book issue. So the consequences were no more bothersome than invisible leakage and private unhappiness. Furthermore, such clergy as might be well disposed to the traditional liturgy had to face the fact that in a more and more centralised organisation the enclaves of independence were being mopped up and their own chances of preferment diminished.

The second issue, with much less immediate bearing on the Eucharist was disagreement over the scope and style of social activism and political comment. Certainly social activism had a strong base among clergy, so that in England they were more likely to be *Guardian* readers than their parishioners and in the USA much more likely to be Democrats. But the ideological alignments between those who protested over the liturgy and attitudes to social activism were quite loose, and these attitudes did not lead back to the control of sacred space. If individual clergy altered the text to ensure it was politically correct that certainly irritated some and distracted others, but has not so far broken out into full scale cultural warfare. The nub of the problem lies in a difference of view between conservative men and women in the congregations and clerical committees tilted in the other direction, well defended against traditional pressure groups, but defenceless against change.[14]

Many issues of cultural politics remain segregated at a safe distance. Clergy may, for example, derive various communitarian stances from the structure of the Eucharist, but these do not impinge directly on people who think otherwise, or on the majority who are unlikely to have any idea what is going on. In these segregated areas what has been a collusive avoidance of quite serious differences behind the protective screen of (hitherto) shared words and gestures can still be maintained, provided the participants know how to steer their way past symbolic flashpoints.

There remains one line of demarcation close to the altar where tensions over liturgy are experienced quite acutely, and that lies between reformist clergy and lay participants in the ritual, notably vergers, thurifers, cross-bearers and the like. Without these lay participants everything would collapse. Moreover, such people care passionately about minutiae as well as about due reverence and propriety. Their liturgical views are very conservative but rarely taken into account, though clergy do recognise it is unwise to ignore them entirely.

The reasons for such a demarcation probably lie in different kinds of satisfaction derived from the liturgical role. For lay participants their performances are simply immense privilege and pleasure, whereas for many clergy neither liturgy nor pastoralia offer an exhaustive or fully satisfying account of what they believe they are about. Some of them have become chronically bored or dissatisfied with liturgy or pastoralia or both, and that breeds the itch for change. Social activism then provides a sense of breaking out of the clerical sub-culture and achieving some impact on "the world", in which case liturgy has to be "retooled" for the job in hand.

The main argument of the foregoing lays stress on the dynamics of the clerical sub-culture as crucial. Only by some understanding of that can one gauge properly the problems encountered by lay protest. After all, the aims of that protest were modest and reasonable enough. Protesters asked for no more than the maintenance of the Prayer Book in the mainstream where sufficient numbers desired it. Most of them recognised the genuine gains brought by the liturgical movement and were simply shocked by the blank refusal to listen. As the Archbishop of Sydney commented in personal conversation, "What you ask is entirely reasonable but I have to say the clergy are bolshie about it". Similar quotations could be multiplied. "The bit is in their teeth", as the Dean of Canterbury put it to me. "In a clerically led Church we decide", said a London suffragan.

The problem is that those committed to the sacred ministry under-standably seek a reason for the indifference they encounter about which something can be done, and being human they also need to have a sense of going somewhere. That sense is reinforced by the increasingly managerial structure and language of a Church which received from secular culture a version of its own notion of "mission statement", as well as the "action plan". Proposals for advancing "mission" and "moving forward" are generated in the national and international bureaucracies and handed down for imple-mentation by the local overseers. These make no attempt at rational suasion but operate through managerial discourses, backed up by a low-level thera-peutic vocabulary. Since the Church is a religious organization, policy has to be advocated as "the way the Church is going" under the providential guidance of the divine will. Appeals to the Holy Spirit become particularly emphatic when policy is driven by the politics of ecumenism.

What is too painful even to entertain is any suggestion that the Church remains "wrapt in the old miasmal mist" and is churning round and round on its propellers rather than voyaging anywhere in particular. Though it is blindingly obvious that new translations, fresh liturgies and linguistic adjust-ments are not remotely commensurate with the contemporary problem, never-theless, they have to be represented as relevant responses to modernity. They are "experiments" instituted and justified by the need to appeal to the "unreached tribes" of post-modernity, but immune to empirical test or to reversal if unsuccessful. Nor is there much of a welcome for the idea of niche marketing, though that is palpably what is happening in practice. Niche marketing implies that the proposed adjustments are ad hoc and the Holy Spirit favours horses for courses rather than the one true solution. Though the proponents of change speak officially in favour of pluralism, they make sure pluralism ends with them. The "People of God" need to be adjured to "pull together" and encouraged by such manipulative blandishments as piety can supply.

The Church represents a master-disciple relationship which in the early centuries was reframed as a relationship between the believer and hier-archically managed channels of grace. Today in "established" situations it continues to operate as a "divine service" station for millions of intermittent "customers". To secure compliance over liturgical alterations it has to rely on a decent willingness on the part of worshippers to trust that clergy know their own business, assisted by the fleeting character of any direct contact, plus Anglican social tact and manners. In any case, lay people recognise that there are many clergy who exhibit high levels of dedication and social and pastoral service, as well as some who are equipped with profound scholarship. Decency decrees it is unfair to burden such people with complaint or contention and it appears downright cynical to suspect their operations of being more Trollopian than evangelical. It is also dangerous to undermine those who hold in trust one's existential vulnerabilities.

The language of faith is consolatory and denunciatory; it establishes solidarities and mutualities; it conveys the profundities of redemption, penitence and reconciliation and prescribes the journey from alienation to acceptance. Faith pronounces and remits. What such a language cannot do is create the neutral spaces needed for rational and civil debate and disagreement.

Thus in the recent local dispute in which all colleaguely consultation was avoided, and all dialogue over compromise rejected, I had to mark up and explicitly bracket my own conscious shift away from the obfuscatory unction of "Christian" exchanges to the criteria governing academic debate. The transition is difficult to achieve because such criteria are alien to a clerical world hovering between institutionalised charisma expressed in aggressive assertions of episcopal authority and managerial bureaucracy. No doubt that is the reason that lay consultants called on to help from time to time on commissions, such as Philip Larkin, Ian Robinson or P. D. James, have experienced such frustration. There seems no sense that the issues involved call for precise and informed judgement in literary matters and indeed questions of sociology. What was not dogma was dismissed as taste and opinion.

Maybe over two decades of involvement in the issue, together with the renewed impact of recent dispute, have worn away the psychic tread, reduced the resources for eirenic judgement and brought on a mood of cynicism. It is very possible.[15] In any case, the combination of "dumbing down" with managerialism is equally evident in the BBC, the broadsheets and the universities. Yet on another issue, fought over three decades, criticism has found its target: the Labour Party has tackled the teaching profession and reintroduced tables. Perhaps the Church too may awake from what one senior cleric calls "its waking dream".

NOTES

1   I had no objection to the RCL as such but to the total lack of consultation in its imposition by the canons residentiary and their refusal even to make known or discuss or compromise with respect to the options within it. See Note 13.

2   George Steiner, *No Passion Spent* (London and Boston: Faber and Faber, 1996), p. 57.

3   Adrian Hastings, *The Construction of Nationhood: Ethnicity, Religion and Nationalism* (Cambridge: Cambridge University Press, 1997).

4   Diarmaid MacCulloch, *Thomas Cranmer: A Life* (London and New Haven: Yale University Press, 1996), ch. 14. Cf. Colin Buchanan, Trevor Lloyd and Harold Miller (eds) *Anglican Worship Today* (London: Collins, 1980), p. 128 et seq.

5   Roger Homan and David Martin (eds) *Theological Colleges and the Book of Common Prayer: A Survey* (St. James Garlickhythe, London: Prayer Book Society, 1985).

6   Roger Homan, "Noli me tangere. Management skills of the Parish Priest", in David Martin (ed) *Poetry Nation Review 13: Crisis for Cranmer and King James* Vol. 6, No. 5. (Manchester: Carcanet Press, 1979).

7   David Martin, (ed) *Poetry Nation Review 13: Crisis for Cranmer and King James* Vol. 6, No. 5. (Manchester: Carcanet Press, 1979).

8   Michael Perham, (ed) *Model and Inspiration: The Prayer Book Tradition Today*, Essays by Colin James, P. D. James, David Martin and David Stancliffe (London: SPCK, 1993).

9   For an analytic and descriptive account cf. Barry Spurr, *The Word in the Desert* (Cambridge: Lutterworth Press, 1995). Also cf. Charles Sisson, *Is There a Church of England?* (Manchester: Carcanet Press, 1993), and Brian Morris, (ed) *Ritual Murder* (Manchester: Carcanet Press, 1980).

10 David Martin and Peter Mullen, (eds) *No Alternative: The Prayer Book Controversy* (Oxford: Blackwell, 1981).

11 Gerald Hammond, "English Translations of the Bible", in Frank Kermode and Robert Alter, (eds) *The Literary Guide to the Bible* (London: Collins, 1987), pp. 647–666.

12 A critique of superficial Catholicising over a base of sixties' ideology, and of the downgrading of penitence and redemption, all summed up in the "false smile" of celebration, is provided in Paul F. M. Zahl, *The Protestant Face of Anglicanism* (Grand Rapids, MI: Wm. B. Eerdmans Publishing Company, 1998).

13 A recent sermon in Guildford Cathedral on the Feast of St. Paul (January 25) attempted to soften up resistance to the abolition of Cranmer's collects and the Authorised Version at Sung Eucharist by saying that while some suffering—the holocaust—was inexplicable, other kinds, such as Paul's loss of his old identity at conversion, and childbirth, are required by a "dynamic God" as a prelude to joy. Hence, by analogy, a "baffling" resistance to liturgical change would likewise pass through suffering to joy in the adoption of the new lectionary.

14 An amusing if very minor example of this tilt occurred at Westcott House, Cambridge, in 1982 when as a prospective ordinand I was reproved by the Principal for reading from the Authorised Version while the Committee for worship in the chapel somehow got away with the abolition of Matins for a period in favour of meditation around a coffee table.

15 Traces of comparable frustration are to be found in Kieran Flanagan, *Sociology and Liturgy* (New York, NY: St. Martin's Press, 1991) and *The Enchantment of Sociology* (London: Macmillan, 1996), as well as in Ian Robinson, *Prayers for a New Babel* (Worksop, U.K.: Brynmill Press, 1982) and in C. A. Anthony Kilmister, *When will ye be wise?* (Wimbledon: Blond and Briggs, 1983).

AFTERWORD

EAMON DUFFY

The Duke conference on the Eucharist produced an extraordinarily rich cluster of papers, ranging over many aspects of the Eucharist and its ecclesial and biblical context. Mary Douglas's dazzling exposition of the symbolic arithmetic of the Book of Leviticus's provision for bread-sacrifice provided an enormously illuminating context for Christ's own Eucharistic interpretation of his death. Catherine Pickstock and Herbert McCabe's elegant papers, so different in idiom and approach, converged in a common insistence on the reinsertion of Eucharistic meaning—and hence of Eucharistic presence—into a broader understanding of how meaning is arrived at at all, and how any linguistic sign works. Sidney Griffith's deeply affecting exposition of the sacramental idiom of the hymns of Ephraem the Syrian, in the midst of a conference devoted to often very abstract and demanding technical discussion, immersed us in liturgical poetry of great immediacy, depth and richness, beautifully communicated.

We were earthed to the social and political dimension of Eucharistic worship by Bill Cavanaugh's witty and challenging attempt to work out a contrast between the rival universalisms of Globalisation on the one hand, and, on the other, the *Catholica*, constructed round, and by, local Eucharistic communities. We were also confronted by more disturbing reminders of the social reality of Eucharistic belief and practice in David Martin's painfully personal narrative of how "reverence before the condensed symbols of love is always turning into deference before authority", and in Miri Rubin's dark paper on the role imposed on the Jews of Europe in the Middle Ages, as the enemies of the Eucharist. Thereby, Christ's own people, his flesh and blood, became an incarnate *otherhood* that could be targeted in order to underpin the Christian community's sometimes fragile and strained sense of *brotherhood*.

The patterning of the papers produced some real surprises, not least the extraordinary fact that a conference of this sort should have devoted so

Eamon Duffy
The Divinity School, St. John's Street, Cambridge CB2 1TW, UK

much time and skill to exploring the notion of transubstantiation—in Fergus Kerr's characteristically searching but also user-friendly teasing out of the attempts of the British philosophers Elizabeth Anscombe and Michael Dummett to construct non-metaphysical accounts of Eucharistic presence, in the centrality of transubstantiation in Catherine Pickstock's paper, and the attempt to construct a more sophisticated and fire-proof version of transignification in Herbert McCabe's paper on transubstantiation. This is all the more remarkable given that Catholic discussions of the Eucharistic presence since the 1960s have often displayed marked embarrassment about the doctrine of transubstantiation: it was therefore a surprise to discover, to borrow a phrase from Shakespeare, that the old man had so much blood in him.

The element I missed in the conference, however, was any detailed engagement with questions of Eucharistic rite and practice, though it is surely here above all that questions of Eucharistic theology impinge most directly upon the majority of Christians. The revision of the Eucharistic rites of all the major churches of the West over the last thirty years has had profound implications for every dimension of Eucharistic belief and practice, and beyond that, for the self-understanding of those churches, and their stance toward and involvement with the "world"—society, politics, culture. Within the Roman Rite, in particular, the post-conciliar transformation of our Eucharistic experience has been, quite simply, revolutionary. The heart of this revolution has been, of course, the translation of the Mass from Latin into the vernacular, but as I have argued elsewhere, far more was going on in the move from Latin to common speech than mere translation.[1] The revision of the Missal of Paul VI was greatly influenced by a set of theological and historical assumptions which now look naive and simplistic, chief among them the notion that the Canon of the Mass was, despite its venerable antiquity and its centrality as the defining prayer of the Latin theological tradition, a decadent and disordered form of an earlier, simpler and more theologically stream-lined "primitive" pattern, best represented in the Eucharistic prayer of Hippolytus. The Roman Mass thus needed to be "restored" by a process of simplification and elimination, involving the smoothing away of "needless" repetitions and other signs of the process of historical accretion which had obscured the simplicity of the primitive model. Because the Roman Canon itself proved resistant to any such "restoration", three alternative Eucharistic prayers were devised to supplement it, and these have in fact effectively dislodged the Roman Canon from its central place in the tradition: in most parish churches it is now seldom used.

Catherine Pickstock has brilliantly demonstrated the theological poverty of the theological assumptions underlying these developments. In *After Writing* she argued that attempts to produce a rite embodying a simple linear movement towards God, eliminating repetition and linguistic redundancy, sprang from a failure to grasp that the "liturgical stammer" of the ancient rite in fact embodied a profound and vital theological perception. She argued that the address of fallen humanity to the divine necessarily involves the "constant rebeginning" which the older rite embodied.[2] Every true Eucharistic rite must enact within itself both the simultaneous possibility and impossibility of access to the heart of God, the paradoxes of contingency gathered into eternity, of the material as the vehicle for spirit. In eliminating or muffling these tensions, the newer rites crassly rush in where, quite literally, angels fear to tread.

In a similar way, Denys Turner argues in his paper that the Eucharist makes present the future, but does so "necessarily under conditions of absence, for the kingdom, as such, is not yet with us". At the heart of Holy Communion is an enactment of "that failed communication which is our consort with the Father through Jesus". The Eucharistic word of power, which makes Christ and his kingdom present to us, is also a failure of speech, in which we are conscious of our distance from, as well as our closeness to, the Mysteries we handle.

The difficulty which the Church shaped by the new rites has in coming to terms with and living these tensions is everywhere evident in the ICEL versions of the short presidential prayers—the Collects, Offertory and Post-communion prayers—which are one of the great glories of the Latin liturgical tradition. I have argued elsewhere that these ICEL versions consistently betray a drift towards a pelagian dumbing-down, in which the tension and paradox which gives these brief prayers and the Roman Rite itself their depth and complexity, is emptied away, and our relationship with God is consistently presented as straightforward and untroubled. These tendencies can be illustrated quite literally at random from the Missal, and any three or four consecutive Sundays will provide a cluster of examples. To demonstrate this, I take the prayers for the Sunday nearest to the time of writing these remarks, the 24th Sunday in ordinary time, and the weeks immediately following.

The Prayer After Communion for the 24th Sunday is a characteristic Roman prayer, which explores the transforming effect of reception of the body and blood of Christ in terms of a divine seizure of a reluctant nature: in the prayer grace is imagined as a divine commando-raid which, despite ourselves, liberates us into new life.

"Mentes nostras et corpora possideat, quaesumus, Domine, doni caelestis operatio, ut non noster sensus in nobis, sed eius praeveniat semper effectus: per Iesum ..."

A literal translation of this might run

Lord, may the working of your holy gift seize possession of us, body and soul, so that the effect of that gift may always prevail within us, and not our own inclinations.

The ICEL version is breathtakingly pelagian: out goes the sense of Divine seizure, the cry that God may force his way into our reluctant hearts. Instead, the prayer becomes a mild prayer for advice and guidance. The path to God is easy and open: all we need is a word of advice.

Lord, may the Eucharist you have given us influence our thoughts and actions. May your spirit guide and direct us in your way.

The same disastrous softening is at work in the versions of the prayers for the following Sunday, the 25th in ordinary time. The Collect for this Sunday is a no-nonsense prayer which takes as its starting point the gospel summary of the Law "Thou shalt love the Lord thy God with thy whole heart, and thy neighbour as thyself".

Deus, qui sacrae legis omnia constitua in tua et proximi dilectione posuisti, da nobis ut, tua praecepta servantes, ad vitam mereamur pervenire perpetuam.

A literal translation might run

God, you made the whole of your law to stand in the love of you and of our neighbour: grant that, following your commands, we may come at last to eternal life.

Notice that the weight of the prayer falls on the idea of the Law, and its quite specific summary in the requirement that we should love God and neighbour: we ask for the grace to obey God's command to love him and our fellow mortals, and so to be made worthy of eternal life. Eternal life is something which is reached towards, by an obedience which is itself the gift of grace—"Da nobis". The ICEL translator was evidently uneasy with all this talk of laws and precepts, and once again, direction and obedience are softened into the following of advice.

Father, guide us, as you guide creation according to your law of love. May we love one another and come to perfection in the eternal life prepared for us.

Notice here both the elimination of the specificity of original prayer's allusion to the Gospel story of Christ and the summary of the Law, and behind that, of the Old Testament law, and also the disappearance of any sense of struggle towards eternal life, implicit in the verb "pervenire". Now, the outcome is not the result of obedience to precepts but of the following of guidance, and the goal is perfection in an eternal life "prepared for us"—in the bag in fact. The abrasive, slightly dangerous edge of the original prayer has been sandpapered away.

The effect of such softening is the elimination of any sense of distance, tension, dialectic in our relationship to God and his Kingdom. This revulsion from any such dialectic is manifest throughout the more specifically

Eucharistic prayers for these Sundays. The prayer over the gifts for the same day, for example, is an uncomplicated but characteristic petition that God may accept the gifts so that they become a vehicle for hidden realities.

Munera, quaesumus, Domine, tuae plebis propitiatus assume, ut, quae fidei pietate profitentur, sacramentis coelestibus apprehendant.

This can be translated

Lord, we beseech you, favourably to accept the gifts of your people, so that what they profess by faith, they may grasp in the heavenly mysteries.

This prayer simultaneously celebrates and beseeches, it articulates the difference between the people's offering and the realities which God gives us through it, while it asks that this offering may, by God's gift, become the means by which the people of God lay hold on realities which they know only by faith. For all its brevity, the theological wisdom of the Roman Rite's "liturgical stammer" is fully in evidence here. By contrast, the ICEL translation turns the prayer into a bland expression of the congregation's faith, in which God is asked for nothing, in which the gifts are no longer the vehicle for the heavenly exchange, a means by which, through the gracious will of God, we pierce the veil of contingency and lay hold on the future. Instead, they are reduced to being an expression of *our* belief and love:

Lord, may these gifts which we now offer to show our belief and love be pleasing to you. May they become for us the Eucharist of Jesus Christ your Son.

Much the same theological collapse is evident in the brief prayer over the gifts for the next Sunday. In this short prayer, the distance between the gifts on the altar and the heavenly realities they symbolise and communicate is emphasised.

Concede nobis, misericors Deus, ut haec nostra tibi oblatio sit accepta, et per eam fons nobis omnis benedictionis aperiatur.

This translates as

Grant to us, merciful God, that this offering of ours may be acceptable to you, and through it, may the fountain of all blessings be opened for us.

Notice here that the offering itself is not the fountain of all blessings, but the means by which it is asked that that fountain should be opened. The prayer respects the sense of presence through the mode of absence which Turner has emphasised as inherent in any account of Eucharistic presence. Predictably, the ICEL version simply eliminates this distance.

God of mercy, accept our offering and make it a source of blessing for us.

The effect of this elimination of distance is the same as that in the version of the "Ecce Agnus Dei" prayer in current use when the priest holds up the host before communion. Instead of quoting St John the Baptist literally from St John's Gospel *"Behold* the Lamb of God", the priest says *"This is* the Lamb of God". Here, however, we need the distance implicit in the word "Ecce", "Behold", a word which points, as John himself points, to a future not yet fully present. When applied to the Eucharistic elements, "behold" points us beyond the elements themselves to a beholding by faith, to the coming of the kingdom and the marriage supper of the Lamb. It affirms the identity of the sacred species and the realities they communicate, yet it preserves also the necessary eschatological distance between promise and fulfilment, between the Eucharist as "pignus" or token, and the consummation of all things, when rites and shadows have their ending.[3]

This sort of exercise could be endlessly extended, and the hammering of the ICEL translators is in danger of becoming a particularly sadistic form of blood sport. But what I am pointing to is more than the disastrous inadequacies of the English versions of the Eucharistic prayers of the largest Christian communion now in use throughout the English-speaking world. The tell-tale theological consistency in these versions is a symptom of a disastrous failure of the Eucharistic imagination of Western christendom. The power and indispensability of the Eucharist is that it punches a hole in the wall of contingency, that it allows us to glimpse and to touch the eternal. It thereby allows us to hope, because it opens the prison doors, it enables us to shape this world towards the eternal. But a glimpse and a touch are not the same as tranquil and safe possession. We live *in via*, the Eucharistic church is a people "perigrinantem in terra". The calamity of the new Mass in its English guise is that it constantly occludes the provisionality of the present world order, constantly nudges us towards a smugly pelagian sense that we possess the mysteries we celebrate with longing. During the conference, one American participant told me that the nun who had prepared his children for first communion had taught them to say not "Domine, non sum dignus" before reception, but "Lord, I *am* worthy to receive you". One laughs and cries at the same time in the face of such crassness, but there is no mystery about it. The church's acknowledgement of the wound of being, the limitations of contingency and mortality, of the gulf between the created and the eternal which is so miraculously and marvelously bridged in the Incarnation and in the Eucharist, has been psychologised as just another case of low self-esteem, and has been idolatrously trivialised in the process. But the rite we now live with is hospitable to such trivialisation, and if the Christian imagination of the Latin Church is to survive, something drastic will have to be done.

That is why Sidney Griffiths' moving exposition of the liturgical poetry of Ephraem the Syrian was for me so timely and necessary an element in the conference. Ephraem's constantly reiterated image of the bread of the

Eucharist as a burning coal, an ember, manages marvelously to convey both the sense of joy at the power, love and condescension of God in giving to us mortals what angels dare not handle, and the element of danger, of the consuming radioactivity of the holiness of God revealed in Christ, and the practical demands which that holiness makes upon us. Any Eucharistic worship which does not speak of both elements of this dialectic has nothing true to tell us of God, and deserves to be struck dumb.

NOTES

1 E. Duffy, "Rewriting the Liturgy: The theological implications of Translation" *New Blackfriars*, January 1997, pp. 4–27, reprinted in S. Caldecott (ed) *Beyond the Prosaic: Renewing the Liturgical Movement* (Edinburgh: T & T Clark, 1998) pp. 97–126.
2 C. Pickstock, *After Writing: On the Liturgical Consummation of Philosophy* (Oxford: Blackwell Publishers, 1998), pp. 170–266: for a brief summary of her argument, "A Short Essay on the Reform of the Liturgy", *New Blackfriars*, February 1997, pp. 56–65.
3 These points are elaborated, using different examples, in "Rewriting the liturgy" passim.

Index